Daughter of the Goddess: the Sacred Priestess

DAUGHTER OF THE GODDESS:
THE SACRED PRIESTESS

Naomi Ozaniec

Aquarian/Thorsons
An Imprint of HarperCollins*Publishers*

The Aquarian Press
An Imprint of HarperCollins*Publishers*
77–85 Fulham Palace Road,
Hammersmith, London W6 8JB

Published by The Aquarian Press 1993
1 3 5 7 9 10 8 6 4 2

A catalogue record for this book
is available from the British Library

ISBN 1 85538 280 6

Typeset by Harper Phototypesetters Limited,
Northampton, England
Printed in Great Britain by
Mackays of Chatham, Kent

Contents

To all women everywhere who seek themselves

Acknowledgements

I should like to thank Caitlín and John Matthews who allowed me to use their wonderful library, the exteriorisation of the akashic records, and encouraged me throughout.

I should like to thank the staff of the Chandler's Ford library who, with great dedication to duty, tracked down the most obscure documents in true Sherlock Holmes fashion.

I should like to thank all those who so kindly permitted to me use their personal testaments.

I should especially like to thank Jerome who always found the time to share ideas with me.

I should not forget my children who have patiently awaited the end of the book.

I should like to thank Dolores Ashcroft-Nowicki and the Aquarian Press for allowing me to include the rite, The Star Hall of Isis.

I should also like to thank the following publishers for permitting me to reproduce illustrations: Rider and Co for the Vestal Virgin from *The History of the Vestal Virgins of Rome* by Sir Cato Worsfold; Weidenfeld & Nicolson for the illustration of the Neolithic figurine from the *Roots of Civilisation* by Alexander Marshak; Routledge for the Agia Triada sarcophagus; HarperCollins for the Vulture Shrine, from *The Language of the Goddess* by Marija Gimbutas; Dover Books for the illustration of Isis and Nephthys from *The Gods of the Egyptians* Volume 2 by W Budge; the Alinari/Anderson collection and the Mansell Collection for the Isian Procession.

I should like to thank the Athens Museum for the 'Bear of Artemis', the Iraq Museum for the Mesopotamian priestess and the Berlin Museum for the illustration of the Vulci cup.

Preface

I have always been interested in the human quest for meaning and justification. I have always found the comparative search for the absolute, deeply fascinating. Each civilisation, indeed each society, offers its own truth as being the only truth. The broad historical sweep of this work has enabled me to become immersed in some of the many explanations of the human-divine relationship. I am still fascinated, perhaps even more so by the belief structures which uphold civilisations.

This book has not been an easy one to write. I set out with many questions. I have not found all the answers. Documentary evidence for civilisations long dead is incomplete and more often non-existent. Artefacts and archaeological sites reveal the bare bones of a people. The moving spirit of a civilisation is far harder to touch and describe, it is as elusive as perfume upon the air. Yet it is this invisible essence which breathes life into actions and most especially ritualised actions.

I am interested in the role assigned to women by differing societies generally, but I am particularly interested in the differing functions assigned to women who play a sacred role for others. I deplore the lack of women in sacred office in the world today.

My own interest is more than academic or historical. I have witnessed mediation, conscious mediumship at close quarters. It is powerful, it can be awe-inspiring. I have mixed with women who currently fulfil the role of priestess with great devotion. The priestess is alive and well at the end of the twentieth century.

I have enjoyed the detective work imposed by the task of

researching this book. It is still incomplete. There are still many unanswered questions. I have become deeply interested in the matter of polarity which has reappeared unbidden through various civilisations. It seems that the sexes are still at war one against the other.

I am interested in the past and the present but most of all I am interested in the future. How will the undeniable re-emergence of the Goddess tradition develop? Will it flower into a movement which has something genuine to offer humanity in the twenty-first century, or will it wither on the vine, starved by its own narrow interests.

I have been immersed in this study both by day and by night. My dream life has reflected my work, throwing up goddesses and bee maidens alike. A dream of Isis released me from a deep, agonising paralysis of spirit which afflicted me midway through my work. I had fallen into gloom and was convinced that the fruits of my labours would only meet rejection by women so attuned to another note.

I feel that I have merely scratched the surface of the issues which I have found to be pertinent. Hopefully others will follow. There is much still to be discovered.

Introduction

In the history of religions priests and priestesses represent high sacral personages. Their specific character consists of being invested by a community as supernaturally authorized mediators to the transcendental world for the performance of the public cult rituals.

J MARINGER, Priests and Priestesses in Prehistoric Europe

The contemporary perspective of society makes it difficult for us as a group to recognise and respect the role of the priestess as a sacred ministrant and mediator of divine presence. The Church of England is being riven asunder by the question of women's ordination. Imagine the reverberations if these women were demanding recognition as priestesses of Christ. The fact that these women seek to be priests rather than priestesses is a measure of male dominance within Christianity.

The priest is an all too familiar figure. We understand his functions as personal counsellor, theologian and as the official representative of sacred power at religious ceremony only too clearly.

The priestess is an unfamiliar figure to society at large, a leftover from the ancient world, dragged up from the depths like the rediscovered coelacanth. Such is the power of androcentricity, the male-centred society. However, the priestess was not always an unfamiliar figure.

Priestesses were prominent in the vanished civilisations of Sumer, Babylon, Egypt, Crete, Greece and Rome. Priestesses in shamanic guise were important throughout oriental history. They were significant in Celtic lands and in Old Europe. The priestess was a familiar and accepted figure in the ancient world. The priestess of Demeter enjoyed such high prestige that she was accorded a special place at the Olympic games. She sat upon a raised dais and was treated as a semi-divine person. Plutarch dedicated his study, *De Iside et Osiride*, and a second book, *Brave Deeds of a Woman*, to the priestess Clea. Sacred women played a definite and particular role in many varied societies.

We cannot doubt the existence of these women, but we should not make careless assumptions about their functions. We have to permit these past civilisations to speak for themselves as far as is possible. Imposing twentieth-century values and assumptions on cultures long dead is dangerous and facile. It is only too easy to superimpose current feminist values onto the past. Superficially at least, there would seem to be a harmonious resonance between the intentions of modern women's spirituality and the practices of the ancient female priesthoods. Yet if we are not to be simply glib in our comparison, we must be prepared to look beneath the surface presented by the past. We need to ask many questions. Who were the women who became priestesses? What function did they fulfil? By what authority did they hold office? What was the nature of their work? What kind of daily lives did these women lead? It is possible that we will not find the answers which have simply been lost in the intervening morass of history.

The term 'priestess' has now appeared in contemporary feminist vocabulary, indeed the priestess has reappeared in person. It is simply assumed that current usage is identical with past meaning. The shamanic priestess, medium, and mediator are not identical in psychic function. The initiator into women's blood mysteries and the initiator into the transcendent mysteries are not identical either in function or intention. Yet both ministrants might be called priestesses. We will have to be prepared to look further than simple labelling if we are to understand what these women meant within their own time.

The feminist movement has done much to reclaim the history of women. This is a powerful corrective to written history which has been little concerned with the contribution and value of women. It is undeniable that the male historical perspective is at best incomplete and at worst distorted. Women themselves feel that it is time that the balance was redressed. The process is ongoing and open ended. Feminist theologians and writers have revealed the uncompromising androcentric thrust of cultural development.

Feminists have done much to uncover both the overt and covert ways in which women's freedoms have been restricted in the past. Their work has also significantly contributed to a revival of interest in the Goddess-based religions of the past. The worship of The Great Mother presents a powerful antidote to the male-dominated religions of this present Great Age in which so many women feel excluded, and even reviled. It has also contributed significantly to a renewed interest in the role of the priestess.

The image of female deity is compelling for we are each born from the mother. It is not difficult to envisage the prime creative principle in female form. Historically, the creator was worshipped as the Great Mother long before the notion of the Father God existed. We are in a position to look back through history and observe the results and consequences of these two contrasting belief systems. We find ourselves at the close of two thousand years of patriarchy, confronting enormous problems of global proportions. The ecological and environmental crises that loom large seem to speak for the failure of a way of life proffered by a male deity. Under the aegis of a Father God, the Earth has been robbed, pillaged and raped, not as simple acts of godlessness but because the Father God offers creation for his children to use as they will. The Father God offers supremacy to his sons. It is their manifest destiny to master the Earth and to conquer. The Earth has been conquered but the victory is manifestly hollow.

There is no doubt that many women feel the Goddess is reappearing. Women are again working with images of the Divine Feminine to discover themselves. Wherever and whenever the Goddess manifests, women will turn towards Her in service as priestesses.

The eventual demise of the priestess coincided with a profound change in sacred belief. The whole edifice of the ancient world was dismantled as God replaced Goddess and the sons of the father supplanted the daughters of the mother. The Nymph of the Grove, in *The Golden Fleece* by Robert Graves, reacts to the spread of the Father God with alarm and disbelief: 'Who may a Father God be? How can any tribe worship a father. What are fathers for but the occasional instruments that a woman uses for her pleasure and for the sake of becoming a mother?'

The Goddess was dethroned, the priestess was removed from sacred office. Womanhood fell from grace to disgrace.

As we set out to look into the history of our race to search for the priestesses of the past, we are brought face to face with the difficulty of the task. In truth we need to examine the spiritual and cultural history of every civilisation in order to seek out the threads which bind woman and Goddess together, watching as it is torn away to prise woman and Goddess apart.

The attempt to examine the historical role of the priestess is not an easy one. Nonetheless the search has value. In finding the past we might just come to understand the present a little more clearly.

Chapter 1

THE FALL FROM GRACE

To make priestesses of women is an error of heathen godlessness, not a commandment of Christ.

APOSTOLIC CONSTITUTION III, 9

THE PRIME SEPARATION

The current move for women's ordination has brought a deep-seated and well-disguised misogyny out into the open. The Church as an institution has always repressed women both as worshippers and potential power holders. This misogyny is so pervasive as to be practically invisible, woven into the very fabric of institutional thinking. Female sexuality lies at the root of the issue.

It is virtually impossible to pinpoint when and how body and spirit became theoretically separated. Once engendered, however, this division ran through all fundamental aspects of life like a wildfire, polarising human endeavour and behaviour into two irreconcilable categories. Women, sex, nature, the body and the emotions came to be seen as the inferior, dark and wayward aspects of human life. The culture of men, the mind, the spirit, the life of reason were the hallmarks of the superior path. The lower had to be transcended, temptations had to be overcome. The prime division between all things material and all things spiritual had profound and devastating consequences for all the activities, endeavours, ways of expression and people so categorised. We are still suffering from this schism today. The holistic movement has finally emerged, bringing a sense of unity to mind-body-spirit and a sense of common humanity to both men and women alike.

The prime separation between the things of the body and the things of the spirit is now invisibly integrated into society, created by centuries of reinforcement and cultural conditioning. Like creeping tentacles these notions have strangled both structures and human relationships with a choking grip. Reconciliation cannot take place until we are able to see the twisted, even ludicrous, logic used to divide matter from spirit.

If we are to look at the gradual process through which the spiritual and the sexual became hopelessly estranged one from the other, we will have to untangle a complex web of human ideas and institutions. The simple and biological act of intercourse between a man and a woman has proved to be anything but simple. Within the human family the sexual act has produced profound sociological, economic, legal, political and religious consequences. Sex is natural to all life, shared by the human and animal kingdoms. It is this fact which supposedly-civilised men found so hard to bear. How could divinely created man share the same functions as the beasts of the field! How could a man be subject to nature's powerful passions, no different from the ox and the ass? To prove himself better than the beasts, as being above and separated from the animal passions, the instinctive drives and animal urges had to be rejected and suppressed. It was only woman who dragged him back into the grip of feelings, passions and irrational desires.

Greek society was deeply repressive in all its dealings with women. Intercourse was always thought polluting. Aristotle, whose thinking influenced the philosophical foundation of Western thought until the end of the seventeenth century, wrote widely on physics, chemistry, biology, political theory, ethics, logic, rhetoric and metaphysics. In the biological studies he naturally included the reproduction of the human species. He attributed four causes to the origin of human life. Of these, three were contributed by the male, the fourth and the lowest, the material womb, was contributed by the female. He explained that life was created by the meeting of sperm and 'catamenia' – female discharge. He defined both sperm and catemenia as 'seed', except that, 'catamenia are semen not in a pure state but in need of working up.'[1] Aristotle believed that it was the female's colder blood which prevented her from completing the necessary transformation into semen. 'Semen then is a compound of spirit and water.'[2] Furthermore, 'semen both has soul, and is soul potentially.'[3] Male seed is divine. However, 'catamenia has an affinity to the primitive matter.'[4] He defined woman as 'a mutilated male, and the catamenia are semen only not pure; for there is only one thing they have not in them, the principle of soul.'[5] In the Aristotelian world, 'the male is by nature superior, and the female inferior, the male ruler and the female subject.'[6] In line with contemporary Greek thought he equated women with matter and regarded matter as being inferior to spirit.

Western cultural values were derived in many ways from the Greek model. Aristotle's words were taken to heart by the churchmen of later centuries. They made sure that the inferior of the species were kept firmly in their allotted place.

HATRED OF THE BODY

He that has intercourse in marriage as he would with a whore commits adultery with his own wife.

CLEMENT OF ALEXANDRIA, PAIDAGAGOS 11: 10; 99; 3

Questions of sexual conduct preyed heavily on the minds of pre-Christian thinkers. Pythagoras believed that men should devote themselves to sex in winter, not in summer, and in moderation only during the spring and autumn. Sex was in any case injurious at any time of the year. Sexual activity was widely thought to be dangerous to health, a squandering of male energy. Women were not thought to be weakened by sex as they sustained no loss of bodily fluids. Hippocrates believed that the retention of semen was the key to physical strength. Soranus of Ephesus, personal physician to the Emperor Hadrian, asserted that only permanent celibacy was health-giving and that reproduction was the sole justification for sexual activity.

A new note was introduced into the debate by Stoa, the founder of Stoic philosophy. He rejected the pursuit of pleasure altogether. Seneca, a leading stoic, adopted the maxim, 'Nothing for Pleasure's Sake'. Celibacy was promoted as the ideal state of being. Marriage was only a concession for those too weak to resist the carnal passions. When tutor to Nero, Seneca wrote a treatise on marriage. 'The wise man causes reason, not emotion to prevail when loving his wife. Let him resist the onset of passion and not be rashly impelled to the conjugal act.'[7] When writing to his mother Seneca stated,

> When you consider that the sexual urge is bestowed on man, not for his enjoyment, but for the reproduction of his own kind, then, provided that you remain untouched by the noxious breath of sensual pleasure, every other form of craving, too, will pass you by without touching you. Reason fells all vices at a stroke, not just some of them. Its victory occurs only once and is universal.'[8]

Seneca was giving voice to the already current belief that sexual activity was purely for procreation, never for pleasure. It was a necessary evil and should be treated as such.

Reason, the province of men, was able to overcome vice, the temptation of women. Intercourse was regarded as a test of moral fibre, to succumb to pleasure was to fail, the desire for sex was itself shameful. The celibate life alone was pure, uncontaminated by the defiling touch of a woman. Spirit could only soar above matter when earthly passion had been quelled.

In the Church, the celibate life was to became synonymous with the spiritual life. A train of bizarre and twisted logic began to take shape as official Church policy. First, married priests were asked to be celibate. Canon 13 of the Sixth General Council stated: 'In the Roman Church those who desire to enter the deaconate or the priesthood must undertake to desist from intercourse with their wives.' Canon 48 continued: 'If a man be a consecrated bishop, his wife shall withdraw to a somewhat remote convent but the bishop must provide for her.' Then the laity were separated from such sinful priests. Gregory VII forbade laity on pain of excommunication to attend mass by married priests, calling it a *crimen fornicationis*. It was only a matter of time before priests were forbidden to marry. Finally, Pope Innocent II, at the Second Lateran Council 1139, declared that marriage was forbidden to priests and any marriage after ordination was invalid. Priest and woman, man and wife, matter and spirit had to be separated.

Perverted logic spawned perverted conclusions. The cold intellect produced absurdity heaped upon absurdity. Mysogyny reigned in the guise of theological debate. Holy hatred compounded fearful fascination. Men convened in pompous and self-important assembly to discuss women, women's bodies, women's bodily fluids, women's unsuitability for the spiritual life, women's weakness and ultimately the inherent sinfulness of the female of the species. Of course, no woman was ever permitted to contribute to the all-male party: that would have been like having a leper to tea.

Spirituality and sexuality were conceived to be extreme polar opposites, mutually exclusive principles. The spiritual life was the chaste life. Christianity took its lead from both the Greek philosophers and Judaic tradition, picking up the theme of women's sinfulness with self-righteous glee. The Church sat in serious and solemn debate to discuss whether sex had occurred in the Garden of Eden. Gregory of Nyssa concluded that it had not. John Chrysostom too believed that an asexual form of procreation occurred. 'There was no desire for intercourse, neither was there conception, nor birth pangs nor parturition nor any form of corruption, they dwelt in pure virginity as in heaven.'[9] St Augustine also debated the old question, had Adam and Eve engaged in sexual intercourse in paradise? He too concluded that their union was asexual and envisaged means by which this might have taken place. Adam and Eve might have 'had children without intercourse in some other manner, as a gift from the Almighty Creator who had after all created them without parents.'[10] Later, he revised his opinion, believing that genuine intercourse had taken place. Eve was, after all, not fitted to be a helpmate to Adam in matters spiritual so it can only have been as a helpmate in matters generative that she was there at all.

Having decided that sex had occurred in the Garden of Eden it was important to decide whether sexual desire had existed too. On this issue Augustine was quite clear: although the act had taken place, sexual excitement of any kind was quite absent. He argued that as some people may waggle their ears and 'others may even move the entire scalp so before man sinned by rebellion and punishment, his human organ, without the excitement of lust, could have obeyed his human will for the purpose of parenthood.'[11]

By the age of 29, Augustine had an 11-year-old son by a mistress whose name he never mentioned. She was finally sent back to Africa without her son. His mother arranged for a new and more socially-acceptable bride. Augustine could not wait out the allotted two years for his new wife. 'Since I was not for two years to obtain her who I sought, I would brook no delay, being no lover of marriage but a slave to lust. Consequently, I procured myself another woman.'[12] However, after his conversion Augustine set about rooting out all the sins of the flesh with all the passionate fervour that only the newly-reformed can muster. His long-time friend Possidius wrote of him, 'No woman ever set foot inside his house. He never conversed with a woman save in the presence of a third person and outside his parlour. Not even for his elder sister and his nieces, nuns all three would he make an exception.'[13] The Mad Hatter's tea party continued.

The Church could not reconcile sexuality and spirituality. Animals engaged in acts of sex, men were not animals, men could not willingly engage in sex. Theological contortions and logical acrobatics without number were undertaken to keep men and women, sex and God, as far apart as possible. The Church viewed women not merely as inferior but as impure, defilers of the sacred space.

To limit the effects of the walking, breathing pollution, the Church laid down rules of conduct, dress and behaviour. Clement of Alexandria wished to cover up the offensive female. 'The woman should be completely veiled save when at home. By covering her face she will tempt none to sin, for it is the will of the Word that it befits her to be covered at prayer.'[14] The Apostolic Constitutions laid down that women could not take communion except when veiled. Pope Nicholas in a letter to the Bulgars in AD 866 insisted that women even cover their hands. 'A woman may not receive the Eucharist with bare hands.'[15]

Ambrose urged women to walk in the streets veiled. 'Let the woman veil her head, that she sees her chastity and modesty assured, even in public.'[16]

Women were forbidden to hold ecclesiastical office by the Apostolic Constitution. 'We do not permit women to exercise the office of teacher within the church; they are only to pray and listen to teachers.'[17] The same Apostolic Constitutions claimed that as Mary had not baptised Jesus, women were obviously unqualified to perform baptism or other priestly functions. The Synod of Laodicea Canon 44 forbade women to officiate at the altar: 'Women may not approach the altar'. The Synod of Nimes debarred women from 'priestly office'. A letter from Pope Gelasius to the Bishops of Luciana in AD 494 stated: 'We have learned to our annoyance that even women, so it is said are ministering at holy altars, and all that entrusted exclusively to the ministrations of men, is being performed by the sex not entitled thereto.'[18]

The Synodal statutes of St Boniface forbade women to sing in church. The Synod of Elvira decreed that woman should neither receive nor write letters in their own name. Pope Gregory advised bishops not to share their homes with mothers or sisters. The Synod of Paris AD 856 decreed that no woman might enter premises occupied by a cleric.

WOMEN, DAMNATION AND SIN

Who can be unaware that marital intercourse can never take place without lascivious ardour, without the filth of lust whereby the seed conceived is sullied and corrupted.

POPE INNOCENT III

These absurd restrictions which continued to spew forth as official policy represented institutionalised fear. Men truly believed that they were in danger of damnation should they succumb to female temptation, so insidious were the moral teachings of the Church. The Church wriggled continuously on the single dilemma of its own making. Sex was justified solely for the purpose of procreation – after all, biblical text was very clear: 'be fruitful and multiply'. Pleasure during this act was, however, a sin, Augustine had even declared that sexual pleasure was the vehicle through which original sin was transmitted from generation to generation. The celibate life remained the ideal. Marriage was the remedy for those who could not live up to the ideal. Marriage itself was but a poor substitute for the continent life. Sex was forbidden in marriage during holy festivals, during pregnancy, menstruation and on Sundays. Pope Nicholas I sent a letter to Boris, Bulgaria's newly-converted ruler, and reminded him in no uncertain terms of the Christian obligation. 'If one must abstain from worldly labour on Sunday, how much more must one be aware of carnal desire and all bodily pollution.'[19]

Unnatural positions, that is any position in which the woman did not lie beneath her husband, were considered to be sinful as such positions were thought to prevent conception. An anonymous thirteenth-century codex stated that a wife's acquiescence in deviation from the normal coital position was as grave a sin as murder. Theologians were concerned to establish precisely which parts of the sex act carried the most sin, thereby enabling them to save the immortal souls of their sinning parishioners. Simon of Tournai asserted that the conjugal act could be commenced without sin but not completed without it. Cardinal Robert Courson decided that the greatest sin was in the middle part, 'during which the whole man is ruled by the flesh'.[20] Anselm of Laon postulated that it was the intensity of a man's sexual desire which determined the gravity of his sin. Theologians even debated which was more sinful, the lust for a beautiful woman or an ugly woman. Petrus Cantor held that the sin was the greater with a more beautiful woman as it was more delectable. Alanus ab Insulis differed in his conclusion: the sin was less with the beautiful woman because 'he is more overcome by the sight of her beauty', and therefore by implication less responsible.

Cardinal Huguccio of Ferrara, tutor to Pope Innocent III, devised the perfect solution, sinless intercourse, the restrained embrace, *amplexus reservatus*. Quite simply the husband retained his semen, for it was at this moment that a man gave way to pleasure. 'I can so render my wife her due and wait in such a manner that she assuages her desire.'[21] The restrained embrace only saved the man from sin, however – should the woman experience an orgasm, also thought of as an emission of semen, a mortal sin was hers. The *amplexus reservatus* was not invented as a means of contraception, itself regarded as a sin, but as a means of avoiding the sin of pleasure. In practice it is difficult to see the difference between the *amplexus reservatus* and *coitus interruptus.* Theologians, however, distinguished one from the other by the splitting of even finer hairs. *Coitus interruptus* has always been treated as a grave sin, whereas *amplexus reservatus* found some favour even into this century.

The Church's continuous attempts to save the faithful from the sins of the flesh have been as remarkable in their ingenuity as they have been absurd in their detail. Women were consistently defined as defilers of the sacred. Menstrual blood was a contamination, childbirth was proof of carnal knowledge, female orgasm thought to be the emission of female semen was a sin, desire was a sin, pleasure was the means of transmitting original sin to the next generation. Sexual thoughts were sinful, sexual desire was sinful, sexual pleasure was sinful. If a man could not be celibate let him marry and perform pleasureless sex if he must. Sin was never more than a thought away for men and women alike. Sin brought damnation and hell, the raging inferno, a little closer. This is the heritage bequeathed to women. Is it any wonder that the question of women's ordination threatens the unity of the Church? This perfidious legacy, like a dark shadow, still lurks in the male group mind. It is the invisible enemy of women everywhere.

Chapter 2

IN THE BEGINNING

Women's history is indispensible and essential to the emancipation of women.

GERDA LERNER, *The Origins of Patriarchy*

THE DISTANT ROOTS

Our quest must begin at a time long before the priesthood, either male or female, had a name. We must attempt to find the roots of our own spiritual history which are deeply buried in the physical earth. It is difficult to comprehend the enormous distance in time which separates us from our ancestors. Historical labelling is only instructive when we also attempt to make a leap of imagination and try to envisage the daily lives of these earliest peoples.

The first humans were the upright, tool-using, tool-making Paleanthropians who survived and evolved for some two million years by scavenging, hunting, gathering, fishing and foraging. We can only speculate on the beliefs and thoughts of these people. 'If today there is agreement on the fact that the Paleanthropians had a religion, in practice it is difficult, if not impossible, to determine what its content was.'[1] We have some documentary evidence: human bones, stone tools, red ochre pigments and objects from burials. Burial practices were an important landmark on the road of evolving humanity and abstract thought – no animal buries its dead. Grave objects indicate a recognition of individuality, red ochre signifies the hope for a new birth.

These early people took another highly significant evolutionary leap with the domestication of fire, first documented at Choukoutien in 600,000 BC. How fire must have revolutionised these lives, bringing the possibility of seared meats, heated foods, warmth and flickering light. Fire also brought change in consciousness and action: supplying the fire with dry material became a vital act. It is no surprise that the hearth is perhaps the oldest symbol of domestication and social cohesion. Only humankind has domesticated fire. The hearth fire evolved into the sacred fire, the altar flame, the bonfire of celebration, the light in the darkness. The flame has become an important human symbol, everywhere tended by sacred ministrants.

These people lived and struggled for thousands upon thousands of years. It is difficult to grasp the enormity of such a time scale. Nevertheless, this is the starting place for the emergence of human consciousness and thought. Our distant roots are here, buried in the ground. 'It is tempting to simply gloss over this huge period of human development.' Eliade points out the dangers:

> To leave an immense part of the history of the human mind a blank runs the risk of encouraging the idea that during all those millennia the activity of the human mind was confined only to the preservation and transmission of technology. Such an opinion is not only erroneous, it is fatal to a knowledge of man. *Homo faber* was at the same time *homo ludens, sapiens* and *religiosus*. [2]

In the attempt to make sense of the mysteries and terrors of life, humankind even in its earliest and most primitive stage was able to develop meaningful abstract concepts to live by. This distant and unknown period, astonishing for its length, forms the bedrock of human development.

The Paleanthropian Age was succeeded and surpassed in achievement by the Old Stone Age or Paleolithic Age. Following in the patterns established by their forebears, the Paleolithic peoples were nomadic hunter-gatherers who refined tool usage, developed burial practices and created both accurate and symbolic representations of their life experiences. Ritualised activity appears, offerings are made, sacred places are evident.

The presence of the Divine Feminine is overwhelming in the consciousness of the Paleolithic mind. Representations of the male are entirely lacking during this period. Extraordinary statuettes and female forms appear. These are the first tangible expression of transcendence. Eliade remains cautious as to their exact use. 'It is impossible to determine the religious function of these figurines. Presumably they in some sort represent feminine sacrality and hence the magic-religious powers of the goddess.'[3] Symbolic activity represents the quest for meaning. It is the search to make sense of life experience. The Paleolithic life experience revolved around the basic need for food, shelter and safety. Human life existed amidst a vast and often dangerous landscape, co-existed with other animals and survived against elemental weather. The forces of sun and moon, wind and water, cycles of summer and winter, autumn and spring, were ever-present realities. The life of the great herds, their movements across vast empty terrains, the birth of animals, the power of the bear, the terrifying bulk of the mammoth, were part of European Stone-Age consciousness. The Paleolithic mind also knew the magic of fire, the power of a stone implement, and the extraordinary event of human birth from the body of a woman who, just like the animals of the herds, became swollen with young.

SACRED STORIES AND RITUAL ENACTMENT

It is difficult to imagine our lives without the stories of others. We learn in infancy to be human by imitation.

TSULTRIM ALLIONE, *Women of Wisdom*

The abundance of female imagery in a variety of forms represents the first attempt to make sense of life experience, to explain the process and events of nature through the process of womanhood. 'The periodic and regular female processes and their stories served as the basis for storied equations, explanations and verifications for comparable periodic processes in nature.'[4] The Goddess unified all life experience. Her stories were the first stories told by humankind to each other.

The Feminine was an implicit part of Paleolithic life, present throughout all activities and most especially at moments of major import: childbirth, death and initiation. A pre-literate society like any other has the inner need to teach the young in the ways of the group, to unite the group in its intention and understanding of the world. Without written language which is specialised communication, the enacted story – ritual – becomes the means of transmission. The validating stories evolved by the group are not told passively but enacted dynamically. This method becomes the basic humanising intellectual and social skill, the primary tool and technique of developing culture. The ritualised story becomes an integral part of group memory. Younger members learn the ways of the group and of the world outside the safety of the homebase. Enactment naturally moves from the recounting of personal experience, to portray the great impersonal forces of fear, danger and death. Ritualising the powerful and threatening themes of birth, death and renewal projects these fearful powers into a realm which is safeguarded by costume and disguise. The enacted story can encapsulate the past, portray the present, point to the future, bring together possibilities, reveal dangers and establish the accepted pattern for different groups: boys-becoming-men; girls-becoming-women; mature women; mature men. Sacred drama is rooted here, in the emerging process of human development. It is the framework in which the sacred representative is born. The Goddess is made present in the lives of the people through her stories.

We have little evidence for the existence of priestly function in Paleolithic times. Yet we have abundant evidence for Paleolithic drama, the enacted story, ritual. It is not difficult to understand the psychological and spiritual factors at work. Life was harsh and unpredictable, mysterious and full of danger. Vital moments, leaving and returning from the hunt, initiatory rituals, births and deaths, seasonal earth bonding and celebrations called out for the presence of the Mother.

The commitment and passion shown to the Great Earth Mother must have been echoed in rituals and worship which sought her active presence in daily life, the safe delivery of a child, a successful hunt, safe passage, recovery from sickness and sound

27

decision making. Cave art is highly suggestive of shamanic trance practice. In the trance state the empowered individual leaves the world of the mundane and travels to the world of spirit, directly to the world of the Goddess. Her guidance must surely have been sought, an answer was awaited probably through an intermediary, the sacred representative who spoke for the people, articulating their needs before deity.

The sacred representative need not be a formalised role belonging to only one person. In any gathering when deity and group come together in reciprocal relationship, the group awaits a response. How will the response be known? Will the Goddess show herself through a sign, an omen, perhaps a dream? An individual may feel inspired to give advice, offer comfort, take a decision. The Goddess may show herself through anyone or in any manner, but certain of the group, for whatever reason, may be especially open in themselves to the voice of inspiration. They naturally and spontaneously take up the mediating role. Eventually over the generations the role becomes more specialised. The priestess is born.

The abstract quest for the meaning of human life, indeed all life, begs the question of origins and destinations, beginnings and endings. Creation myths explain the particular relationship of the group to the creator and establish a framework for dealing with the world and each other. There is no reason to suppose that the Paleolithic mind did not grapple with such abstract thought. The answer was self-evident: new life came from females, both women and animals. Woman, the being with rounded breast and swollen belly, was the life-giver, the one who gave all things birth. The mythological tale and the sacred image were born together. The sacred story does not need to be told in words: movement, sound, and action convey meaning. Group enactment makes the meaning clear to all. The story created by the group to explain its own being becomes the structure into which all experiences and processes come to find a place. Seasonal changes, patterns and cycles are contained in the nature of the primal mother. She encompasses all. Her stories unite humans and animals, demonstrate the powers of nature and the place of people. Marshak understands this relationship very well.

The group could participate regularly in her story and through her, in a continuing understanding and re-telling of the meaning of nature and process; the group became part of the story in which she was a mother. They themselves entered into the family of nature and animals, they were part of her story and her family, they acted in terms of obedience, offering, sacrifice, prayer and taboo.[5]

ICONS AND STORIES

The image came first.

BUFFIE JOHNSON, *Lady of the Beasts*

The story of the mythical ancestor has many chapters. The mythical ancestor, the creatrix, holds the past and the future in her stories. Women are seen to pass through many changes, the flat-chested girl, the fertile woman and the full-breasted mother. Paleolithic female images are remarkably varied. It is a great mistake to think only of the classic Venus of Laussel as being typical of feminine representation. Female images took many other forms, some being highly stylised and impersonal. The Magdelanian reindeer-hunting society in south-west Germany near Switzerland produced a dozen tiny figures sculpted in black coal. These tiny, holed figurines, shorter than the length of a finger, have become highly polished from handling. They may once have been part of a necklace or individual pendants. They have neither face, arms, nor breasts yet they are clearly female in shape with exaggerated rounded buttocks. These tiny figurines are typical of a class of depiction which emphasised female buttocks in isolation to all other female characteristics. 'The buttocks silhouette is found so frequently that it must be considered a purposeful convention.'[6] These enlarged buttocks have been the source of much speculation in the past. Buffie Johnson suggests simply, 'It is in the buttocks that the cosmic egg is stored'. Doubtless, Paleolithic peoples saw new life hatch and likened the rounded buttocks to eggs. This idea was fully realised in the egg-bearing bird deities of the subsequent Neolithic period. Another figure from the same site is quite different, microscopic analysis showing it to be quickly but deftly made. It shows a full figure with breasts, stomach and marked lines to distinguish the legs. It has neither arms nor feet and the head is no more than an angled block. It was not designed to be worn. It bears no evidence of wear and was probably used for a single event, possibly related to pregnancy.

Again from the same site comes a baton of reindeer antler, about 16cm in length. It shows a rounded belly and inscribed breasts. This piece was clearly intended to be held. The handle is small, suggestive of a woman owner. It shows no signs of wear or use. It too was probably used for a single occasion.

The East Gravettian culture of Czechoslovakia produced a group of quite different female images – rods embellished with breasts. There is no attempt to humanise the form. It is stark and simple: the rod and breasts are marked with notches, in all probability a lunar count.

From Dolni Vestonice comes a series of eight beads in the form of a pair of breasts. Each bead is holed. Each breast is notched around the edge. 'It would seem that breast images were used and worn . . . by women or else by a shaman or ritual person performing for women, helping them participate in the story whose symbol was the flowing breast.'[7]

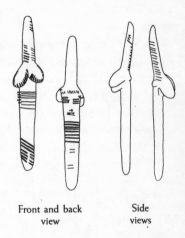

Front and back view   Side views

Figure 1. A stylised figurine with lunar notation. Was this made and notched by a woman acting in a ritual capacity?

Yet another female image appeared in the stylised fork-like pendant from the same environment. It has none of the fullness normally associated with goddess images, lacking breasts, upper limbs, full belly or buttocks. More like a full wishbone with splayed legs and vulval slit, this image can only be one of girlhood. Perhaps such an image was worn or owned by a young girl before menstruation. The abstracted vulva was a widespread image –

more than a hundred painted vulva symbols exist in France alone. These images appeared in oval, triangular and circular settings. The vulva was both stylised and realistically portrayed, placed in graves and inscribed upon cave walls. 'It is not the anatomic "sexual organ" that is being symbolised, but the stories, characters and processes with which the symbol has become associated.'[8] We find this symbol in a wide variety of contexts. This symbolic code must have conveyed an immediate message to the onlooker, as obvious and clear as the written word. The vulva image may have been used to indicate the birth of animals, or a particular time of year when young animals appeared. It may have been used as a sign for birth in the most general sense, or of personal rebirth through the portal of death.

The extraordinary wealth and variety of female images indicates a rich symbolic code. Marshak rightly points out that the variety of female images must lead us to ask:

> . . . which aspect of the female process or myth is being depicted, symbolised or given story? Is it the menstrual, pubertal, copulative, pregnant or the milk-giving? Is it a specialised or a general aspect of the myth or story? Is it the general image of the mother "goddess," the ancestress of the tribe? Or is it the female aspect which is related to birth and rebirth in all life and nature and, therefore to a "female property"? Is it related to biological or seasonal cycles? Is the image related to the lunar cycle via the story of birth, death and rebirth and by comparisons between the lunar and menstrual cycles? Was the image made to be used for a specialised purpose as one aspect of the wider myth, or was it a long-range image?[9]

These images, whether carved as statuettes or inscribed upon cave walls, had a practical purpose. They were used with intent either by an individual or by the whole group. Different types of images clearly had a different purpose, carrying a specific set of symbolic associations. The pre-pubertal girl lived by a different story from that of the post-pubertal young woman. The pregnant woman and the post-pregnant, lactating woman each experienced a different aspect of womanhood that is lived out through a different story.

We know that the natural biological processes follow one upon the other quite automatically. Our ancestors could not be so certain. Without biological knowledge menstruation, conception, birth and lactation are mysterious and even frightening events, unconnected to specific causes. Ceremonial and ritual acts serve not only to prepare the individual for the coming change but also through sympathetic magical enactment to promote and seemingly bring on these important but nevertheless uncertain events. A young girl might be prepared for menstruation by the ritual showing of female images, perhaps an exchange of personal signs, a girl's pendant for a woman's pendant. Perhaps accompanied by an older women a girl might be taken to a cave to paint her own female image alongside other symbolic signs and marks. Perhaps she would understand that her own blood would bring life. Older women would have learned that flat-chested, slim-hipped girls who did not bleed never had babies. We are of course deep in the realm of speculation.

Pregnancy was part of life, perhaps partially understood in relation to other animals who also gave birth. The swollen belly and full breasts were sure signs of forthcoming life. Perhaps women whose bellies were beginning to fatten carved an image of the Great Life Giver, hoping for protection and a safe birth. Perhaps women who wanted the belly to fatten with child made an image and presented offerings. We can only guess and speculate yet again. Some images were probably personal, others related to the group as a whole. An unusual female image comes from Predmost in Czechoslovakia. The symbols are engraved on a mammoth tusk. Egg-shaped breasts reach as high as the head. There is a circular stomach with navel, and an oval womb. The imagery is stylised but clear. Perhaps this image represents the divine tribal mother in all her aspects. The tusk is heavy; perhaps it was the central point of group ceremony.

A heavy slab from the Magdelanian period at Fontales is inscribed with two female images and a number of animals along with notational markings. This stone is one of a type found in Germany at Hohlenstein and throughout the Dordogne. Each stone has been used over a long period of time, being overengraved with new female images and marks.

Whatever the precise meaning of the feminine figure: some things are certain, it was made periodically and repetitively, it was a symbol that had a traditional story and use, it was engraved on stones that were not carried about much and therefore served as records of a sort in the habitation site. The engraved images on the Hohlenstein slab were not long-term but imply a specialised, repeated short-term use. [10]

It is possible that the image was related to menstruation or the cessation of menstruation, and initiation into the months of pregnancy. This may have been but one aspect: these images were also related in story to other processes, to the seasons, the animals, the seasonal habits of the animals and to rites and ceremonies surrounding them. Perhaps we have a record of the lives of the women in the group, the potential fertility being rendered by buttock images, the actual child-bearing record being represented more abstractly with marks and signs. Animal images might represent a time of year in which the other recorded events took place. This of course is pure speculation. Whatever the spectrum of meaning in these female images of the Upper Paleolithic the tradition of the image was carried into the Mesolithic and Neolithic cultures that followed. It was part of the tradition that prepared the way for agriculture. Images which were to belong to the whole group might be accorded group recognition, possibly by marking the inception with a ritual or gathering of importance. The image when completed represented the powers that were valued and needed by the group. It was an epiphany of the Goddess, symbolising all the qualities attributed to her. An image might be permanently displayed in a prominent place, possibly near the group hearth in a protective stance. Other images might be shown only at certain times or in certain relevant circumstances, perhaps at times of decision-making, celebration or even group sorrow. The image might acquire a keeper, possibly the maker, or a group of keepers who were responsible for it in some way. The powers inherent in the cult image might also be seen to be present in the keepers who were recognisably like the Great Mother herself.

PAST, PRESENT AND FUTURE

Time itself was probably first measured by the moon's phases.

SHUTTLE AND REDGROVE, *The Wise Wound*

The Paleolithic age covered a vast span of time from 700,000–10,000 BC. This was an enormous period, millennium piling upon millennium by the hundred. Paleolithic lives were spent in savage circumstances, living in elemental weather and a wild and dangerous landscape. It is clear that these people developed a sound practical knowledge from observing the animals, watching the moon and harmonising with the progress of the seasons. We need to place the Great Mother in her cultural context.

Small groups lived and struggled together, moving on as circumstances dictated. Each generation was unconsciously indebted to that which came before, perhaps adding to the store of practical knowledge for those to come. Tools were simple but each had to be individually crafted; a poorly made tool could mean failure. Expertise was doubtless recognised and valued. The skills of cutting flints, making pigments, tracking game, finding water, knotting fibres or catching fish were each hard won from the world, gained only through careful observation and applied thought. There were comparatively sudden outbursts of activity when new skills were acquired and applied. There were phases and periods characterised by the expression of a new idea or the development of an old one. But for the most part, cultural peaks were slow set against the ponderous and relentless march of time, millennium after millennium. Apart from an improving competence in tool-making and survival skills, these people also drew abstract concepts from their surroundings, developing sophisticated concepts of notation and time.

The ability to recognise the concept of time and to record its passing is yet another uniquely human characteristic. The past can only be placed in order, the future envisaged in sequence, when the passage of time has some meaning. Women have an instinctive sense of passing time, the months are punctuated by the natural biological clock. Repeating events such as lunar and menstrual cycles were probably the first time-markers recorded upon bones and stones. These small and easily observed cycles led to an understanding of greater cycles, the passing of the seasons and the passage of a year.

The emergent timekeeping of the Paleolithic peoples formed an important bridge between the hunting-gathering life and the birth of agriculture. Timekeeping preceded agriculture by thousands of years, developing through a long, slow development of observational and notational knowledge through a 20,000-year period from the early Paleolithic to the late Magdelanian period. This developing function was important for both the practical and ritual calendar. Decisions needed to be taken about initiations, migrations, celebrations, possible meetings with other groups. Timekeeping, or mark-making as a record of observable events, began as a lunar and a menstrual count and developed into a sophisticated notational system, passing from simple tallying to elaborate animal signs as seasonal markers.

Initially different marks were used to record lunar events. Typically, a mammoth tusk from the Ukraine was marked with multiple signs at different angles. An angle containing a tiny mark represented the hidden moon. An open angle stood as a sign for the beginning of a series. An additional angled stroke possibly represented a day in which there was no observation. Extra-long lines represented evenings of clear observation. Marks above the horizontal represented something about the month as a whole or marked the completed period. All this came from a Paleolithic mind without written language. This tusk was found to be a record of a four-month-plus period beginning at one season and ending at another.

A bone from Aurignacian layers at the Abri Blanchard site in the Dordogne was marked with dots. One face of the bone represented two months of observation, sixty-three edge marks stood for three months of observation.

Other suitable surfaces including pebbles were marked with geometric markings and cross-hatching. Groups of lines and angles each carried a particular meaning. A group of six pebbles with geometric designs included a pebble which had been engraved on two faces with cross-hatching and with linear marks enclosed by other lines. It presented a total of fifteen lunar months.

As these time-markers evolved in both sophistication and complexity, animal images appeared as seasonal delineations. Reindeer, mammoth, bison and horse, among other creatures, appeared beside the older geometric compositions. The site of Montgaudier in a Magdelanian cave complex produced a reindeer bone with a single hole at one end, engraved with realistic creatures, two seals and two serpentine forms, obvious signs of the spring. This bone represented the birth of the new year.

At La Vache in the Pyrenean foothills, comes a spatula marked with the head of a doe and wavy lines looking like snakes or water. Below these images is the head of an ibex. There are also two flowers, representing early spring and summer. On the reverse is the head of a bison, with open mouth and tongue out in a rutting pose. There are also plant forms but without flowers and bare branches representing autumn.

This timekeeping function was an important aspect of Paleolithic culture, revealing an increasingly complex system of thought and time-factored activities, including ceremonial and ritual encounter. Paleolithic timekeeping practices passed into the Neolithic future. The tradition of the small personal timepiece, the marked bone or pebble, was superseded by the vast stone calendar – circles and stone markers which encapsulated the cycles of moon and sun. The great communal ceremonies which accompanied the path of the year evolved as knowledge of the cosmic patterns developed. These cosmic patterns were also incorporated into the life of the Divine Feminine. The major events in the life story of the Goddess – her puberty, union, childbirth and death – became the markers of the year, ritually enacted by the community and led by sacred intermediaries.

DEATH IN LIFE – THE HUNT

The hunt itself, therefore, is a rite of sacrifice, sacred and not a rawly secular affair.

JOSEPH CAMPBELL, *The Masks of God*

Paleolithic people were quite advanced technologically by

comparison with their own predecessors. Tool-making had evolved into weapon-making. A sharpened flint made an effective blade, a stone attached to a handle made a formidable hammer. These new weapons changed both outlook and social behaviour. The Paleanthropians had survived by foraging, collecting and scavenging with probably little division of labour across the sexes. The ability to kill with a weapon brought the possibility of the chase and of group effort. Gradually, over thousands of years, a new pattern emerged, men took on the responsibility of hunting larger animals over a wider territory, women took on the responsibility for hunting smaller game, foraging and collecting. There is no reason to assume any diminution of status for women.

The relationship between hunting practices and the Mother Goddess was a significant aspect of the social and spiritual framework. The organised kill had a direct effect upon the evolution of belief and sacred practice. It is facile to assume that the hunt was a natural expression of innate violence.

The hunt assumed spiritual qualities as the body of the animal was transformed into the life of the people. The abundance of animals, like human life itself, was seen to come from the Great Mother who had the power to replenish and renew. The cave of animals hidden deep in the earth was perceived as the belly of the mother, perhaps seen as the magical source of all animal life. Rites held here perhaps justified the kill and atoned for the animal life, glorying not in the death of the beasts but sanctifying the passing of life, the transition through death to the realm of the animal spirits. To take life created by the Great Mother might be a dangerous exercise unless correctly undertaken through ritual preparation and due observance to the spirits of the beasts themselves.

The hunt pin-pointed the precarious nature of life, both of animals and people. The act of the kill focused the mind very clearly on the value of life and death and underlined the sacred relationship between humans and animals. Rituals and taboos doubtless developed to preserve the balance between the hunter and the hunted, to show respect for the spirit animals and their sacrifice. These complex totemistic acts created a relationship between people and animals which extended far beyond the hunt itself. The hunting realm belonged to the Lord of Wild Beasts, not as a creator deity but as a Master of the Hunt who established certain rules which permitted the taking of life. Choice offerings and ceremonial respect atoned for the death of the beast. Hunters might not take more than was needed. The selected bones of the slain beast, when laid out with due ceremony, permitted regeneration. Enacted stories preserved the essence of the beasts and honoured their spirit. A reciprocal relationship between humans and animals was preserved. The richness and complexity of the religious ideology of hunting peoples must never be underestimated. Since we cannot reconstruct his religious beliefs and practices, we must at least point out certain analogies that can illuminate them, if only indirectly.[11]

Recent hunting groups such as the Inuit or the Plains Indian reveal the complexity of the hunting code. They remained ever mindful of the need to conduct the hunt with a good heart, even waiting to be summoned in a dream by the animal itself. Group rituals, songs and stories preserved the delicate balance between the needs of the humans and the needs of the beasts. Breaking the rules of the hunt imperilled all, bringing failure, disaster and dishonour.

The degree of sophistication and complexity revealed by later hunting societies is indicative that the hunt was not solely a matter of feeding the group, nor even of social organisation. Hunting has its lessons and skills to teach. The hunt demanded the physical qualities of strength, stamina, speed and stealth. It also required an understanding of the animal's life cycle through observation and close contact. Modern Aboriginal hunters impersonate the nature of the quarry by imitating the posture and sounds of the animal not only as a means of acquiring a disguise, but as part of the process of totemistic empowerment. The Paleolithic hunter dressed ceremonially in the pelt of an animal was doing nothing different.

Hunting societies invariably depict the animals that they hunt through art, song, dance and storytelling. The hunter comes to know and respect the ways of his quarry, even to celebrate and impersonate these qualities. The beasts become teachers offering non-human models of strength, bravery, power, cunning and endurance.

The beliefs of the group would be reflected in social organisation and ritual practices. Hunting parties would follow the rules evolved by the group to safeguard the hunt, the kill would be celebrated but dues would also be paid to the spirit realms. The social life of the group would be enriched through gatherings to enact the story of the hunt with its dangers. At other times the group might meet to celebrate their relationship with one particular animal or to initiate a young member to full adult status through a hunting scenario.

Paleolithic groups hunted over a long period. It would be most unlikely if during that time succeeding generations failed to evolve and pass on some degree of hunting law. Younger members of the group invariably would learn their skills at the hands of more experienced group members. It is feasible to suggest that the hunting skills could be taught though physical games, tests of strength and trials of ability between older and younger members, culminating in an initiation into group life. It remains very likely that these caves were the places of adult initiation into the hunting code.

> When the hunter was brought here into the secret dark and the light was suddenly flashed on the pictures, he saw the bison as he would have to face him. He saw the running deer, he saw the turning bear, and he felt alone as he would feel in the hunt. The moment of fear was made present to him. [12]

Joseph Campbell also supports the initiatory function of these caves. All the elements of classic initiation ceremonies are to be found here. The youthful candidate would be led by an adult or probably a group of adults through a strange and foreign territory to the specified place of trial. The candidate would undoubtedly experience a high level of fear which might only be countered through trust, obedience and physical bravery. At the site itself, the candidate would encounter the great beasts, often painted life size. The adult might impart tribal hunting lore to the future hunter before leaving the youth alone in the cave to dwell on the beasts and possibly receive a vision or some private experience. Admission into adult life would depend upon successfully surviving such an ordeal. Final acceptance into adult status would be overtly celebrated. Imprints of feet moving in a circular motion, probably dancing, have been found. Some 55 representations of men dressed in skins, often in dancing postures, have been discovered. The dance is a universal act of celebration.

If boys-becoming-men were initiated into the hunting code in the subterranean chambers, girls-becoming-women were also initiated into the mysteries of their own womanhood in hidden chambers. Ritual conveyed the essential meaning of the transition through ceremonial language, enactment, symbol, testing and final celebration. Older adult group members functioned as initiators by establishing rites of passage for the new generation, instinctively performing the social aspect of a sacred role.

The cave sanctuaries were hidden and inaccessible, sometimes miles underground. Pigments, ropes, ladders, lights had to be transported into these dark underground chambers. The achievement was social, artistic and sacred. The labyrinthine Cabarets Cave demands a long and tortuous journey in order to reach the site itself. The painted walls in the Trois Frères and Niaux caves are set hundred of metres into the earth. At Lascaux, the lower gallery can only be reached by descending through a shaft some six metres deep. There can be no doubt that the great beasts were painted with foresight, planning and intent.

The famous Venus of Laussel is to be found at the mouth of a cave. The inner walls reveal animal figures, a doe and a horse and also a fragment of a male figure with uplifted arms. The cave clearly served as a sacred place. 'This sanctuary served the covenant of man and beast.'[13] Campbell also reminds us that 'the figure must have represented some mythic personage so well known to the period that the reference of the elevated horn would have been readily understood as, say, in India a lotus in the hands of the Shri Lakshmi or in the West, a child at the breast of the Virgin.' The Mother Goddess with upraised crescent, whether horn or moon, ultimately presided over the rites enacted within the cave, standing at the threshold like a guardian.

The Trois Frères cave complex was discovered a few days before the outbreak of the First World War. The figures in this cave are unique. One wall is marked with a series of painted red dots, probably notational. Animals are changed into others through intentional overpainting, a reindeer cow is given the legs of a web-footed creature, a second reindeer has the head of a bison. From top to bottom a whole wall is covered with engravings of mammoth, rhinoceros, bison, wild horse, bear, wild ass, wolverine, lion and musk ox. The smaller animals are also represented: snowy owls, hares and fish are clearly drawn. Above them all at the far end of the sanctuary, some five metres above the floor, is the image now called the Sorcière of Trois Frères, a shamanic figure clearly male, perhaps in the role of the Lord of the Wild Beasts as instructor to the hunters, guardian of the beasts. He wears the antlers of a stag, the tail of a horse, the paws of a bear. This sanctuary is his domain.

Men's mysteries may have begun here rooted in rites of atonement, genuine reverence, genuine fear. The Lord of the Wild Beasts was not a creator; only the Goddess could create.

LIFE IN LIFE – THE SEED

Food plants are sacred, since they are derived from the body of a divinity.

MIRCEA ELIADE, *A History of Religious Ideas*

Paleolithic peoples were both hunters and gatherers, depending on circumstance. Meat formed only a part of the Paleolithic diet. Foraged and gathered plant material was just as important to the day-to-day life of the group. Foraged food accounts for between 60 to 70 per cent of the total diet of modern foraging groups. It is impossible to estimate accurately whether this represents a typical Paleolithic diet as plant foods leave little visible remains. Foraging is better suited to those carrying and looking after children: women. Collecting is a more reliable, though undramatic source of food. Women probably collected fruits, nuts, leaves, roots, bark, rhizomes, bulbs, fungi, water plants, possibly seaweed, lizards, turtles, insects and eggs. This contribution was absolutely vital, bringing a varied daily diet. The hunt was not always successful and not always possible. It is significant that in the few remaining modern foraging-hunting societies women share an equal status with men.

The activity of gathering food brings a quite different set of values from the hunting code. There is none of the high drama of the chase or the evolution of a taboo system which surrounds the kill. Instead, those gathering plant life are brought into direct proximity to, and reliance on, the changing seasons and the cycles of growth. Women became sharp observers of the natural world: recognising different plant varieties, learning and teaching what might be poisonous, discovering the various properties of plants and finding seasonal food.

Women entered into a close relationship with earth and its bounty. Small groups of women possibly with young children acquired social and indeed technical skills. Accumulated food requires containers. Plants need deft fingers for picking and preparation. Honey-gathering requires courage and planning.

Natural forces such as rain and the waters which clearly permit life took on a vital significance. Growth, cyclic change and renewal fused together as a sacred constellation. Women could see growth taking place in an immediate way: the quickening of the child inside; new shoots waiting to be plucked; hatching eggs and emerging babies.

Women made their own shapes in stone and bone to project what they felt, to express what they needed, to ask for what they wanted, to celebrate what they had. Unlike Men's Mysteries, which in part share the collective blood guilt, Women's Mysteries share secrets of life-blood.

THE GREAT AGE OF THE GREAT MOTHER

Nowhere in Neolithic Goddess culture is there any sign of warfare.

ELINOR W GADON, *The Once and Future Goddess*

As the millennia passed so the nomadic cave dwellers gradually settled into new patterns. The climate warmed. Animals were gradually domesticated. Sheep were domesticated at Zawi Chemishanidar by about 8000 BC. Spinning and weaving consequently developed. Milk, milk products and meat were on hand. The goat was first domesticated in Jericho in about 7000 BC bringing milk, meat and leather. The domestication of the pig in around 6500 BC gave a regular and varied meat supply. The domesticated dog at Stan Carr in about 7500 BC brought an unusual development: the animal companion, worker and ally.

Village life replaced cave life. At first villages were temporary affairs, simple dwellings easily constructed and easily abandoned. Gradually the village took root, everything was on hand. There was no need to follow the herd.

A new rhythm of life was created, based around the cycle of the seasons, the planting and the harvest, the seed and the crop. A settled life brought new requirements. There were developments in architecture and building, construction and form. The first created temples appeared in the late Neolithic period, doubtless served by the first temple personnel.

The discovery of pottery brought together the utilitarian and the sacred, the ritual and the mundane. Vases, jugs, pots, dishes containers, querns, bowls, ornaments, figurines and animal figures appeared. Images of female divinity were manifold. The Goddess appeared in many guises, as bird goddess, snake goddess, cow goddess. Serpent imagery was abstracted into spirals to decorate, enhance and emphasise the nature of figurines and statuettes. Bird and snake together symbolised the mystery of birth and took on a cosmic significance. The egg, another ancient cosmic symbol appeared in egg-shaped vases and figurines with bulging buttocks. It was also abstracted into decorative designs. New life was observed to hatch from the egg resulting in a profound constellation of associations between woman, egg and emerging life. It was expressed through varied representations: the bird goddess; an egg-bearing bird-woman; the beaked-faced female. This idea was current late in Paleolithic times but was elaborated by more sophisticated Neolithic peoples. Neolithic figurines became increasingly complex, representing bird-women – strange hybrid beings with human heads, tail feathers and twin eggs bulging within the buttocks. Indeed the famous 'Venus of Lespugue' is such a hybrid with clearly-incised tail feathers. Holes were often pierced at the top of the head so that feathers might be inserted for ceremonial occasions.

Animals and creatures – fish, bears, bees, deer, dogs, birds, butterflies and caterpillars – frequently appeared as decoration or carving. These widely various symbols were often combined one with another to express abstract cosmic ideas. The symbols were widely used to decorate dishes, cult vessels, figurines, and even the walls of houses. Geometric patterns stylised symbolic motifs. Images of rain and waters were abstractly symbolised – parallel lines, zig zags, chevrons and meanders represented water in different forms. The cross, encircled cross and decorative derivatives appeared as symbols which connected the four directions. Triangles appeared as signs of female generation; dots within lozenges indicated the seed of life. Lunar crescents and crescent-shaped bulls' horns appeared as decorative motifs. The richness of Neolithic artefacts reveals a sophisticated level of abstract thinking, a well-developed imagination, refined practical skills and a settled way of life, all under the watchful eye and protective arms of the Mother Goddess. The overwhelming impression is of a people for whom nothing was profane.

This period produced the world's earliest permanent settlements. In the Near East between 9000 and 6000 BC a series of small townships developed, based upon the spiritual foundations of female divinity. The Anatolian town of Catal Hüyük represents the peak of this process.

Catal Hüyük is situated in modern Turkey. When excavated by James Mellaart it revealed twelve successive layers of habitation dating from 6500 BC–5700 BC. The site covers some 32 acres and is still largely unexcavated. It is the largest Neolithic site in the Near East standing as an extraordinary testament to the richness and complexity of its dwellers.

The buildings were constructed from sun-dried brick with wooden beams set into the walls and roofs. The walls and floors were replastered annually and decorated with images including geometric patterns, parallel lines, crosses, four-pronged flower-like symbols, horns, animal and human representations, birds, human hands and horned pillars. Hand prints were often made directly onto walls. Integral features, similar to those found in modern adobe houses, were built into the houses giving raised surfaces and niches. The overall town was planned and laid out in a regular fashion. 'The regularity of the town plan indicates a sophistication seldom visible on other sites.'[14] Catal Hüyük is quite remarkable for its rich spiritual tradition; images of the Goddess abound and penetrate all aspects of daily life. There were a large number of specialised buildings, one to every four or five houses, clearly not intended for personal habitation, each decorated with extraordinary cosmic images. 'The Red Shrine', so named by Mellaart, had a red-burnished lime plaster floor which had been twice relaid. The walls were painted red, except for one wall which was decorated with an image of a circle with a marked centre. A straight line and wavy lines were superimposed on the image. Another wall contained a moulded porthole which enabled a person to see into the room from the adjoining shaft. Moulded platforms and benches were also painted red. Long red plastered runnels ran along the edge of the platforms. A raised platform resembling an altar or table stood in the centre of the room. Mellaart himself was unable to explain the function of this room. It took a woman's eye to recognise these images. Dorothy Cameron, one of Mellaart's team, suggested that this was the birthing room. It was coloured red and decorated with relevant images. The circle represented the cervix, the line represented the umbilical cord, and the pouring wavy lines depicted the gently flowing amniotic fluid.

The setting-aside of a special place for birth represents the importance granted to this event. Birth took place under the aegis of the Goddess. Female attendants probably served as midwife-priestesses.

In Catal Hüyük female anatomy appeared as architectural embellishment, breasts were carved in rows. Rows of carved bulls' heads filled walls or sat atop pillars. Few of these bulls' heads have clearly depicted eyes. These images are not in fact true bulls' heads but representations of the reproductive system. The womb and fallopian tubes with flower-like openings bear a remarkable resemblance to the outline of a bull's head with upswept horns. The people of Catal Hüyük might easily have gained a working knowledge of anatomy as it was their practice to leave bodies exposed for excarnation before burial. Mellaart suggested that interment took place only once a year when the remains were buried beneath the sleeping platforms of the family. Males were buried under the northeast corner platform, females were buried

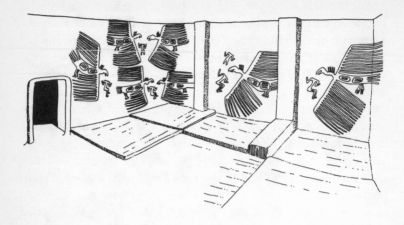

Figure 2 The vulture shrine in Catal Hüyük. Did women, perhaps
dressed as vultures, perform funerary rites here?

beneath the larger platform to the south of it. Children were
buried beneath the platform bed of the mother.

A shrine for the dead was decorated with enormous vultures
accompanying headless human beings. This clearly referred to the
process of excarnation. The vulture was universally recognised as
a scavenger and purifier, ever present amidst the process of decay.
It is probable that final burial rites focused on vulture imagery.
Images show that women disguised as vultures performed the
funerary rite, acting as priestesses of the dead. We cannot know
the words or ritual movements which accompanied the last rites
of these peoples. It is tempting to speculate that disguised as
vultures the priestesses imitated the bird's movements in dance,
offered thanks for receiving the bodies of the dead and finally
acted as overseers at the final burial. We cannot know, we can only
guess. It is interesting to note that the Egyptian hieroglyph for
vulture also signifies 'mother' and 'compassionate'. The Hebrew
rhm meant, 'pity' or 'compassion', but also 'women' and 'vulture'.
The vulture crown was worn by the Egyptian queen in her role
as mother. Mellaart was impressed by the level of civilisation
which he discovered. He concluded that, 'the Neolithic
civilisation revealed at Catal Hüyük shines like a super nova

among the rather dim galaxy of contemporary peasant cultures.'[15] The people of Catal Hüyük produced a wide range of artefacts displaying the highest standards of skilled craftsmanship and indicating a specialisation of skills. The wall paintings and relief figures are unparalleled at this time. Clay was used for pottery and figurines. Artefacts included open bowls and containers, seals for stamping patterns onto textiles, bone spoons, obsidian beads, mirrors and various items of jewellery. Grave goods included stone mace heads, obsidian lances, flint daggers, copper finger rings, bone belt hooks and eyes, jewellery, beads, pendants, cosmetic palettes, obsidian mirrors, bone spatulas and ladles. Mellaart found Catal Hüyük to be sophisticated and settled. 'Its numerous sanctuaries testify to an advanced religion, complete with symbolism and mythology; its building to the birth of architecture and conscious planning; its economy to advanced practices in agriculture and stock-breeding; and its numerous imports to a flourishing trade in raw materials.'[16]

Another cultural basin flowered between approximately 6500–3500 BC extending from the Aegean to the Adriatic. This Old European culture contained five different groups, the Aegean and Central Balkan, the Adriatic, the Middle Danube, the Eastern Balkan and the Moldavian West-Ukrainian. Each evolved its own character, all were united in the name of the Great Mother. Marija Gimbutas describes this culture as 'matrifocal, probably matrilinear, agricultural and sedentary, egalitarian and peaceful'.[17]

The Old European culture, though widespread, was remarkably homogeneous – animal husbandry, artefacts of bone and stone, ceramic bowls and jars, the cultivation of wheat, vetch, lentils and peas, copper and gold work, tool-making and pottery. Trade took place by boat along inland waterways. These people had completed the changeover from a nomadic hunting-gathering life to an agricultural way of life.

The spread of agriculture had a profound impact on spiritual practice and philosophy, shifting focus from the fertility of the beasts to the fertility of the land itself. Religious relations with the animal world were supplanted by relationships to the world of vegetation and the principles of growth. The universe was now presented through sacred images taken from the natural process of growth, the World Tree replaced the Lord of the Wild Beasts. Planting was seen to be akin to planting the human seed. Human fertility and sexuality was likened to the fertilising powers of nature. 'The sacrality of sexual life, and first of all feminine sexuality, becomes inseparable from the miraculous enigma of creation.'[18] The agricultural pattern establishes 'a complex symbolism, anthropocosmic in structure, associates women and sexuality with the lunar rhythms and with the earth.'[19] These themes were not new. In addition, 'women and feminine sacrality are raised to the first rank.'[20]

The people of Old Europe developed a rich spiritual life. There were sanctuaries, temple buildings and a wide variety of ritual objects, libation vases, partitioned bowls, ladles, altar pieces, ritual artefacts, bowls and tiny lamps. Votive offerings included figurines, spindle whorls, miniature vessels, even tiny chairs, thrones and stools modelled in clay. Seasonal change was now marked with agricultural festivals to emphasise the importance of planting and harvest. A collection of late Vinca figures from about 5,000 BC reveals individuals dressed in ceremonial costume. 'The richly clad figurines are probably not meant to depict ordinary villagers; they are more likely to personify specific goddesses or gods or represent worshippers or priests attending rites, garbed appropriately in masks and festive costume.'[21] Additionally, the costumes are too elaborate and impractical for everyday work. Female figures are shown with long, closely-fitting dresses, sometimes with a long skirt and blouse. Others wear aprons attached by broad hip belts. It is possible that we are seeing the forerunner of the costume of the Minoan priestess with flounced skirt, apron and open blouse. Women wore necklaces with beads of stone, bone, copper or clay. Bracelets and arm rings of shell, bone and stone were worn by both men and women. Pendants were worn by both sexes. Men wore belts and chest bands but were otherwise often naked.

Ritual costumes and ceremonial masks have a long history beginning in the Paleolithic period with the ritual wearing of animal pelts. The wearer took on the powers of the animal, impersonating it through movement and sound while preserving anonymity. Impersonating the spiritual powers is a dangerous business; the disguise brings safety.

These settled Neolithic people experienced a security and stability in the seasonal renewal of crops unknown to their Paleolithic forbears. It is not difficult to envisage the Neolithic enactment of myth at seasonal festivals, the sacred scenario through which a group remembers its own past and anticipates the future. 'Myth and seasonal drama must have been enacted through the medium of the idol.'[22] The idol or figurine was probably the first representation of the deity. As the process of representing the gods evolved, an individual or group of individuals as much like the deity as possible, came to represent the divine by playing the part of the deity. The role would have changed according to ritual and time of year, as planting and harvest necessitate quite different epiphanies. In effect, the role could have been filled by different people at different times. While in the act of impersonating the deities, the actors in the sacred drama would have been treated as epiphanies of the deities themselves, possibly asked to bestow a blessing or give an oracle as the deity. Here lies the key to the mediating function of priesthood; when the individual identifies totally with the deity, the personality becomes transparent, the deity is made real.

The role of the priesthood in all probability begins to emerge as a recognisable function, even if it was shared by a number of people. The establishment of temples, shrines and a variety of ritual objects points to more specialised keepers of both sites and sacred items. Perhaps shrines were looked after by a series of people on a regular basis. These attendants might have taken care of votive offerings, lit lamps, cleared away old offerings, regulated sacrifice. Perhaps they sat quietly seeking inspiration from the deity. Votive offerings, copious ritual equipment and the tiny models of domestic furniture indicate that it was possible to enter into a personal relationship with the Goddess. We cannot really know what was in the minds of these distant peoples as they met and worshipped her.

The mythology of agricultural peoples is quite different to that of hunting and gathering communities. The classic myth of cultivators involves the death and dismemberment of the divinity;

plants multiply when they are broken into pieces and placed in the earth. The creation of regular seasonal festivals enabled the participants to experience the cyclic renewal of life. The world is renewed each year. The year itself is born. The Paleolithic lunar count evolved into the Neolithic calendar. 'The central theme in the re-enactment of myths obviously was the celebration of the birth of the infant.'[23] The newborn spirit of the vegetation appeared in a variety of guises. The year-child was all things bright, fresh and young. The new cycle, the new crops and the child of the mother came together in spring celebration. For the first time, however, representations of the phallus and iphthyphallic male figures appeared. This awareness of the male as impregnator began to modify the role of the Great Mother. Belief in parthenogenesis gave way to an understanding of sexual union, represented and enacted in the sacred marriage, a ritualised act in which the pair, impersonating the deities, undertook cosmic impregnation on behalf of the whole group. A statuette from the East Balkan Chalcolthic Gumelnita complex from the fifth millennium BC shows a male and female figure side by side almost conjoined like lovers.

The sacred marriage represents a move away from the concept of the female creatrix who gives birth of herself. The male principle makes an appearance as the consort, the fertilising one who like the vegetation will last only for the season. The Mother Goddess is undying, her consort is ever-dying. The fruit of their union is mythologised in some tales as the newly-discovered cereal crop. Mother Earth has united with the god of the sky or the atmosphere. The archetypal sacred marriage was depicted in myth. It was undoubtedly enacted in reality.

The great age of the Great Mother passed as Neolithic cultures gave way to dynastic empires and the rise of the city state. The Great Mother did not die but was succeeded by her daughters, individualised manifestations of her many powers, the Goddesses Inanna, Isis, Hathor and many others. The role of the priestess emerged.

Chapter 3

MESOPOTAMIA – THE BETROTHED

I say 'Hail'! to the Holy One who appears in the heavens!
I say 'Hail'! to the Holy Priestess of Heaven!
I say 'Hail'! to Inanna, Great Lady of Heaven!
Holy Torch! You fill the sky with light!
You brighten the day at dawn.
I say 'Hail'! to Inanna, Great Lady of Heaven!
Awesome Lady of the Annuna Gods! Crowned with great horns,
You fill the heavens and earth with light.
I say 'Hail'! to Inanna, First Daughter of the Moon.
Mighty, majestic, and radiant,
You shine brilliantly in the evening,
You brighten the day at dawn,
You stand in the heavens like the sun and the moon,
Your wonders are known both above and below,
To the greatness of the holy priestess of heaven,
To you, Inanna, I sing!

HYMN TO INANNA

THE FIRST PRIESTHOOD

Neolithic life passed away only slowly, generation after
generation. Change was inevitable. The technology of metals
appeared, specialisation and hierarchy grew. A new social order
emerged. The supremacy of the Great Mother was diminished.
Gods and goddesses spawned like greedy offspring, each claiming
a portion of inheritance. The rise of the city state brought a new

set of values. Matrifocal, matrilinear social organisation was over, superseded by patriarchy, defended cities, the clash of iron and the force of arms. The Great Goddess was ousted by many deities both male and female, each presiding over a separate domain. Specialisation appeared in daily life. A formal priesthood appeared. For the first time we know the names of individual priestesses. We know something of their lives, duties and functions.

In the post-Neolithic culture of Mesopotamia, priesthood became a highly-structured and hierarchical body of administrators and cult officials based in a permanent home, the temple. Its functions and duties were defined and encoded.

Within this priesthood women exercised a formal role. Nevertheless, understanding the role played by women may not be straightforward. It is difficult to enter the mindset of a civilisation long dead. We need to ask many questions. To whom did these women minister, on what occasions, and in what manner? What was the nature of the relationship between the priesthood and the political-religious structure? Who were the women who acted as priestesses? What was the functioning relationship between the priesthood and the deities they served? What was the meaning attributed to their function? We must be prepared to let the civilisation speak for itself. We need to constantly remind ourselves that Mesopotamian cviivilisation, through its successive phases, Sumerian, Akkadian and Babylonian, stretched over some four millennia. Social and religious change was gradual, evolutionary and organic. It adapted in response to intrinsic factors possibly closed to us. We remain outsiders attempting to glimpse the workings of the collective Mesopotamian psyche. We should not forget that.

The Sumerian civilisation was rooted in the land now known as Iraq, lying between modern Baghdad and the Persian Gulf. The area was settled by a series of peoples. The Ubadians arrived in the fifth millennium and established the village settlements which in time became Ur, Eridu, Abad, Isin, Larsa, Uruk, Nippur and Kish. The Sumerian people arrived in Abad in the second half of the fourth millennium. Their arrival led to a cultural and ethnic fusion which became a major creative force in history. Here were the first walled cities, the first written language, the first kings and the first formalised priesthood. A great deal had changed since the agricultural economies of the High Neolithic. Society was now highly structured, organised and hierarchical. Religious life too was also highly structured with official positions, functionaries and state ceremonials. Cultural life flowed from the temple which housed the deity, no longer the Great Mother Goddess but a pantheon of many deities both male and female.

Mesopotamian religion was filled with a great assembly of gods, each representing different aspects of the natural world. These deities were often envisaged in polarised relationships. The first member of the ruling triad was An, the sky god (from the Akkadian 'Anum'). According to one tradition, he was polarised with a goddess also called An (from the Akkadian 'Antum'), who personified the rains flowing from her udder, the clouds. An was also polarised with Ki, the earth, and with Nammu, the power of the riverbed to produce water. Later, as Inanna's star rose in the pantheon she was partnered with An, eclipsing the earlier goddesses.

Next in importance we find the god Enlil or Nunamnir, Lord of the Wind, most especially the moist productive winds of spring. He was polarised with Ninlil or Sud the grain goddess. Their son was Ninurta or Ningirsu, god of the plough and of spring thunderstorms. The third member of the ruling triad was Ninhursaga. She has many names – Ninmenna, Ninmah, August Lady, Dingirmah, Aruru, Germ-loosener, or Nintur. She originally represented the numinous power of the stony soil, the foothills of nearby mountains. She was called, 'Lady of the Foothills' and 'Lady of the Stony Ground'. She was also the mother of the living creatures of the foothills. She was most often called Nintur, 'Lady Birth hut', 'Lady of Form Giving' and 'The Lady of the Womb'. Nintur was also called the midwife of the country and 'Lady of the Embryo'. In one tradition she was polarised with Shulpae, King of the Wild Beasts. In another tradition she was polarised with Enlil. As Ninhursaga she suckled kings with her pure milk. Enki was included late in the ruling group, enlarging it to four members. His domain was the numinous power in the sweet waters of rivers, marshes or rain. The firstborn son of Enlil was Nanna, or Suen, the moon god. Nanna's children were Utu, god of the sun, the foe of darkness and thereby of injustice; Ishkur, god of rain, and Inanna, the personification of the storehouse. This complex genealogy of generations and powers provided the background to Mesopotamian religious life and the life of its temple personnel.

These gods and goddesses represented the individualised powers of nature as experienced by the Mesopotamians. The waters, winds, storms and stones and were imbued with divine status and envisaged with a specific gender. Male gods had by now supplanted the Great Mother. The sky god had taken precedence over the earth mother. This process can only have been gradual, reflecting changing social circumstances and power structures within the post-Neolithic period. The discovery of meteoric iron by the Sumerians may also have contributed to a shift in ideas. Meteoric iron fell from the sky. It was called 'sky fire', *An Bar*. This type of iron was scarce, its use remained principally ritual. The discovery of 'sky fire', however, presented a philosophical quandary. These magical stones were not of the earth, they were known to fall from the sky. As earth and sky were opposite in every respect, the 'star metal' was clearly a gift not of the goddess but of the god. It is highly significant that the Sumerian word for water and semen are the same, no wonder then that An the sky god was also called the Fecund Breed Bull. The bellowing of the regular spring thunderstorms and the warm rain were visible signs of the fecundating activity of the sky god himself.

It is against this philosophical and religious background that we must set the development of Sumer. By the third millennium, Sumer consisted of a dozen or so walled cities surrounded by villages and hamlets. The previous millennium had been mainly peaceful but the third millennium was marked by banditry and raids. Disorder was the order of the day. The walled city was a defensive response to an offensive situation. Robert M. Adams showed that the network of open villages which had characterised central Sumer in the early dynastic period disappeared as villages amalgamated into larger cities for security.[1] Contemporary Sumerian literature also reflected the fear of enslavement by an enemy.

Each city had its own patron deity. The outstanding feature of each city was the temple, the ziggurat, the stepped mountain. It was the tallest building of the district. Inside the temple precincts lived its many servants, both male and female. The Sumerian and Akkadian word for temple denotes a house with all the emotional closeness of a home and owner. The priesthood, like the staff of any great house, served the owner faithfully, catering for every need.

The Sumerian priesthood is best compared to a civil service of administrators, officials and cult personnel. The highest spiritual position was held by the *en*-priestholder. This prefix was used by servants of either sex. Some individuals now proven to be priestesses were for a long time mistakenly believed to be priests. The *sanga* was the temple's administrative head. He was in charge of agriculture, industrial works and the temple accounts. The *guda* priests looked after the gods in the manner of personal servants. The *ishib* priest was in charge of drink offerings, the *gala* priests were singers and poets. There were different classes of priestesses, mainly hierodules who were dedicated to the god. As a significant cult activity, sacred prostitution was regulated through law which created prohibitions and freedoms for quite different classes of hierodule. The *qadistu*, 'a woman whose womb is taboo', was described by the term *nu gig*. The term *nu* translates as 'sexual organs' and *gig* translates as 'taboo', an apparent contradiction in terms. However, it refers to the fact that certain classes of hierodule were forbidden to have children. The Sumerian counterpart of this term signifies 'the interdicted womb'. In other words the *quadistu* might not bear children even though marriage was permissible.

Hierodules dedicated to gods were generally forbidden to have children. Ishtar herself was called, 'the hierodule of the great gods', *Istar qa dis ti ilani rabuti* and also the, 'hierodule of An', *nu gig an na*. She was herself childless. The term hierodule was a high title, possibly the throne name of the queen-consort of Mesannepadda.[2] Perversely enough it seems that the hierodules of Ishtar, the *Istaritu* could, however, have children. The *naditu*, whose sign denoted an unsown field, 'who let their womb live in wisdom', were also theoretically forbidden to bear children.

However, we also know that some *naditu* women did have children. Another class of hierodule, the *kulmasitu*, 'pure of semen', were described by the sign *nu bar*. The term *bar* is equivalent to the term *mas*, meaning 'ritually pure'. These hierodules probably practised *coitus interruptus*. The class of hierodules called *ugbabtum* were also known as *assinatum*, that is the female equivalent of *assinnu*, the male class of sodomite priests. The term *nin-dingir*, 'the lady who is a deity', was sometimes used for a chief priestess but mostly for priestesses of the *ugbabtum* class. The omen literature is clearly unfavourable in the event of a *nin-dingir* priestess conceiving. Intercourse with a priestess of one's own god was forbidden.

The collection of laws which proscribed the activities, rights and penalties for different class of sacred hierodule probably evolved from the mythological story of Atrahasis. In an Akkadian myth, a flood was released against a noisy humanity. The gods were horrified at the destruction so wrought. Enki and Nintur conferred to find a solution to the noise problem. Their deliberations created a scheme for birth control, introduced a type of barren woman and established several categories of priestesses forbidden to have children. This story seems to reflect a fear of overpopulation which may have been genuinely felt. Myth became reality as regulations and bizarre justification divided sexuality from reproduction.

The term *en* was used in both a political and religious context. In Uruk it was used as the ruler's title. The word was also found in many divine names such as Enki and Enlil. It was also used as a prefix in the names of those who served the gods such as Enheduanna. Rulership was seen as being essentially divine, embodied in the deities, followed by the physical ruler, upheld and interpreted by the servants of the gods.

Temple life was regulated and formal, its purpose was to serve the gods in every respect. The deity was believed to inhabit the temple, immanent within the cult statue. Cult statues were dressed and fed, bathed and escorted to bed. Four meals were offered daily, laid out in a precise manner according to instruction. The interchange was reciprocal, the deity was served by the people, the people were served by the deity. Prayers and petitions accompanied by offerings were placed before the deity for consideration. We have a clear presentation of the function and duties of the Sumerian priesthood. We have a great deal of literary and archaeological evidence from a variety of Mesopotamian sources including tablets, cuneiform cylinders, hymns, prayers, temple sites, excavations and artefacts.

A surviving text preserved from the Seleucid period from Erech outlines the rites of the prerogative of Anu, the divine office of Bit-resh, Esh-gal, E-Aanna and the temples of Tiranna, the ceremonies of kingship, and 'the proceedings of the enchanters, the conjurers, the singers and the craftsmen all who are in the company of the foremen, not counting all that pertains to the students of divination.' Unfortunately for us, only the directions for the daily meals of the god are preserved. The gods took four meals a day, called the great and the little meals of the morning and the evening. There were also special food offerings at particular times. The regulations were most precise. The table of Anu was set with eighteen cups. Seven were laid to his right with two kinds of beer, seven were laid to his left with a variety of beverages and four cups were laid in front containing wine. All aspects of religious practice were formulated and regulated in just as precise a manner.

We cannot understand the functions of feminine priesthood without reference to the way in which the state viewed itself.

SUMERIAN KINGSHIP

The impact of the new ruler concept on contemporary thought can hardly be overestimated.

THORKILD JACOBSEN, *Treasury of Darkness*

If we are looking for the roots of patriarchy, we will find them here between Neolithic agrarian economies and the emergence of the city state. Kingship, not queenship, emerged as the dominant political and religious model. The king became the head of the country, either divine or divinely appointed. This should not come as a surprise when force of arms could win or defend the day. Sumerian kingship began as a temporary office laid down when the need diminished. During the third millennium the emergency was long standing. Kingship simply became permanent.

The concept of kingship developed considerably through Sumerian use, moving from the early idea of governorship denoted by the term *ensi*, to kingship, the *lugal*, 'big man'. The idea of dominion was extended successively with new kings. The title, 'The King of the Land' was used first by Lugalzaggesi. His successor, the Akkadian Sargon, expressed his kingship in a new title, King of the Four Quarters.

Each aggrandisement needed to be justified by the gods. For the Sumerians all state decisions and choices had to take place with the consent of the gods. The royal office holder had to be seen as the blessed servant of the deities, to be acting in accordance with the will of the gods.

Kingship, still newly hatched, began to develop a complex philosophy, expressed through rites and ceremonials. The king had to be seen to be justified in the eyes of the gods and the people. The thoroughly masculine institution of kingship evolved some complex and subtle relationships with the Feminine represented by mother goddesses and their representatives, daughter-priestesses. The king stood in a particular relationship to divinity, often perceived as a divine son, divinity incarnate or an appointee of the gods. If divine authority and power was vested in the gods, the king had to be seen to be empowered by the gods themselves. The king ever needed to legitimate his authority and position. He sought this through the Sumerian birth goddesses. The crowning achievement of the birth goddesses was represented as the birth of kings. Theology and political power became inextricably linked.

> *Giving birth to kings, giving birth to lords*
> *is verily in her hand.* [3]

In another hymn to Ninhursaga, the birth mother we find:

> *to give birth to kings, to tie on the rightful tiara,*
> *to give birth to lords, to place the crown*
> *on (their) heads, is in her hands.* [4]

The same is said about a related figure, Ninmug, 'Lady of Vulva', in *Enki and the World Order*. In a passage concerning the origin of mankind in 'Creation of the Hoe', Ninhursaga is called 'the lady giving birth to lords, giving birth to kings'.[5] She is called Ninmenna, 'Lady of the Diadem'. According to an Old Babylonian investiture ritual from Uruk, The Lady of the Diadem was empowered to place a golden crown firmly on the head of the 'lord'. We may speculate that her part would have been taken by one with the authority of the birth goddess invested in her: a priestess. An inscription tells us that Rimsin 11 was invested by the goddess Nintur, also called Ninhursaga of the city of Kesh and by her local name Ninmah, which means 'August Lady'.

The most powerful man of the kingdom was openly empowered by the Feminine. Nintur, however, did not develop a political function while An obviously did. Tensions and power struggles in society were mirrored by battles among the gods themselves. Eventually it was the sky god An who ritually proclaimed the king chosen by the assembly and conferred the insignia of kinship upon him. It was the Akkadian king Sargon who introduced a new element into this political-religious synthesis by installing his daughter Enheduanna as High Priestess of the moon god in the temple of Ur and possibly as High Priestess of An at Uruk. This combination of royal and priestly roles set a precedent. It was a pattern which was to last for several centuries.

The installation of Enheduanna was doubtless politically inspired. As a military conqueror Sargon needed to consolidate his position. He needed the approval and acceptance of the gods. As a sign of good faith and in the hope of gaining the favour of the gods, he gave his daughter as the bride of the God Nanna at Ur and his 'sister' to the god An at Uruk. It is unclear if the sister referred to textually is in fact a separate person or Enheduanna herself by another title.

Sargon's background is obscure. He came from Kish. His origins were humble. By tradition it was said that Sargon in the guise of a gardener had won the love of Ishtar. His father, whose name is unknown, is also termed a gardener, an epithet applied to a king or his substitute taking part in the sacred marriage. His mother, according to tradition, was a Sumerian priestess. This is a fascinating enigma. Could Sargon have been the offspring of a sacred marriage? If this was indeed the case his claim to kingship would have been unusual yet insistent. It was a military victory over Lugalzaggesi which brought dominion over Ur and Uruk. Sargon, however, turned military victory into the foundation of a dynasty. He could claim Ishtar as his mother and justifier. His own daughter would have particular reasons for identifying with and exalting Inanna, as she certainly continued to do throughout her life.

The Sumerian Inanna, the Akkadian Ishtar, could be seen as the guiding deity of the family line. The rise to power of her father could be viewed as the will of Ishtar-Inanna herself. The rise of the family to prominence would have been the opportunity, divinely bestowed, to exalt the name of this goddess before the people, to raise her status in the pantheon of deities. When Sargon defeated a rebellion late in his reign, the rebels were forced to accept and acknowledge Ishtar. As Sargon rose to prominence, Inanna's star also rose. It was during the patronage enjoyed by Sargon and Enheduanna that Inanna was exalted to an equal rank with An. Enheduanna wrote the following:

> *You are the senior queen of the heavenly foundations and zenith.*
> *The Anunna have submitted to you.*
> *From birth on you were the 'junior' queen.*
> *How supreme you are over the great gods, the Anuanna.* [6]

Enheduanna's career as High Priestess reveals a complex mix of political aspirations and cultic obligations. We glimpse her performing rites and arising from the couch of dream divination. Yet political power is an ever-present theme in her life. When her father died she was banished. We also see a new element in the evolution of Sumerian kingship at work through the office of the High Priestess.

Sargon's practical establishment of the Sumerian-Akkadian empire and Enheduanna's theological exaltation of Inanna brought about what has been called the 'dynasty of Ishtar'. Inanna-Ishtar became the wife of An, supplanting Ki. The city of Uruk became th *ki-nin*, the queen place. Enheduanna became *muru*, 'the female-in-law of An'. Sargon took the title *pa-ses-an-na*, 'older brother-in-law of An', or simply, 'male in law of An'.[7] We also find the Middle Babylonian king Adad-apal-iddina called 'father-in-law of Nanna', when his daughter was priestess and bride of the moon god at Ur. These dynastic families intermarried with the gods, an astounding piece of political and religious thinking. The marriage and newly-created kinship ties between the royal daughter and the gods of principal city states created a familial pattern across the human-divine divide and served to legitimate the king and his heirs.

Kings followed the pattern established by Sargon for some five centuries. The king's daughter became the reigning High Priestess and wife of the god. This is the extraordinary foundation which supported the cradle of civilisation. Kings were the in-laws of the gods, royal daughters became the wife of a god. Kings became gods by marrying into the family of the gods.

ENHEDUANNA

In the person of Enheduanna, we are confronted by a woman who was at once a princess, priestess, poetess, a personality who set standards in all three of her roles for many succeding centuries, and whose merits were recognised in singularly Mesopotamian fashion, long after.

W.W. HALLO AND J.J.A. VAN DIJK, *The Exaltation of Inanna*

We know Enheduanna by this her formal name. This is not a personal name but her official title. The name Enheduanna is probably constructed from the priestly title *en* combined with *Heduanna*, a manifestation of the moon god Sin. Her name may also be an epithet of Dumuzi, as were the titles Ennungalanna and Ensipazianna. These names bear a remarkable similarity to the names taken by two later priestesses, Enmegalana and Ennirziana. Enanedu, the last of the dynastic priestesses in all probability, means 'priest(ess whom) An has adorned.'[8]

The title taken by the moon priestess at Ur was constructed upon the root *en* denoting rulership, followed by additional signs, and completed by the name of the moon god Nanna in some form, giving the formula En(d)Nanna.[9] Different cities used different

Figure 3 The face of a Mesopotamian priestess looks across the centuries at us.

titles. The High Priestess combined both political and spiritual power. In her dual capacity she was regarded as wife of the god, possibly given in symbolic marriage. Enheduanna was herself married to the moon god Nanna. The title *nu-ge-gal* probably means wife of the principal god of the city. We know of the use of this title, though we are not able to show its connection specifically to the moon cult. Enmenanna, who was successor to Enheduanna, styled herself 'spouse of Nanna, High Priestess of Suen'.

The laws of Hammurabi established a severe punishment if a man should spread false and slanderous rumours about a man's wife or a *nin-dingir*, 'the lady who is a deity'. In other words it was punishable to slander either the personal wife of another or the wife of the god.

As symbolic wife of the god, the priestess would have identified herself with the goddess, as Enheduanna did so forcefully.

Enheduanna herself was clearly identified with Inanna and also with Ningal, the mother of Inanna who was married to Nanna the moon god. These priestesses were not without power. Gadd writes, 'so important and sacred was the dignity of these priestesses at Ur that they were often able to retain office undisturbed by dynastic changes in the civil government of the city.'[10] High Priestesses were frequently long serving. Enheduanna was intelligent, gifted and politically astute. She also has the honour of being the earliest recorded poet in history. The importance she gained during her life was matched after death when she underwent apotheosis. Her name is found in a long succession of epithets of deities in a long hymn to Dumuzi. She was in effect counted among the deities. Her picture is preserved on a limestone disc excavated from Ur. She wears the tiara appropriate to her office and a flounced robe. She is shown in the company of other women, probably priestesses, making an offering. After the death of her father she was temporarily removed from power through the revolt against her nephew Naram-Sin. The removal of a High Priestess from office was unusual. Enheduanna, however, was especially vocal and may have made herself unpopular with enemies of her father. She wrote of this injustice:

> *I cannot appease Ashimbabbar.*
> *Lugalanne has altered the lustrations of An and all his other rites.*
> *He has stripped An of his temple Eanna.*
> *He has not stood in awe of An-Lugal.*
> *That sanctuary whose attractions are irresistible, whose beauty is*
> *   endless,*
> *That sanctuary he has verily brought to destruction.*
> *Having entered before you as a partner, he has even approached his*
> *   sister-in-law.* [11]

Enheduanna clearly depicts 'Lugalanne' as defiler of the sacred. The name Lugalanne was not the personal name of any particular King: Enheduanna was probably being cautious. It is possible, however, that the person referred to as 'Lugalanne' offered an illicit sexual advance to Enheduanna herself, a heinous crime in view of their cultic relationship. The verb used here is elsewhere used in connection with adultery. The term *muru*, often translated as sister-in-law, more accurately means female-in-law. Lugalanne as *en* of Uruk would have been the *dam-inanna*, that is bridegroom of Inanna. Enheduanna as *en* of Ur was *dam-nanna*, bride of Nanna. Since Inanna was the daughter of Nanna, Lugalanne would have stood in a cultic relationship to Enheduanna. She cursed Uruk, calling it 'a malevolent rebel against your Nanna – may An make it surrender'.

Enheduanna's poetry combined theology with the political events taking place around her. Her own story was intertwined with that of Inanna. Enheduanna's poems praise Inanna: 'you alone are exalted'. We again find reference to the relationship between the deities which would have been mirrored in that of the cult representatives. She calls Inanna 'beloved of An', 'hierodule of An', and 'beloved bride of Ushumgalanna'.

Let us now let Enheduanna herself speak to us across the thousands of years.

THE BANISHMENT FROM UR

Verily I had entered my holy giparu at your behest,
I, the high priestess, I Enheduanna!
I carried the ritual basket, I intoned the acclaim.
(But now) I am placed in the leper's ward, I even I, can no longer
*   live with you!*
They approach the light of day, the light is obscured about me,
The shadows approach the light of day,
It is covered with a sandstorm.
My mellifluous mouth is cast into confusion.
My choicest features are turned to dust.

INVOCATION OF INANNA

You of the appropriate me's,* great queen of queens,
Issued from the holy womb, supreme over the mother who bore you,

---

* me = divine essences

Omniscient sage, lady of all the lands,
Sustenance of the multitudes, I have verily recited your sacred song!
True goddess, fit for the me's, it is exalting to acclaim you.
Merciful one, brilliantly righteous woman, I have verily recited
  your me's for you!

INANNA AND THE ME'S

Lady of all the me's, resplendent light,
Righteous woman clothed in radiance, beloved of Heaven and Earth,
Hierodule of An, you of all the great ornaments.
Enamoured of appropriate tiara, suitable for the high priesthood,
Whose hand has attained all the 'seven' me's.
Oh my lady, you are the guardian of all the great me's!
You have picked up the me's, you have hung the me's on your hand,
You have gathered up the me's, you have clasped the me's tightly to
  your breast.

We find some reference to Enheduanna's cultic duties in the poems:
  Lines 66–67

Verily I had entered my holy gipaur at your behest,
I, the high priestess, I Enheduanna.
I carried the ritual basket, I intoned the acclaim.

This refers to the bringing of grain and other offerings recorded for Bau and other deities. It is possibly related to the sacred marriage.
  Lines 118–19

My hands are no longer folded on the ritual couch,
I may no longer reveal the pronouncements of Ningal to man.

Line 136

One has heaped up the coals in the censer, prepared the lustration.

The precedent established by Sargon continued with a line of dynastic priestesses. The High Priestesses who followed Enheduanna held individual office for remarkably long periods of time. Ennirsiana held office for a mere 19 years compared with Enanatuma who probably held office for some 47 years. It was common for a single High Priestess to remain in power through the reign of one or more kings, riding out any political storms. We have some information about these women, though some confusion still remains in certain areas. It has been suggested that there were two priestesses with the same name, Enanatuma I and II who between them covered an otherwise extremely long period of office, although this may still have been held by one person.

Ensakiajanna was elevated to priesthood at about 15 years of age. Her installation took place in year 23 of Simuilium's reign. This event was important enough to be chosen as the name of the following year. She held office for 43 years. Her father's reign was followed by Nur Adad who ruled for 16 years, Sin Iddinnam who ruled for 6 years, Sin Eribam who held office for only 2 years, Sin Iquisam who was king for 5 years and finally Silli Adad. It was not until the fifth year of Warad Sin that a new priestess was appointed. Ensakiajanna was still alive and joined Enanedu in making an offering. Enanedu was the last of these dynastic priestesses. She undertook considerable reconstruction at her temple. We have a record of her work inscribed in cuneiform on two columns on the base of a cone now in the British Museum. The inscription reads, starting at line 28:

> *En-an-e-du*
> *the priest(ess) truly called by that exalted name*
> *child of Kudur-Mabag, I*
> *the pure ge-par on its old foundation I laid its brick true and firm*
> *I made its wall exact to the touch of a finger*
> *that house I created anew.*
> *at the time the space Ses-ban-an-Du, the clear ground, the portion*
>   *for the ancient priestesses*
> *its place a wall did not border: its thorn its bushes I felled*
> *a watch had not been set, its place had not been cleansed*
> *but I, in my wise understanding sought the place of portion, the*

clear (ground) at the back
beyond the lying-places of the ancient priestesses
I made a wide space
in its place (where it was) fallen I heaped up a great (protective wall)
a strong watch I set, that place I cleansed
in order to proclaim the name given to my priesthood I put the structure into place
inscribed full many foundation records of my priesthood
I laid them in . . . . . .
(of) that wall I called its name 'He that respects me . . . shall be praised. [12]

This cone was discovered for the first time by king Nabonidus. During his reign there was an obscuration of the moon, reason enough to consult the oracle. The state books recorded that the moon god desired an *enitu*. Here is another indication of the relationship between the god and the priestess. At first Nabonidus suggested that a daughter of the royal clan should be appointed. The oracle refused this suggestion. His own daughter was put forward and accepted. The text states, 'I paid attention to the decree of her great lord Sin, my god who engendered me, and to the utterance of Shamash and Adad, and I raised my daughter, my own offspring, to the enu-priesthood.' She was ceremonially raised to the priesthood in a sacral area which first had to be cleared. It was during this clearance that two stela were found. One stele showed a priestess in ritual ornaments and dress, the second recorded the building contribution of a predecessor, namely Enanedu. This would have been regarded as a most favourable omen and a vindication of the oracle. Nabonidus even incorporated a little Sumerian phraseology to gain historical and religious credence. Following her example he instituted a rebuilding programme.

The concept of sacred woman as betrothed of the god took another form under the Babylonians who developed a unique institution, the *naditu* women. *Naditu* means, 'fallow'. This institution may also have evolved as a response to the myth of Atrahasis which laid down several categories of barren priestesses.

The *naditu* women lived celibate cloistered lives in the service of the sun god Samas in Sippar, northern Babylonia, and in the service of Marduk and Ninurta in Nippur. This institution is recorded from 1880–1550 BC. It had special links with the rulers of the first Babylonian dynasty, its heyday being under Hammurabi and his son Samsuiluna. The earliest record of the cloister can be traced back to Immerum, one of the three local rulers of Sippar in the early nineteenth century BC.

Possibly only those in Sippar lived in a closed community. *Naditus* of Marduk could marry but were not allowed to bear children. These *naditu* women were permitted to arrange a second wife to act as child-bearer for the husband and servant for herself. This arrangement was so curious that it can only reflect what was felt to be divine sanction.

The *naditu* were called *kallatum*, a term which referred to a young girl living with and provided for by her father-in-law. It means betrothed. Virginity is implicit in this status. The goddess Aja was also called *kallatum*. The *naditu* was probably seen as the betrothed of Samas and the daughter-in-law to his father the moon god Sin. The position held by the *naditu* was probably symbolised as the betrothed virgin of the god. There is little evidence to suggest that these women were temple hierodules. The *naditu* lived in the *gagum*, the locked house. They were well supported with female domestic staff of cooks, weavers and millers, a granary and purely administrative staff, probably male. During the reign of Sin Muballit between one hundred and two hundred *naditu* lived within the cloister at a time. The cloister as a whole was under the jurisdiction of the temple.

This institution drew wealthy and even royal candidates. Three princesses became *naditu*: Ajalatum, daughter of Sumulael; Iltani, a daughter of Sin-Muballit, and a second Iltani, daughter of Simsuiluna or Abi-esh.

The *naditu* women were required to be in constant attendance upon Samas and Aja, in their temple adjacent to the cloister. It would have been customary to offer food before the cult statue and to attend to its dress. Offerings were made twice daily. The *piqittum* was a special offering of meat and beer made on the 20th of each month. Apart from this festival there were probably six other festivals of which we know very little. All offerings were supplied from individual estates.

Entry into the cloister was decided at birth. Often it fell to the oldest daughter to be, 'raised to the gods'. Such a decision was reflected in the birth name, Amat-Samas, 'the servant girl of Samas', or Eristis- Aja, 'Aja's desire'. Formal entry into the cloister finally took place through a ceremony of initiation when the girls were about fifteen. This took place once a year, on the first days of the tenth month *Tebet*, December–January. It was not unlike a marriage settlement in form. The cloisters incurred the expense of the initiation, paying for a betrothal gift of food, drink and silver items. The girl received a dowry. One list mentions 9 slave girls, 24 garments, 42 headdresses and a shroud. Other items include furniture, jewellery, crockery, weaving equipment, cows and sheep. The candidate was also given 'ring money' over which she had full rights. During the ceremony, the thread of Samas was placed in the young girl's hand. In a letter, a young woman referred to her first entry when she saw the face of her lady, an indication that she was led into the presence of the goddess Aja, probably a cult statue. When the youngest Iltani was initiated she was sprinkled with holy water. This was probably only performed for the high-ranking *naditus*. Economic transactions between the head of the family and the cloisters also took place.

The *naditu* women were given considerable economic freedom, engaging in trade and commerce. They conducted business in silver and barley. They leased fields, houses, orchards, barns and shops. A particular *naditu* traded in tin, another employed over one hundred workers. The law 178–180 stated that her share of the paternal estate could either be managed by her brother, or she could bequeath it to who she liked. If she received no share, she would share equally at her father's death with her brothers.

These women, betrothed of Samas, lived much like nuns, apart from their economic activity which was without doubt extensive. But we should not forget that the daily offerings for the god were financed from the personal estate of the individual. These women were wealthy as a group, their wealth served the god just as they did. This unique combination of spiritual status and economic activity remains unusual. We still do not have a full account of the functions and duties of these women. It is certain that they served the god as betrothed in the same capacity as that symbolised by the presence of the goddess Aja. These women were married to the god, their celibacy in theory was lifelong, their seclusion within the locked house was total.

In Mesopotamia we find an astonishing range of sacred functions. The priestess played the part of temple hierodule, chaste wife and empowerer. Royal daughters served this institution by marrying into the family of the gods and becoming celibate and faithful wives. At the sacred marriage, the priestess as goddess empowered the king. Wherever we look, we find paradox.

GLOSSARY

Dam-inanna, the spouse of Inanna
Dam-nanna, the spouse of Nana
En, a term denoting rulership
Ensi, a term denoting governorship
Enitu, a concubine of the god
Ishib priest, priest in charge of drink offerings
Gagum, the locked house where the naditu lived
Gala priest, singers and poets
Guda priest, personal servant to the gods
Kallatum, betrothed
Ki-ni, the queen place, the name given to Uruk
Muru, the female-in-law
Naditu, celibate women dedicated in the service of the god
Nin-dingir, 'the lady who is a deity', title of a class of priestess
Nu-gig, a class of hierodule
Pa-ses-ana-an, male-in-law of An
Piqittum, the offering meal made by naditu
Qadistu, a class of hierodule
Sanga, the administrative head of a Sumerian temple
Ugbabtum, a class of hierodule

Chapter 4

EGYPT – THE EPIPHANY

Egypt is the very home of the goddess: for all that exists and is
produced in the world is in Egypt.

HERODAS

NETER AND HM NETER

Egyptian gods were generally described by the term *neter*. This is
difficult to translate: it implies a renewing power. Goddesses were
described by the term *netert*. The ordinary class of the priesthood
were called *hm neter*, servants of the gods.

The role of women in the spiritual life of Egypt has generally
been underestimated by scholars. This is in part due to Herodotus
who stated that, 'no woman exercises the priestly office either for
a god or a goddess, but men in all cases'.[1] Herodotus, however,
has been called the Father of Lies. In fact, women played an
integral part in the spiritual life of Egypt.

In order to understand what this meant we have to examine the
complex relationship between the temple, the priesthood, the
deities and the pharaoh. The priesthood tended the deites, the
deities upheld the pharaoh, the pharaoh served the people. There
was but one pharaoh, many deities, a large number of temples and
numerous cult personnel.

Egyptian political and spiritual life was unified, a single
manifestation of divine kingship. The pharaoh was both head of
the state and its high priest. He was divine, the son of Re, the
living Horus.

As we attempt to unravel the complex and at times contradictory Egyptian religious practices, we need to remember that we are dealing with an immensely long-lived civilisation. Its thirty dynasties conceal a rich history, change and permanence, stability and upheaval. Its religious life, ever complex and subtle, cannot be separated from the political foundation. Our knowledge of this civilisation remains incomplete despite temples, tombs and treasures. We may have discovered architecture and artefacts, but what still eludes us is the Egyptian mind. We are attempting to piece together a jig-saw of the living past, although we do not have all the pieces. The mistake, as ever, is to assume that we may simply transfer our own values, beliefs and even hopes about women's roles onto this distant culture.

When we look at Egypt, perhaps the archetypal home of the priestess, we again find paradox and certainly mystery. Like the civilisations which preceded it, Egypt lived by its sacred stories. Its cult personnel enacted the sacred dramas in exactly the same manner as their Neolithic forebears, although the Egyptian story was quite different. It was precise, formulated, committed to text, no longer held in folk memory. The setting was more spectacular, sophisticated by comparison with cave sanctuaries and underground chambers. Now the stories were enacted upon the sacred lake, through the processional avenues and in the great halls. The principle was still the same however.

Women were never absent from religious life in Egypt. They were included in the active religious and ceremonial life of Egypt from the earliest times – there were priestesses of Neith in the Old Kingdom. She was called 'The Great Lady', 'The Mother Goddess', 'The Lady of Heaven' and 'Queen of the Gods'. Sadly we know very little of this cult and its organisation. The cult of Neith maintained close ties with the cult of Hathor, yet we know almost nothing of this long-lasting relationship. Priestesses sometimes served gods, although the reasons for this are unclear. An Old Kingdom queen was a priestess of Thoth, and there was also an Old Kingdom non-royal priestess of Ptah.[2] Musician-priestesses and funerary priestesses are mentioned from the Old Kingdom onwards. We find the cult title 'Wife of Min' from a tomb at Akhmim, probably dating from the Heracleopolitan period.[3]

Here are the main threads which together form the basis of the female priesthood of Egypt: sacred musician; funerary practitioner, and Wife to the God. In all of these roles the priestess was identified as an epiphany of a particular goddess.

As we explore the historical role of the Egyptian priestess, we need to put the much-fictionalised image to one side. The role of the priestess was laid down in the mythology. Cult acts, functions and rituals were determined and established by the nature of the individual goddess. As Isis and Nephthys mourned Osiris, mourning became a cult function given over to women. The tradition of the funerary priestess was modelled upon Isis, Nephthys and sometimes Hathor.

MIDWIVES TO THE DEAD

I raised my lament to high heaven, a wailing reached the residents
of the nether world.

PYRAMID TEXT

Isis and Nephthys provided the archetypal model for lamenting and mourning women. Funerary priestesses took on the mantle of Isis and Nephthys who mourned for the dead Osiris. In the Old, Middle and New Kingdoms, two female officiants impersonating Isis and Nephthys took part in the procession to the embalmers where they participated in certain ceremonies. On the day of burial they also took part in the procession to the tomb. Isis herself had an underworld aspect as Amentet, the hidden goddess. Ceremonial mourners were sometimes called, *drt*, kite. Isis and Nephthys were called the 'great kite' and the 'little kite'. In the *Book of the Dead*, Nephthys addressed the deceased, 'O daughter of Hathor, art made to triumph, thy head shall never be taken away from thee, and thou shalt be made to rise up in peace.'[4] At the annual re-enactment of the embalmment of Osiris, two priestesses, 'pure and with the hair of their head and bodies removed', impersonated the mourning Isis and Nephthys.

Women held posts of responsibility as funerary priestesses from the Old Kingdom onwards. The funerary tradition continued right down to the Ptolemaic period when female libationers

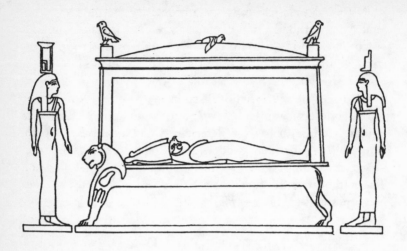

Figure 4 It was customary for two priestesses to impersonate Isis and Nephthys at the resurrection of Osiris.

played the role of the *ka* servants of the earlier times. They were responsible for the upkeep of tombs, the safety of mummies, and the ceremonies which it was believed were of importance to the dead. Female officiants could perform the funerary liturgy, a tradition which, in all probability, dated back to the earliest dynasties. Funerary priestesses received from tomb endowments just like male priests. Goddesses as givers of life were also the receivers of the dead. Hathor, in the form of a cow, gave new life to the deceased. 'She shall make thy legs to walk with ease in the Underworld in her name of Hathor, lady of Amentet.'[5]

The image of a goddess, often Nut, was inscribed on the coffin lid. The deceased was placed in the embrace of the goddess whose outstretched arms received the newly departed. The coffin was both womb and tomb.

Funerary office could be purchased. In the year 136 BC a certain Taesi made over to Shakhpere in return for a sum, 'the emoluments, the tombs of the persons which have fallen to me'.[6]

WIVES, MOTHERS AND HIGH PRIESTESSES

Egyptian priests and priestesses not merely exercised the functions
of divinities; they sometimes actually impersonated them.

BLACKMAN, *Priest and Priesthood, Egyptian*

The relationships defined in Egyptian myth set the pattern for
cultic practice. Accordingly, as Isis was the mother of Horus, the
queen took up the mantle as priestess of Isis, mother of the
pharaoh-to-be. As Hathor was the wife of Atum, her cult
representative was also wife of the god immanent in the pharaoh,
and mother of the god yet to incarnate. The highest cult
representative, the High Priestess, was identified with the wife or
mother of the god to whom the temple was dedicated. Her major
identification was as Hathor and in this capacity she made music
and danced and fulfilled cultic duties. Each office holder was
identified with the local divinity.

At Elephantine the High Priestess bore the title 'Satet', the wife
of Knum, the god of the locality. The High Priestess of Horus
of Edfu was called, 'She who is upon the Throne', *hryt nst*, a
reference to Hathor of Edfu. The High Priestess of Horus of
Hierakonopolis was called 'wife', *hbst*. The High Priestess of Horus
of Athribis in Lower Egypt was called 'Protectress', *hwyt*, which
was also the name of the local Hathor. The High Priestess of
Horus of the Letopolite Haroeris was called 'Mother of the God',
and was again identified with Hathor.[7]

At any one time there were many women throughout the
country holding the office of High Priestess. The office holder
was often the wife of the High Priest. Typically, Pepi-ank was
monarch of Cusae, and his wife was a musician-priestess of
Hathor bearing the title of High Priestess. The chief of the
concubines of Amun was often the wife of the High Priest,
occasionally a sister or daughter.

The High Priestess was appointed to office by the king. King
Aspalta appointed a member of the reigning family to be High
Priestess of Amun of Napata, as his predecessor King Analman
had also done.[8] Below the office of High Priestess, sacred
appointments were made by the local governor, purchased,
conveyed by deed, transferred or bequeathed.

The High Priestess was authorised to fulfil cult duties such as lustration, purification, the offering of sacrifice and libation. In this capacity she was empowered to be present in the most sacred inner shrines and attend the central cult rites. A relief from Luxor shows the High Priestess of Amun Re standing behind a male officiant. Her hands, like his, are raised in adoration as the deities are summoned. The Ethiopian queen mother Nnsrws and her daughter Hb both filled the office of High Priestess of Amun of Napata. They are each shown pouring out libation. The princess Nebttowi is shown consecrating an offering in the Valley of the Queens, an act normally performed by the king himself. The Decree of Canopus also directs musician-priestesses to present ears of corn to the deified image of Berenike, in itself a distinctly cultic act.

Priestesses were paid for their work. The prophetship of the daughter of Nekonkh who lived in the Fifth Dynasty, was endowed with five arouras of land as were the prophetships of ten out of her twelve brothers. She and her brothers were also given equal shares in the donations from the temple. Nitemhe, prophetess of Khons of Teuzoi received yearly, as did the rest of the prophets at that temple, a one hundredth part of the income derived from the temple endowments. There were also occasional fees of linen, oil, bread, ox flesh, goose, beer, lamps, herbs and milk which were offered to the deity first. The High Priestess of Amun of Napata received a daily allowance from the temple storehouse. This amounted to ten loaves of black bread, five loaves of white bread and a monthly allowance of fifteen jars of beer, a modest stipend, in fact. By contrast the stipend of the High Priestess of Amun in Saitic times was 3,300 arouras of land situated in seven nomes in Upper Egypt and four in Lower Egypt. She also received a daily quantity of bread from five sources. From the daily temple offering she was apportioned two khar of spelt (wheat), eleven hin of wine, cakes and bundles of vegetables. Additionally, she received three oxen, five geese and twenty jars of beer each month.[9] We learn from the Decree of Canopus that the wives of priests were granted a daily allowance of loaves called the Bread of Berenike. In addition, daughters of priests were, from birth, assigned rations from temple endowments.

THE BEAUTEOUS ONES

The priestesses of Hathor took on the essential cult role by taking on the mantle of Hathor herself.

MARIANNE GALVIN, THE PRIESTESSES OF HATHOR

Hathor was renowned for her beauty. It was written that she was called 'the beautiful, the lovely one who stands at the head of the "House of the Beautiful", the gods turn their heads away in order to see her better.'[10] Her priestesses were her living representatives.

The cult of Hathor reached popularity in Old Kingdom and peaked in the Sixth Dynasty. Queen Hatshepsut's identification with Hathor brought renewed cult prominence again in the New Kingdom. The cult was served almost entirely by women but also included priests in small numbers. They fulfilled a purificatory role and were possibly responsible for the daily toilet of the cult statue. Men held all the hereditary administrative posts as overseers and inspectors.

Hathor was possibly first thought of as a patroness of the falcon folk, perhaps a personified totem. She first appeared upon the pear-shaped palette of king Narmer, sacred to Horus. By the Fourth Dynasty she was considered a fully-fledged being with a complete cult of her own. She was worshipped at three main centres: Saqqara; Denderah, and Cusae.

The name Hathor is derived from *ht hr*, meaning 'the House of Horus'. Patricia Springborg is not alone in suggesting that this should be understood as the 'womb of Horus'.[11] As the womb of Horus, Hathor stands as mother to both Horus and his living counterpart, the pharaoh. A text states, 'inside her body; inside her a house of Horus is being prepared, hence her name is Hathor'.[12]

To unravel the mysteries enfolded in the being of Hathor we have to turn to Egypt's fascination for symbolism which both reveals and conceals. Hathor was depicted both in bovine and human form. The Hathor head itself, often appearing atop a column, was the personified uterus with its curling wig, like the 'curiously antennary uterus of the heifer'. Hathor was also depicted as a woman wearing a horned disk upon her head like her sister Isis. Her nature was clearly bovine, personifying fertility, nourishment and protection. She was also a guide to the land of the dead. Initially, she served only royalty. Later, she served the general population. The Hathors, her priestesses, extended these same benefits through cult acts. What was performed firstly for the pharaoh, through state ritual and ceremonial was eventually enacted symbolically on behalf of others.

The Hathor chapel at Deir el Bahri yielded a collection of both male and female sex organs in the form of baked clay figures. Statuettes of broad-hipped women, sometimes featured on a bed, were recovered from the Eighteenth-Dynasty shrine here. Hathor jars from the same period were excavated by Petrie from the temple of Min at Coptos, built by Thutmoses III. The group consisted of five vessels joined together at the front. Several jars had arms with hands holding the breasts. Here is Hathor as nurturer and stimulator of fertility. These jars were similar to the vessels from which milk was poured in the processions described by Plutarch and Apuleius.

Hathor was a patroness of fertility and sexual love as the following poem indicates. It is a hymn in which Hathor is invoked, praised and entreated for 'the gift of a sister'. The young man offers thanks for a 'sister', a lover.

> *I praise the golden Hathor, I worship her majesty,*
> *I extol the Lady of Heaven;*
> *I give adoration to Hathor,*
> *Laudations to my mistress!*
> *I call to her, she heard my plea,*
> *She sent my mistress to me;*
> *She came by herself to see me,*
> *O great wonder that happened to me!*
> *I was joyful exulting, elated,*
> *When she came, the young man bowed,*
> *Out of great love for her.*
> *I make devotions to my goddess,*
> *That she grant me my sister as a gift:*
> *Three days now that I pray to her name,*
> *Five days since she went from me!*[13]

THE CULT OF HATHOR – THE GOLDEN ONE

The priestesses of Hathor who danced in her honour consciously impersonated her. They partook in consequence of the nature of the Goddess and were able to impart her qualities to her devotees.

BLACKMAN, *The Position of Women in the Egyptian Hierarchy*

The cult of Hathor was popular and prestigious. It had strong links with royalty and included some royal priestesses. During the Old Kingdom and First Intermediate Period a total of 469 persons held some Hathoric title, including purely administrative officers.[14] Of this group, 339 individuals recorded some biographical detail in their tombs. These details provide a glimpse into the familial relations of the group as a whole. Only a small number from this group had relatives who were also holders of a Hathoric title. We have details of 105 mother-daughter relationships. In this group only nine titles were held by both mother and daughter. At Saqqara, 49 women holding Hathoric titles had daughters, only two of whom went on to become priestesses. At Dendera, 10 women had one daughter or more, only one of whom served as Priestess of Hathor, Mistress of Denderah, and held the title *bkrt-nsw-wtt*, 'King's Only Jewel'. The evidence indicates that service in the cult of Hathor was not necessarily hereditary, even though it might be on occasion. Clearly there was no injunction against marriage in the Egyptian priesthood. Of 220 Priestesses of Hathor who recorded biographical information about their husbands, 18 were married to men with Hathoric titles, 78 Priestesses of Hathor are recorded as having one or more daughters. Mrr-rn-nfr-Ibi had four daughters and three sons; unusually all four daughters held the title of Priestess of Hathor. The priestess Nfrw-rn-nfr-Ffi, who also held the title *bkrt-nsw*, 'King's Jewel', had one daughter and two sons. Her daughter Hetyah also served as Priestess of Hathor and held the title Mistress of Cusae and *bkrt-nsw*. Hetyah married into one of the leading Hathoric families. Her husband held several Hathoric titles as did many immediate family members. She had three daughters and seven sons, none of whom held Hathoric titles.

Marianne Galvin studied the interfamilial relationships and

found no case for hereditary succession.

> There is no consistent pattern to indicate that Hathoric priestly
> titles were being inherited within female/female relationships. For
> the group of mother-in-law/daughter-in-law relationships, it is
> probable that the high percentage of cases should be viewed as
> a manifestation of the social implications of the cult of Hathor,
> of the community that it formed and the pervasiveness of the cult
> with respect to the lives of its adherents. Hathoric titles held a
> certain prestige that was desirable, and probably were indicative
> of a certain attitude of devotion, respect or that which was
> desirable and admirable. [15]

Priestesses of Hathor could also hold additional titles which were
usually conferred by the Pharaoh. The titles, 'King's
Acquaintance', *rht-nsw*, 'King's Jewel', *hkrt-nsw*, 'King's Only Jewel',
hkrt-nsw-wtt, and 'King's Noblewoman', *spsst-nsw*, were marks of
social prestige and status. The title 'Kings Acquaintance' was held
by 61 priestesses and two priests. The title 'King's Only Jewel' was
held by 52 priestesses. The title 'King's Jewel' was held by six
priestesses. The title 'King's Noblewoman' was held by 11 priestesses. The significance attached to these titles varied from time
to time. 'Kings Jewel' was indicative of a social relationship to the
king. Its usage during the First Intermediate Period increased
while the title 'Kings Acquaintance' became less popular.

In the Fifth-Dynasty tomb of a princess, the inscription over
the entrance to the inner chamber reads, 'the royal daughter,
king's jewel, priestess of Hathor, priestess of King Khufu, Ni-
Sedjer-kai'. On the architrave over the entrance, it is written, 'May
she be buried in the western necropolis in great old age, may she
travel on the good ways on which a revered one travels well.' In
the Sixth-Dynasty tomb of king Ni-hebsed-pepi and his wife, the
text above her head reads 'his wife, his beloved, the royal
ornament, priestess of Hathor'. [16] The phrase rendered as 'royal
ornament' might more closely be translated as 'King's Jewel'.

MISTRESS OF THE SYCAMORE

Cult personnel held additional titles indicating their authority and
position. At Denderah the Priestess of Hathor additionally held

the title 'Mistress of Iwnt'. There were 19 women who held this title in The Old Kingdom and First Intermediate Period. Priestesses bearing the further title 'Mistress of the Sycamore' served in one sanctuary. This was predominantly an Old Kingdom title held by 52 women, 48 of whom came from this period. Priestesses of Hathor who additionally held the title 'Mistress of the Sycamore in all Her Places' had duties in two temples. However, this office had no authority in sanctuaries dedicated to Hathor in her other aspects. Those who held the title 'Hathor in All Her Places', numbering 11 priestesses and two priests of Hathor, fulfilled duties in all temples. All Priestesses of Hathor were responsible to the 'Chief Priestess of Hathor in All Her Places'. Here is evidence of well-organised cult activity in which women played a leading role. There were also connections with other cults, especially the cult of Neith during the Old Kingdom. There were 21 priestesses of Hathor holding the title 'Mistress of the Sycamore' who were also priestesses of Neith. During the Fifth Dynasty the cult of Hathor and the cult of Re were known to have co-existed in Heliopolitan sun temples. The priestesses in the sun temple at Heliopolis were actually spoken of as Hathors.

MENAT, SISTRA AND EPIPHANY

The emblems were recognised as the manifestations of Hathor herself.

MARIANNE GALVIN, *The Priestess of Hathor*

The priestesses of Hathor were clearly identifiable through their cult regalia: the menat and the sistrum. The sistrum was probably derived from dried papyrus heads which rattle when shaken. It is similiar in shape to the ankh, the symbol of life. It may have first taken shape as a sacred box, a simple rattle containing loose objects bearing comparison to the pregnant womb. Not only does the looped sistrum replicate the shape of the ankh, but it also gives us the 'sa' sign, believed by Murray and Selgman to represent the uterus. The sistrum is symbolically complex, a world away from the simple musical rattle it is usually taken for. It too was seen as a manifestation of the presence of Hathor. Like the menat necklace it was an epiphany of the goddess herself. In the room of archives at Edfu, Hathor is called 'Mistress of the sss and the shm sistra'. The rattling sound was supposed to keep evil at bay. At Denderah, the king and queen walked in procession to the temple roof on New Year's morning. The queen rattled two sistra. The accompanying text reads, 'I have taken the sss sistrum, I grasp the shm-sistrum and drive away him who is hostile to the mistress of heaven.'[17]

The sistrum was carried by the Hathors as priestesses of music who accompanied sacred processions. We must not, however, think that the musician-priestesses were simple sistrum rattlers. These women, when bearing the official regalia, were Hathor herself incarnate and present. 'But their functions, even if purely musical, were far from unimportant as might appear at first sight. The musician-priestesses impersonated a goddess namely Hathor and in that capacity were able to confer divine favour and graces on that divinity's devotees.'[18] The priestesses touched the hands of onlookers with the menat and sistra to give long life, stability and happiness.

The menat necklace, the second symbol of Hathor, was the heavy, beaded collar fastened with a counterpoise at the back. It originated in the Old Kingdom. It symbolised fertility, the counterpoise weights probably denoting the testicles. At Denderah, Hathor herself is described as 'the possessor of the Menat'. Her presence was immanent in the menat itself. When the priestess was wearing the sacred emblem she was united with her deity. Marianne Galvin understands this relationship well: 'The priestesses were imparted with the privilege and honour of representing Hathor when she chose to appear in the guise of her menat.'[19]

Priestesses were presented with the emblems of their authority at the Ritual Presentation of the Emblems. This ceremony possibly marks the first bestowing of the emblems upon the priestess. 'It is the ritual in which Hathor herself transmitted the essence of her divinity to the sacred ornaments and actually became those ornaments as they became her. It is the ritual in which the divine essence of the goddess herself merged with the priestess.'[20] We know that the identification between the priestess and the Goddess was complete; the priestess was the living epiphany of the Goddess Hathor and earned the right to bear the title 'Hathor'.

The menat necklace was sometimes also shaken to make a rattling sound. We can see from tomb scenes that the menat symbolised life and regeneration. Hathoric scenes were not uncommon in tombs. The Old Kingdom mastaba of Qar and Idu shows seven women, four of whom are dancing and three are clapping. The text reads, 'Hail to you in life, Hathor, the places of your Ka are propitiated that you should glow in what the nfrw desires.' The tomb of Senbi shows three priestesses with the menat draped over their right shoulders. The beaded part is extended to Senbi: 'For your kas [souls], the menats of Hathor Mistress of Kusae, for your kas, the menats of your mother Hathor that she may cause you to endure the years that you desire. For your kas, the menats of Hathor that she may praise you.' At Deir el Bahri we find a tomb of Queen Neferu from the First Intermediate Period. Here we find a *bas relief* showing four women wearing the menat. We do not know whether Neferu was a priestess of Hathor, but the scene suggests that this was the case, which would not have been unusual.

MUSICIAN-PRIESTESSES

I dispel what is hostile by means of the sistrum in my hand.

INSCRIPTION FROM DENDERAH

The role of musician-priestess was filled by women from all social classes: queens, princesses, noblewomen and perfectly ordinary women of no special status served as priestesses. By the time of the New Kingdom women from all classes could be attached to the local temple as musician-priestess. Kerome, the daughter of king Takelot II, served as musician-priestess in the temple of Amun at Karnak, as did the daughter of a High Priest of Amun. The wife of a Sem priest of Sokar at Thebes, who was the sister of a High Priest of Mont, was also a musician-priestess.[21] By contrast, an unmarried woman of no particular social standing served as a musician-priestess of Osiris. Two wives of weavers and five daughters of a superintendent of craftsmen were all musician-priestesses of Amun, as was the wife of a shoemaker. [22]

Music, sacred song and ecstatic dance were an important part of all sacred ritual. Musician-priestesses were attached to all large temples. They rattled sistra, shook tambourines and sang. An inscription of Ramesses II adapted by Ramesses III refers to 'the great noble ladies of the temple of Ptah and the Hathors of the temple of Atum', who greeted the king with jubilation and the beating of tambourines. From the Fourth Dynasty we meet the *mrt*, a musician-priestess whom we see depicted in reliefs standing at the approach of the king, clapping and giving welcoming cries: 'he comes who brings, he comes who brings'. The *mrt* was especially connected with the Hb Sd festival and appeared in the company of other musician-priestesses called *sdt*. She was also closely connected with the House of Gold, the Sculptors Workshop and the rite of Opening the Mouth which took place there. The term *mrt* predates the Fourth Dynasty, originating in the Archaic Period when the *mrt* were singers: counterparts of the Goddess Meret, a Goddess of music who welcomed the king to his festival of renewal. In the cult of Amun at Thebes, musician-priestesses danced and sang, beating their single membrane drums and shaking the sistra in his honour. They consciously impersonated Hathor as the wife of Atum Re and in turn themselves were called concubines to the god.

The women sistrum-bearers were regarded as musician-priestesses, not simply as musicians. A Middle-Kingdom stela clearly distinguished priestesses from singers and musicians. In the Middle Kingdom musician-priestesses, *hnywt*, were attached to the temple of Osiris at Abydos. In the New Kingdom there were musician-priestesses for Osiris, Isis, Mut and Hapi, Upwawet and Amen Re. Strangely enough, we even hear of concubines, including a Chief of the concubines, attached to the goddesses Mut, Ubastet and Nekhbet. There were five musician-priestesses attached to Denderah in Ptolemaic times.

We should not diminish the sacral aspect implicit in the role taken by these women. 'It must not be concluded however that the priestesses of the Old Kingdom and the Middle Kingdom were merely temple musicians.' [23] From the Middle Kingdom at Cusae and from the Ptolemaic period at Denderah her priestesses were known to perform life-enhancing and rejuvenating acts in public processions. They extended the menat, bestowing a life-giving blessing. During a winter festival, the priestesses of Hathor and the Ihwey priests of Hathor, also from Denderah, together extended her blessing to the populace. The musician-priestesses paraded through the streets, stopping at houses to bless the people, holding out the emblems of Hathor, the sistra and the menat necklace.

Hathor brought joy and beauty to life. Her presence was celebrated with song, dance and delight. From a poem on the sarcophagus lid of Wennofer we can glimpse the atmosphere of a feast of Hathor.

> *Singers and maidens gathered together,*
> *Made acclaim like that of Meret.*
> *Braided, beauteous, tressed, high bosomed,*
> *Priestesses richly adorned,*
> *Anointed with myrrh, perfumed with lotus,*
> *Their heads garlanded with wreaths,*
> *All drunk together with wine,*
> *Fragrant with the plants of Punt,*
> *They danced together in beauty, doing my heart's wish,*
> *Their rewards were on their limbs.* [24]

HATHOR – ROYAL WIFE AND MOTHER

Hathor had a special relationship with the pharaoh

BLEEKER, Hathor and Thoth

The priestesses of Hathor acted as the living epiphany of Hathor herself. The mythological functions attributed to Hathor prescribed the imitative cult functions. Originally Hathor served only royal persons through her priestesses. Only later did her functions serve the people generally. Her nurturing, protecting and fertilising powers were initially reserved for the king. She was depicted feeding the kas of the king. In the city of Apis, the capital of the western or third lower Egyptian nome, the High Priestess was called *snkyt*, 'she who gives suck'. She was depicted offering her breast to the king, impersonating Hathor, offering him life, stability and good fortune.

The pharaoh was the son of Re and the living Horus, both undeniable solar figures, an inevitable identification in a land dominated by the burning sun. Hathor had long-standing connections with the solar cult. She was the Golden One, 'she who nurses the dawn', goddess of the rising sun. She was also the Eye of Horus and the sun-eye of Re. Hathor was the mother of Horus and wife of Atum Re, goddess to the solar gods themselves. Hathor was present through her priestesses at times of royal empowerment, the coronation, the festival of renewal and final apotheosis.

The pharaoh honoured Hathor as divine mother and made offerings to her. This hymn to Hathor from Denderah was sung to accompany the pharaoh as he offered a jug of wine.

> *The king, Pharaoh, comes to dance,*
> *He comes to sing;*
> *Mistress, see the dancing,*
> *Wife of Horus see the skipping*
>
> *He offers it to you,*
> *This jug*
> *Mistress, see the dancing,*
> *Wife of Horus, see the skipping!*
>
> *His heart is straight, his inmost open,*
> *No darkness is in his breast;*
> *Mistress, see the dancing,*
> *Wife of Horus, see the skipping.* [25]

In this second hymn the pharaoh refers to the relationship between himself and Hathor. He is the Horus-child, she is the Golden One.

> *O Golden One, how good is this song!*
> *Like the songs of Horus himself;*

Re's son sings as master singer.
He is the Horus-child, the musician.

He diminishes not your bread,
He reduces not your loaf;
His heart is straight, his inmost open,
No darkness in his breast!

He abhors the sorrow of your ka,
Ha abhors your hunger and thirst,
He abhors the distress of the goddess[26]

In this third hymn the pharaoh reverences Hathor:

O beauteous one, O cow, O great one,
O great magician, O you splendid lady, O queen of gods!
The king reveres you, Pharaoh give that he live!
O queen of the gods, he reveres you, give that he live!

Behold him Hathor, mistress from heaven,
See him, Hathor, mistress from lightland,
Hear him, flaming one, from ocean!
Behold him, queen of the gods, from sky, from earth,
From Nubia, from Manu, from Bakhu,
From each land from each place, where your majesty shines.[27]

The Egyptian Goddess Isis was personified by the throne. Indeed she was the throne as the bestower of kingship. She was said to make the king. It was customary for pharaohs to be called the 'Sons of Isis'. It was also common to depict the pharaoh seated on the lap of Isis, a child on the lap of the mother. The king as high priest made offerings to Isis as his mother and seat of his authority. She was the royal empowerer, the king maker. At Philae we find Ptolemy II Philadelphus offering a sphinx-shaped jar of ointment to Isis. The hymn introduces the officiant:

The king of upper and lower Egypt has come to you,
O Isis bringing to you the myrrh which comes forth from the Punt
and which makes pleasant your fragrance for ever.

It continues:

O Isis, giver of life who dwells in the Pure Island,
take to yourself the myrrh which comes from the Punt,
the lotus (fragrance) which issues from your body,
that your heart may be glad through it,
and that your heart may rejoice every day.
Osiris is in joy. His heart takes pleasure
When the son of the Sun Ptolemy covers for you your head with
*   ungent*
which issues from the Eye of Horus in that its name of 'Ungent'.
The Eye of Horus is the fire which burns the followers of Seth;
Geb gives you his inheritance.[28]

Egyptian kingship was complex. The living King was identified as Horus, the dead king as Osiris. Isis was the mother of the living Horus and the sister-wife to Osiris. She was both mother and wife to the king. As the mother gives life to the son, so the pharaoh was empowered by Isis. She was his mother, his wife, the throne which legitimated his power. At the coronation she was present as the throne itself. In Egypt the pharaoh was all powerful, divinity incarnate, but he was empowered by the Feminine. 'Before the emergence of the polis in classical Greece, the birth of the state was celebrated in the theogonies of ancient Egypt, Sumeria, Babylonia and the Hittite kingdoms. And its mode was female.'[29] The relationship between power holder and power bestower was encapsulated in ancient myth.

The bitter struggles these mythologies recount, of the efforts of patriarchs to suppress siblings and offspring, sometimes pushing them back into the womb, eating them only later to disgorge them, mutilating them and sexually violating them, are signs of the successive struggles of kings against mothers who alone have the power to legitimate kin.[30]

88

Patricia Springborg, senior lecturer in the Department of Government at the University of Sydney, continues.

> The 'birth of the state', no mere metaphor was a symptomatic act in which all the reigning dynasties sought their legitimacy. Scholars have long suggested that the mythologies which have survived the long passage of history from at least the third millennium BC to reach us in the form of literary works, had originally a ritual and performative function that made them central to the state legitimation processes. [31]

Rulers were often depicted making offerings to Isis. On the exterior walls at Philae, Augustus offered myrrh, Tiberius offered a collar, gazelles and geese. In other places Augustus offered wine to Isis and beer to Hathor. Tiberius offered a rattle, mirrors and a breast amulet. Ptolemy II Philadelphus was shown prostrating himself before Isis, offering linen, a necklace and eye paint. In return he received the gift of life.

Engraved upon the temple wall at Philae, Isis speaks to Ptolemy. She is 'The Great God's Mother, Lady of Philae, Lady of Heaven, Mistress of the Gods, Lady of the Southern Lands'. She says, 'I have given you the life span of Re in heaven; I have given you the heaven itself and what is in it; I have given you victory over the south.' [32] Elsewhere in a vertical inscription behind the enthroned Isis the text states, 'O my beloved son, son of the Sun, I have given you the south as far as Kenset, Ta-seti bent down for ever belongs to you.' [33] Another complementary text states, 'I have given you the kingship of Atum on earth; I have given you the land with what is in it; I have given you victory over the north. O my beloved son, king of upper and lower Egypt I have given you the north as far as heaven, the Great Green, bowing heads for ever, belongs to you.' [34]

We find the king reciting a hymn before Isis.

> *Praise to you Isis-Hathor,*
> *God's mother, Lady of Heaven,*
> *Mistress of Abaton, Queen of the gods.*

You are the divine mother of Horus,
The mighty bull, avenger of his father,
Who causes the rebels to fall.

Praise to you Isis-Hathor,
God's Mother, Lady of Heaven.
Mistress of Abaton, queen of the gods.[35]

Egyptian kingship was held in intimate relationship to the Feminine. As Horus, the pharaoh was spouse to Hathor. As the son of Re he was also the son of Hathor. As Osiris, the pharaoh was also husband and brother of Isis herself, closely identified with Hathor. This network of relationships appears at times contradictory. The pharaoh was identified as the son, brother and husband to Isis under varied circumstances. He was also the son and husband to Hathor. These complex relationships formed the basis of Egyptian kingship and its empowering rites.

We find goddesses represented by priestesses at all the vital transitions of royal power, succession, coronation and apotheosis. The pharaoh was ritually initiated into each of the successive roles of kingship which placed the mantle of the gods upon him.

THE PLAY OF THE SUCCESSION

The succession of the crown prince took place immediately upon the death of the old pharaoh, commencing at dawn on the following day. The Egyptians found lapses in continuity impossible to bear. The pattern of cosmic order had to prevail.

A text states, 'I am a legitimate ruler, not a usurper for I occupy the place of my sire, as the son of Isis since I have appeared as king on the throne of Horus.'[36] The pharaoh travelled to a number of cities to perform the play during the period of transition. At the succession we find the myth of Horus and Osiris enacted. It represented the transition of power from father to son. A ritual text, in effect the 'script' of the play, dates from the reign of Sesostris I, the second king of the Twelfth Dynasty. The players included royal princes, officials, craftsmen, priests and priestesses. It consists of 46 scenes each introduced with a brief narrative followed by an explanation, recited by the reader.

The drama enacted the death and burial of the departed king and the coronation of the new king, 'the king who will rule'. The new king is Horus, the departed king is Osiris. As the father ascends to a new life, so the son ascends the throne. During the proceedings the Djed pillar was erected symbolising the resurrection and rebirth of the old king. This was also a subtle allusion to the birth of the new king. The Djed pillar was Hathor pregnant with the Horus child. A ladder was set up for the ascent of Osiris by Horus. Isis appeared as a principal mourner at the death of Osiris. The new king was crowned. His first act was to dispense bounty symbolised by the distribution of bread. Now that the earthly transition of power had taken place, the departed king was made ready for a transition to a new life. The new king donned a *queni*, a stomacher which fitted around his chest and back symbolising the essence of the departed king. It effected a mutual embrace between father and son. The late king was 'supported' in his moment of transition by the vital forces of his son, the son was imbued with the ka of kingship from his father.

Plans for the burial now commenced. Two priestesses represented Isis and Nephthys in their traditional role of funerary attendants, brought food to summon the Spirit Seekers who then conveyed the spirit of the late king to a new abode. Two further priestesses later appeared, taking the part of Isis and Nephthys singing the dirges and lamentations over the body of Osiris. The drama finally ended with the conveyance of necessary items for the cult of the dead king to the divine chapel and resting place.

The king is dead, long live the king.

RENEWAL AND REGENERATION

The concept of renewal was deeply embedded in Egyptian religious thought and deed. The language was remarkably rich in terms denoting this concept: to renew, to become new, to make new, to rejuvenate, to be rejuvenated. The renewal of the cosmos, community and individual was effected by cultic ceremonial, especially the festival of the Hb Sd, the renewal of the king's vitality, often mistakenly called a jubilee.

The Hb Sd was symbolised by a hieroglyph showing two chapels placed side by side, representing the two halves of Egypt. Each contained an empty throne placed on a dais. The Hb Sd was celebrated at irregular intervals marking 'a critical phase in the people's relationship with the gods and aimed at a reintegration, a readjustment or a renewal'.[37]

The series of dramatic rituals which made up the Hb Sd usually began on the first day of the first month in the season of sowing, Tybi. Extensive preparations were required. A Festival Hall, courts, temporary shrines, chapels and buildings to house all ritual regalia had to be constructed. Rites of purification accompanied the arrival of statues, official envoys, and representatives from both halves of the country. Gifts were made to the various deities. These initial proceedings were presided over by the cow goddess Sekhat-Hor, 'She Who Remembers Horus', the divine nurse who suckled the king and acted as the protectress of cattle. She was obviously connected to Hathor. The main celebrations included the reception of deputations and pledges of loyalty, followed by the ritualised crossing of a field representing the whole land of Egypt. At this point the king was faced by Mert who called out, 'Come bring'. We do not understand the significance of this. This role was later taken over by Thoth.

Bleeker upholds the view that *sd* means cloth. The Hb Sd, the festival of the cloth, can be seen as the re-clothing, the re-investiture of the pharaoh. The pharaoh appeared in three costumes, firstly in an elegant and precious robe symbolic of his power, secondly in a short kilt with a tail, finally in a short mantle which could be a prehistoric sacerdotal robe. 'By donning the Sd robe, the king renewed his office and specifically as high priest as intermediary between the gods and mortals.'[38] We find the Divine Feminine present and active in this process. At the Hb Sd of Osorkon, the pharaoh is blessed by the gods Amon, Ta-Tjen, Atum, Kheper, Geb, Isis and Nephthys, presumably through their cult representatives. 'The preparatory rites for the Sd festival of Amenhotep III depicted on the pylon of the temple of Soleb record a role so central for Hathor and her priestesses that it may even include a sacred marriage between Hathor and the sun god.'[39] Hathoric emblems abound here. Lion-masked dancers with arm-shaped wands associated with the cult of Hathor danced and sang before the throne. Priestesses were escorted to the king in order to 'perform the Hb Sd rituals right in front of the throne'. When seated in the chapel, Hathor, through a cult representative, sat behind the king, her right hand on his shoulder. The queen also stood behind him. The earthly wife and mythic wife were both represented. We would certainly expect Hathor's influence at a ritual of renewal and rejuvenation; this was one of her prime functions.

APOTHEOSIS

The Egyptians saw death as a second birth. This applied to all members of society regardless of rank. *The Book of the Dead* contains the funerary spell, 'I live after dying, like Re each day'.[40] It can be said of the deceased, 'today he has arrived in the land of the living'.[41] The deceased was thought to become a being of light. Funerary cults and festivals for the dead assisted the elevation of the deceased to the new life. The death of the ruler was however of special significance. In life the office of ruler was overshadowed by the form of the deity. Death did not break the identification process. Freed from the physical body the ruler was now made ready to walk as a deity in other realms through the rites of apotheosis. Hathor, royal goddess and receiver of the dead, was present in the rites of purification, which prepared the royal soul for astral immortality. In the temple of Soleb, Hathoric song and dance were related to the moment of apotheosis. Six women, in all probability priestesses of Hathor, clapped to a tambourine player, 'opened are the doors so that the god may go forth'.[42]

The soul of the pharaoh was reborn attended by divine midwives.

SACRED QUEENS

It is really astonishing that Egyptologists have so long neglected the Queen.

· BLEEKER, *The Sacral kingship*

Insufficient attention has in fact been paid to the role of the queen. She was called the King's Wife, the Great or Principle Wife. She also carried feminine forms of the titles of the king, translated as 'ruler queen', indicative of power in her own right. Bleeker is unequivocal concerning her position. 'Most scholars have denied the sacral function of the queen but in my opinion this denial is disproved by the facts.'[43] The position of the queen was upheld through powerful mythological identification. She was identified with Mut and Tefnut, Isis and Hathor.

We have evidence for queens offering sacrifice, a significant cultic act. The queen was involved at the important state festivals. She was present at the Hb Sd, the festival of renewal and at the erection of Djed pillar. It was she who 'fills the palace with love'. At the Min festival she had a particular role to play. She was the sole female in the procession representing the stranger, the nomad, a remnant from former times. At this festival she walked around the king. Bleeker regards this as a highly important sacral act. 'It is significant of the sacral dignity of the queen that she performs here an act which is meant to renew the forces of the king. She is in this case not only his equal, but even superior to her husband as she gives him the forces, which he needs for his royal task.'[44]

The queen had extensive powers in her own right. A queen might act as regent in place of a son if there was no heir apparent. She took the title of the Female Horus, King of Upper and Lower Egypt, Daughter of Re. At least four queens ruled in this way. Margaret Murray supports the view that we know too little about the role and function of the Egyptian queen.

> The position of queens in Egypt has been very little studied so far. The divinity of the queen is hardly recognised by modern writers, yet the queen was actually Isis, 'She of the Throne', and as the position of Isis was higher in the eyes of the people than that of her husband Osiris, it follows that to her subjects the queen was as important, if not more so, than the king.[45]

THE GOD'S WIFE OF AMUN

Clearly the God's Wife was a priestess.

GAY ROBINS, The Gods Wife of Amun

From the earliest dynasties the Egyptian king was regarded as divinity incarnate. The divine identification of the pharaoh changed subtly through the centuries. Originally he was closely identified with Horus. The rise of Thebes brought the god Amun to prominence. By the Eleventh and Twelfth Dynasties Amun was associated with Re, the national god of the Old Kingdom, in the form of Amun Re. The cult of Amun of Thebes was solarised, the pharaoh became the son of Amun Re, the wife of the pharaoh became the God's Wife of Amun. Hathor herself bears the titles God's Wife and God's Hand. She is the wife of Amun as state god, outshining Mut the wife of Amun as local patron deity. There was nothing new in the idea of a high-ranking priestess being identified as the wife of the god. It was common practice for the High Priestess of the temple to take a name as wife of the god of the presiding deity. The God's Wife of Amun however became an outstanding institution in its own right. Its most powerful title holder was Hatshepsut who used it skillfully as a power base.

The functions of this office have been misunderstood. It was mistakenly believed that the title was bound up with matters of legal succession which have since proved to be false. The functions of this office were related to the widespread and ancient traditions. 'The nature of the office is made clear by several scenes from the 18th dynasty showing a priestess who is called god's wife functioning within the context of a temple ritual alongside male priests.'[46] Scenes from the Eighteenth Dynasty show the God's Wife Ahmose Nofretary functioning within the context of a temple ritual alongside male priests. She was shown being purified in the sacred lake before entering the temple. She played a role in execration rites, called the god to his repast and burned images of the enemy. Ahmose Nofretary was clearly shown in the close-fitting wig and fillet of a priestess. The God's Wife at Thebes rattled the sistrum and sang in honour of the divinity during the performance of temple services. The God's Wife,

Enkhnesneferibre, was said to be 'pure handed when holding the sistrum', and 'to content Amun with her voice'. She carried flowers into the temple. Temple reliefs show the queen in the role of High Priestess shaking the sistrum while the king burned incense and poured libation. Nefrure, the daughter of Hatshepsut who carried the title God's Wife, was also clearly shown wearing the fillet of a priestess. One relief in the temple of Luxor showed king and queen walking together in a procession with priests carrying clothing for the cult statue. The king consecrated the clothing accompanied by the queen who intoned a chant.

The position is quite clear. 'The Heliopolitan queen as wife of the sun god, would have acted as the sun god's high priestess, and would surely have been identified with the goddess Hathor, the sun God's Wife, both in her capacity of high priestess and also in that of wife of the embodiment of the sun god.'[47] 'We can then see that the office of the God's Wife, although vested in women of the royal family is a priestly office distinct from the role of the King's Principle Wife.'[48] Pharaoh Ahmose is said to have invented the title for his own wife. Ahmose-Nefertari (Nofretary), was legally established in the office of God's Wife. A donation stela was set up in the temple of Amun at Karnak which provided an endowment of goods and land to be handed on in perpetuity to the holders of the office. Ahmose-Nofretary developed this title into a position of religious and economic importance. She took a considerable interest in building works. A significant number of ritual objects dedicated by her have been found at Karnak, Deir el Bahri, Abydos and the temple of Hathor at Serabit el Khadim in Sinai. A large number of scarabs bear her title. Her son, Amenhotep I built a mortuary temple to house her funerary cult. She had the right to three titles: 'King's Wife', 'King's Mother' and 'King's Principal Wife', but she rarely used them, preferring instead to use the title God's Wife. No other queen except Hatshepsut used her title alone like this. The mantle of Ahmose-Nofretary fell not to her daughter Meritamun but to Hatshepsut. Hatshepsut used this office as a base from which to achieve her own ambitions. She made full use of the authority implicit in the title of God's Wife of Amun before she handed it over to her daughter when she took the title of King. It seems that Nefrure in her capacity as God's Wife acted alongside her mother in ritual taking the role normally played by the King's Principle Wife.

The heyday of this institution was during the Eighteenth Dynasty. However, it was revived for a period of some 200 years when Thebes was ruled by a succession of five God's Wives. After the fall of the Twentieth Dynasty in about 1090 BC, Thebes became a more or less independently-ruled principality under the High Priests of Amun. From the reign of Osorkon III of the Twenty Third Dynasty c. 720 BC to that of Psammetikhos III of the Twenty Sixth Dynasty c. 525 BC, power was held not by the High Priests of Amun but by the High Priestess, the God's Wife of Amun.

This was a curious and unique episode in Egyptian rulership. It is difficult to discover the motivating forces of the time. We may safely assume some political expediency was at work. It is difficult to understand the roles played by the competing power bases. The priests were immensely wealthy and influential, the pharaoh was divine yet somehow temporarily diminished, the priestesses were respected but without real power since the rule of Hatshepsut. It is most unlikely that these sacerdotal princesses seized power. It is more likely that power was given over to them in legitimate if unusual circumstances.

The title God's Wife was no longer taken by the wife of the pharaoh but by a chosen princess of the reigning house who was followed by another princess duly chosen and formally adopted as the 'Great Daughter'. The first of these was Shepenupet I, Osorkon III's daughter. She was followed by Amenirdis I, sister-in-law of the Nubian king Pionkh. She was followed by Shepenupet II, who was Pionkh's own daughter and niece to Amenirdis. Shepenupet first adopted Taharka's daughter Amenirdis II, but nine years after the accession of Psammetikhos I, she was forced instead to adopt Nitokris who later adopted Enkhnesneferibre, the daughter of Psammetikhos II.

It is possible that this experiment in rulership was brought to a close due to ensuing power struggles over the rights of succession. The post of the 'Great Daughter' was ripe for political manipulation and intrigue by power-hungry pharaohs who continued to exert substantial influence from the sidelines.

Nitokris, the supplanter of Amenirdis II who never came to rule, was given her titles as God's Wife and additionally Adorer of the God immediately upon her adoption. This was clearly irregular, a manipulation of the system designed to legitimate her position. Enkhnesneferibre more properly received the title God's Wife, Adorer of the God, upon the death of Nitokris.

In the temple of Osiris at Karnak, there is a life-sized statue of Amenirdis I.

> This is an offering for the Theban Amon-Re of Apt, to the god Mentu-Re, the Lord of Thebes. May he grant everything that is good and pure, by which the divine nature lives, all that the heaven bestows and the earth brings forth, to the princess the most pleasant, the most gracious, the kindest and the most amiable queen of Upper and Lower Egypt, the sister of the king, the ever-living daughter of the deceased king, the wife of the divine one Amenirdis may she live. [49]

A text spoke of her work as ruler.

> I was the wife of the divine one, a benefactress of her city Thebes, a bounteous giver of her land. I gave food to the hungry, drink to the thirsty, clothes to the naked. [50]

This was a curious episode in Egyptian history, short-lived and from our standpoint insufficiently researched. These women were certainly not the only queens to rule Egypt but they were unique in ruling in their official capacity as the God's Wife. This tantalising chapter in monarchical rule remains inadequately understood.

These queens were far from insignificant. Hatshepsut, bearer of the title God's Wife, was as powerful and influential as any pharaoh. She identified herself with Hathor and ordered rebuilding work to honour Hathor's name. 'The temple of Cusae which was fallen into dissolution, the earth had swallowed up its noble sanctuary, and children danced upon its roof . . . I hallowed it, built anew, and I sculptured her sacred image of gold.'[51] Her mortuary temple is replete with Hathoric imagery.

Certain other queens also enjoyed special cult significance. Aahames-Nefertari, Nefertiti, Nerfetari-mery-Mut were each divinised. Shepenupet I built a funerary temple for Amenirdis. At Medinet Habu there is a mortuary temple for the three queens, Shepenupet II, Nitokris and Meht-en-wesekht. The accompanying scenes show ladies of Thebes making offerings to the triad of Thebes and the queens, Amenirdis and Shepenupet.

With the fall of Egypt, an epoch came to a close. The age of dynasties was drawing to a close. Egypt was defeated by Alexander. This defeat ended her splendid isolation. Egyptian ideas, themes and images spread abroad. The most notable of these was surely the worship of Isis.

GLOSSARY

Hbst, wife

Hkrt-nsw, a title, 'King's Jewel'

Hkrt-nsw-wtt, a title, 'King's Only Jewel'

Hnywt, musician-priestess

Hryt-nst, a title given to the high priestess at Edfu meaning, 'She who is upon the throne'

Ht hr, Hathor, the house of Horus

Hwyt, protectress

Mrt, a musician-priestess originating in the archaic period

Queni, a stomacher worn by the new king during the coronation rites

Rht-nsw, a title, 'King's Acquaintance'

Snykt, a title given to the high priestess at Apis, 'She who gives suck'

Spsst-nsw, a title, 'King's Noblewoman'

Chapter 5

ISIS ABROAD –
THE SACERDOS PERPETUA

Individual redemption could be attained through participation in her mysteries.

HEYOB, *The Cult of Isis*

ISIS LEAVES HOME

Egypt was defeated by Alexander. The world was changing fast. Egypt's solitary mysteries and strange deities were released from centuries of isolation.

Trade and travel took the Egyptian gods to Athens and Rome. Formal links were established between Italy and Egypt in 273 BC when Ptolemy Philadelphus sent an embassy to the senate. Merchants and Greeks who had served Egypt in military or civilian capacities carried the Egyptian influence with them. The Isian cult spread to numerous Greek cities: Boetia; Phocis; Peloponnesus; Euboea; Epirus; Thessaly; Thrace; Macedonia; Rhodes; the islands of the Aegean and the cities of Asia Minor. The cult was introduced to Sicily in 214 BC. Ostia and Puteoli in southern Italy were soon engaged in trade. Egypt became the granary for Rome.

Wherever the gods travelled, servants and worshippers followed. The cult of Isis travelled from Egypt with small groups of immigrants. An Egyptian priest emigrated to Delos, taking a sacred statue with him which he kept in rented apartments. His grandson provided Isis with her first proper home abroad. Permission to build a hierion of Isis was finally granted in

333/2 BC. The ancient cults were settled in new soil. Adaptations naturally took place which reflected the changed circumstances. The intermingling of Egyptian belief and Greek spirit produced a new synthesis which culminated in the god Serapis, an Egypto-Hellenic fusion. He formed the perfect cultural bridge over which Isis and Osiris walked hand in hand. Isis shared her first home abroad with Serapis.

Ptolemy was well aware of the upsurge in the movement of Egyptian people and religious ideas. He called upon an Egyptian and a Greek jointly to design cult rituals for the newly-imported worship of Isis. He chose Manetho the Egyptian historian and Timotheos of the Eumolpidai clan.

Conventions regarding the worship of foreign gods began to break down. In 135/4 BC the Athenian Demos enlarged the cult personnel on Delos; new buildings and temple precincts appeared; the best families were seen to participate. Involvement in the new cult was clearly prestigious. The headdress of Isis appeared on coins in 110 BC, and Isis was in a position of dominance by the second half of the second century BC in both Athens and Delos.

The religion of ancient Egypt was to flourish in the newly-opened lands of Italy, Greece, Britain, Gaul, Spain and even Germany. Although the worship of Isis and Osiris was rooted in Egypt, it proved to have a universal appeal. The elements of treachery and betrayal, resurrection and salvation were powerful enough to attract a new following. Isis rose to a new prominence to become the saviour of both Emperor and commoner.

Arsinoe, the second wife of Ptolemy II, was also instrumental in taking the worship of Isis to the Greeks. Ptolemaic queens were especially identified with Isis. Dedications were made to Arsinoe as 'Isis Arsinoe Philadelphus'. Sacrificial vessels were inscribed with the words, 'To the Good Fortune of Arsinoe Philadelphus Isis'. At her death she was deified. It was even planned that her temple should have a roof of a magnetic substance so that her iron statue might float mid air as a continuous symbol of her ascension. However, this grand plan was interrupted by the death of the architect. Arsinoe had to settle for her own temple complete with cult personnel. A priesthood was inaugurated for the deified

Arsinoe, being drawn from two families and including both priests and priestesses. The priestess of Arsinoe Philopator was to hold office for life and was not obliged to be of virgin status.

It was not unusual to establish a cult on behalf of a powerful figure. In 211/10 BC Ptolemy Philopator inaugurated a special cult in honour of his mother Berenice II. It was common for the priestess in these eponymous priesthoods to take the name of the cult in which they served. The most common names were Berenice and Arsinoe. Names were often devised to include 'Isis'. Isidora was a hybrid name, being Greek but formed on the Egyptian stem 'Isis'. In 138-7 BC a priestess took the name Thermouthis. A few women took their father's name in feminine form, Aristomache, Nicostrate, Theodoris and Ptolemais.[1]

CANEPHORES AND ATHLOPHORES

In the reign of the young one (Ptolemy V) . . . the priests of Alexander and the Saviour Gods and the Brother-and-Sister Gods and the Benefactor Gods and the Father-Loving Gods and the God Manifest (and) Gracious (Ptolemy V) being Aetus son of Aetus, the athlophore of Bernice Eugergetes being Pyrrha daughter of Philinus, the canephore of Arsinoe Philadelphus being Area daughter of Diogenes, the priestess of Arsinoe Philopator being Eirene daughter of Ptolemy, on the fourth of the month Xandicus, the eighteenth of the Egyptian's (month) Mecheir.

THE ROSETTA STONE

The post of canephore in the cult of Arsinoe was first held by Eirene. She was the daughter of Ptolemaus, a strategus of Cyprus. Her son erected a statue in her honour on the island. She probably held office from the inception in 203 BC until 172/1 BC. Artemo, daughter of Seleucis and sister of Theodorus, held this post from 141/40–116/15 BC.[2] In Alexandria there was only one canephore. It was her job to carry the ritual basket, the *cysta mystica* on her head. She led the grand procession followed by the *prytaneis*, city officials, the *ephebes*, young men and the wand bearers while the population lined the streets in celebration. It was a post carrying some prestige. Bilistiche, the favoured mistress of Ptolemy, was chosen as canephore in 251/50 BC. She was doubtless granted this post as a favour, the usual requirement of both youth and virginity being waived. She was at least thirty and a royal mistress. Later, in 213/12 BC, another royal mistress, Agathoclea, was chosen. Canephores began to appear in Athens by the middle of the first century AD and more commonly towards the end of the second century. At Athens three different canephores were mentioned. Eleven different canephores were mentioned at Delos, the earliest being in 117/16 BC.[3] The office was held for a year.

The office of athlophore, 'prize bearer', was created with the new eponymous priesthood. It is not known what this office involved. Perhaps she carried a particular prize before it was awarded. It was common to give civic prizes at annual festivals. The same woman usually served as athlophore and canephore in successive years. Serving in the cult of the deified dead was a prestigious post. The candidates had to be ethnic Greek and some degree of education was probably important; religious festivals in Alexandria required that some women be literate, and female choirs had to be able to read words and notation. Many post-holders were the daughters of high-ranking men. Thaubarium was appointed priestess in 107/106 BC. She was sister to Helenus, governor of Cyprus. Three daughters of Theodorus, stratugus of Cyprus, were appointed to eponymous priesthoods in one year.[4]

ISIDES SACRORUM AND ISIACI

The true Isaikos is made not by linen clothes and a shaven head but by his pious and philosophical orientation.

PLUTARCH

Egyptian worshippers adapted to the already existing Greek cult associations, *thiasos* or *koinon*. Now new groups appeared, the Sarapiastai, Isiastai and Anubiastai among others. The Isiastai was organised into three levels. The first level contained simple believers: the 'isides sacrorum', a term applied to women mainly belonging to the lower classes (although we have three instances where this term is applied to men). The middle level was composed of devotees called Isiaci, who were organised and directed by a priest. The Isiaci may have performed the duties of the lower priesthood. The third level comprised those who performed functions which were equated with priesthood. It contained initiates, including women. Cyril of Alexandria, showing all the prejudice of his time, could only equate initiation with 'wantonness'. He stated, 'it is the custom of the Egyptians especially for the women to visit temples wearing linen garments, reverently supplying their left hands with a mirror and the right with a sistrum; these women, when they have been chosen among others and have been made initiates of such a religion with difficulty, are deemed worthy of honour – therefore of wantonness.'[5]

The cult groups were small but active in the pursuit of their religious goals. These associations represented a new departure in Egyptian worship now freed from temple discipline, bringing some element of democracy into cult practice. The Egyptian Mysteries had encountered the Greek spirit, resulting in a new fusion of devotion and structure. New cult associations mushroomed in this atmosphere. On Delos the Therapeuti and Melanephors appeared, and were still surviving after 166 BC.[6] One woman is mentioned among the Therapeuti. The Melanephors were at first loosely united but later changed to a closed community. They wore black mourning garments in impersonation of Isis. Another group, the Dekadistai included seven women out of a total group of sixteen.[7] Cult associations continued to be popular, new groups were still appearing at the end of the Hellenistic times. The Navarchs, like a modern-day carnival committee, organised and assisted at the Festival of The Sailing of the Ship. Three inscriptions from Etria from the first century BC indicate that 50 men and 45 women were included in this association.[8] The inclusion of women in these groups is a significant development.

While women do not appear to have formed the majority of the adherents of the cults, they were more involved in the oriental cults generally and in the Isiac cult specifically than in the traditional state religions. Their participation in many instances alongside men and in the same type of priestly office as men was perhaps the reason the ancient authors and after them modern scholars, gave attention to women adherents of the Isiac cult.[9]

SACERDOS PERPETUA

The fact that women played a part at all in the religion was noteworthy.

HEYOB, *The Cult of Isis*

As the cult became established, so cult personnel appeared. However, not a great deal is known about the precise nature of the hierarchy of Egyptian religion as it appeared in the Greaco-Roman world. It seems that the first office holders were native Egyptians who held office for life, followed later by Greek priests and priestesses who followed their own traditional pattern of annual priesthood. This was however not a hard and fast rule. Among priestesses there is evidence for both permanent, *sacerdos perpetua*, and annual duties. It was more common for Greek priestesses to hold office for a year and more common for Roman priestesses to be lifelong. We find inscriptions for priestesses serving in both capacities. An inscription from Chaeronea reads, 'priestess for life of Taposiris Isis'.[10]

Several tombstones from Athens and Rome show women dressed in the garments of a priestess. Presumably these were lifelong priestesses. Dionys served Isis from the age of 15 until the age of 60. Another inscription from the second-third century, from Bracara Augusta in Spain, reveals a woman making a dedication to Isis. She is called 'sacerdos perpetua'.[11] By contrast, an inscription from Thespiae dated from the first century AD indicates that Mnasippa held office for a year.[12] Inscriptions from Imbros in Imperial times, and from Athens dated the mid-third century, both refer to annual priestesses.[13] The inscriptions name 28 women who filled the position of sacerdos. No Isian priestesses held this rank before Imperial times, and there is no known instance of a woman who filled the role of chief priest of a temple. A number of secondary priestesses are mentioned in inscriptions. These included the canephores, the basket bearers, statue bearers, called *pastophores* in Latin and *hierophores* in Greek, and lamp or torch

Figure 5 An Isian procession including priests and priestesses

bearers. A female stolist is mentioned in an inscription from Megalopolis from the second-third century AD. This was an important position with responsibility for dressing the cult statue.

There is evidence for the increasing participation of women as both devotees and cult personnel. The oldest dated inscription mentioning a women devotee comes from Halicarnassus from the end of the fourth century or beginning of the third century BC. It is a dedication made by a husband and wife for themselves and their children to Serapis and Isis.[14] The last inscription by a female devotee comes from Rome, AD 390, and names a priestess of Isis. The oldest inscription from Italy is dated before the middle of the first century BC, and names Ceacillia Polla who made a dedication to Serapis and Isis.[15] All other Italian inscriptions mentioning women date from the centuries after Christ. The greatest number of Isian inscriptions appeared in the first century AD when there were ten. The inscriptions from Athens were also scattered over a broad period of time. The earliest inscription dates from 215/14 BC. A funeral dedication from the Flavian period AD 69–96 shows unmistakable imagery: a woman holding a situla and sistrum. On both sides of the altar there is a basket, the *cysta mystica* from which a snake appears. Perhaps Cantina Procla, for whom the tomb was built, was a basket bearer.[16]

However, inscriptions alone do not give a complete picture of the involvement of women. Statistically, women remained in the minority as both officiants and worshippers. Other archaeological remains show that women did participate in the processions and festivals to a higher degree than indicated by the inscriptions alone. The inscriptions provide an informative but probably incomplete guide to the participation of women.

We know, for instance, that there was a flourishing cult centre at Pompeii in which women played a large part as indicated by the evidence from frescoes. Yet we have only two inscriptions relating to women from this site out of a total of fourteen.

ISEUMS AND CRYPTS

The crypt seems to have been a place for mystery cults.

MAKARONAS, *Water in the Cultic Worship of Isis and Serapis*

The cult of Isis had once been housed in the great Egyptian temples, often sharing sites with other divinities. At Sais, Isis shared a temple with Neith, sometimes thought of as her mother. At Bubastis, she was worshipped with Bast. At Denderah, Hathor's home, Isis too was remembered. The island temple of Philae was shared with Nephthys, Osiris and Hathor.

In the new environment of foreign soil, temples were again built. It was once again common for Isis to share a site with another Egyptian deity, most often Serapis. The days of the vast temple estates was over. Iseum builders had to be content with pockets of land and subscription lists. Nevertheless, these new temple builders were acutely aware of the past Egyptian tradition. On a new small scale they reinterpreted the sacred architecture of the mother land. The crypt, an underground darkened chamber, became a regular feature of the newly built Iseums which sprang up outside Egypt. The crypts were used for a range of activities from the mystical to the prosiac, including the storage of cult equipment and even burial. The old cult had to adapt to new lands and to non-Egyptian peoples. It did so remarkably well.

NILE WATER – THE SACRAMENT OF ISIS

May Osiris give you the cool waters.

CULT FORMULA

The new crypts imitated the mystery crypts of the Egyptian temples. These sanctuaries, though far from home, preserved and adapted the traditions of the mother country. The Nilometer, a common site in the Egyptian temple, was translated into a new form for sanctuaries far away. It was essentially a practical tool for noting the rise and fall of the Nile on a daily basis. However, this simple measuring device had acquired symbolic overtones.

The Nile waters were vital to the prosperity of the land. The river was itself thought of as the god Hapi. Its flooding was connected with the rising of Sirius, the star of Isis. Away from the flood plains, the symbolic meaning of the rising waters outweighed all practical sense. The new sanctuaries in distant shores attempted to reproduce the flood waters in symbolism if not in reality. More than half of the newly-constructed sanctuaries of Isis and Serapis, some 60 per cent, reveal evidence of some sort of permanent water facility. [17] At Delos, a crypt located below the temple precinct was connected directly to the Inpus river. The crypt itself was designed to serve as a Nilometer. Serapeum B, also at Delos, had a similar crypt with no connection to the river. This might have been flooded with rain from time to time. The symbolism of the annual flood was too deeply embedded in the Egyptian psyche for it to be easily forgotten.

The pitcher containing Nile water was the most revered object. It was often carried with veiled hands. It was Osiris himself. 'May Osiris give you the cool water' was a cult formula which symbolically referred to the gift of eternal life. Sacramental Nile water was collected and distributed from two types of cultic pitcher. The urnula, described in *The Golden Ass*, was gilded with a rounded lower portion, was decorated with Egyptian images and had a spout like the beak of a bird and a handle in the shape of an uraeus. No examples of this cultic pitcher have survived, although it does appear in several frescoes. The other basic type, itself a subject for adoration, was the Osiris hydreois. This was a jar decorated with a number of Egyptian sacred objects. Its base was garlanded with flowers, while on the top was the head of the god, the hair arranged in a distinctive crown style. These have been found in five sanctuaries. Pitchers of both types were carried in procession, by an Osiris *hydroies* with hands veiled. There is also a well-known Vatican relief of an Isiac procession. We see a priestess with a lotus flower on her head, a serpent entwined about her left arm and a situla in her right hand. Following her is the holy scribe with a scroll, wearing a falcon headdress. A shaven priest holds a vase enshrouded in his mantle. Another priestess carries a ladle in her left hand and a sistrum in her right.

As the Isian faith and practice spread, sheer practicality meant that some new sanctuaries chose portable containers for water. The passing of time distanced new Isian devotees from the original significance of Nile water. To any native Egyptian Nile water was life itself.

ISIS AT POMPEII

On the basis of the evidence it seems in some localities that at any rate women participated in the Isiac cult in the same capacities in which men did.

HEYOB, *The Cult of Isis*

Pompeii offers the richest representations of Isaic ceremonies that have been found to date. The Iseum was discovered in 1765, and is especially rich in frescoes. Over the central door a scene depicts nine figures including Anubis or an Anubis priest bearing a caduceus. Below this is a panel of Isis with an ankh. Other reliefs show Perseus, Andromeda, Mars and Venus. The crypt itself was typically bare, prepared for heavy rain symbolising the Nile's flood.

In the north west of the precinct, frescoes indicate that some version of the Io myth was enacted. This Graeco-Egyptian mythological fusion represented the triumph over chaos and the liberation of the human soul from bondage and captivity. Perseus, the conqueror of the sea, symbolised victory over the Sethian powers of chaos. The life-giving Nile water symbolised triumph over the saline sea waters. Perseus liberated Andromeda from her bonds. The act of loosening her bonds was taken as a sign of divine power. Those who visited the precinct identified with Andromeda awaiting liberation.

In a badly-preserved painting from the triclinium of the Casa del Centenario, 21 women and one man stand against a mythical background. All but two of these women have white marks on their heads which are possibly traces of lotus flowers, symbols of immortality. Two figures carry a panel with hieroglyphs on it. Another wall painting from the Casa delle Nozze d'Ercole shows a lavish ceremony taking place. On a flight of steps a young woman, probably taking the part of a divinity, extends her hands towards a figure identifiable as Heracles. In the mist of the temple we see Venus, Eros and Priapus. We see two processions, one moving into the temple, the other moving out. At the head of the group is a priestess of Isis with sistrum and situla, who is crowned and wearing several necklaces and bracelets. She is represented on a larger scale than the other figures, possibly to emphasise her importance. Scholars have found no satisfactory explanation for this festival. Some have suggested that it represents the marriage of Heracles. Heyob tells us, 'what is important here is that it was a priestess rather than a priest who represented the Isaic religion at this festival where several other religious representatives were present.'[18] In another ceremony we see three figures. A shaven priest reverently holds a vase with hands covered by a cloak, a priestess holds a sistrum and a second priestess holds a situla and sistrum. In addition there is a choir, perhaps made up by members of a cult association.

Another fresco from Herculaneum shows us a ceremony which includes music making. A dancer is portrayed at the top of a flight of stairs. Behind him are two figures dressed in white; one of them is a woman playing the tambourine. Two persons are kneeling on either side of the altar. The figure on the left shakes a sistrum with one hand while offering a platter of fruits and flowers with the other. She is richly dressed with crown and a fringed tunic or mantle. On the other side, behind the kneeling figure, a woman shakes a sistrum.

At Pompeii we see women performing sacrificial duties. Several paintings depict priestesses carrying offerings platters. Statues of priestesses, one carrying a jar, another genuflecting, have been found at Beneventum.

Priestesses wore the costume of Isis herself, a white linen undergarment, covered by a fringed mantle knotted between the breasts. At times a wide band richly adorned with stars and crescent moons was hung over the shoulder. The garment is remarkably similar to that seen by Lucius in his vision of Isis. The lotus flower, symbol of immortality, was worn at the top of the head for some ceremonial purposes. Priestesses carried a sistrum and a situla which contained sacramental water. This may have been sprinkled, as the situla, an urn, is often shown with a ladle. They frequently wore rings with images of the deities inscribed inside.

In some instances at Pompeii both priestess and priest seem to have been representatives of the cult on an equal basis. The wall painting depicting the reception of Io by Isis includes a male and female figure looking towards Io as if to welcome her. Unusually, both figures hold the sistrum. In addition, the priest holds a caduceus, the priestess holds a baton.

Two engraved silver goblets show both priests and priestesses together involved in sacrificial duties. On the first goblet the priestess is crowned with a serpent, the ancient symbol of initiation. She carries a tray on which there is a cake. The priest carries a censer. On the second goblet the priestess, again with serpent headdress, carries a sistrum and a situla. The priest carries a hydreion, a long-spouted pitcher filled with waters scooped from the Nile.

Outside Egypt the Isian religion reflected changed social circumstances and different spiritual needs. It was a religion which attracted both men and women, and was served by both men and women. The cult myth of Isis and Osiris was now the central theme. The old gods Horus, Hathor and Thoth had remained behind, their stories fading on temple walls. Anubis, the ever faithful companion to Isis, did, however, make the journey. Isian festivals were now more public than ever. The exoteric aspect of the religion was expressed through the festivals. The esoteric aspect was expressed through the Mysteries of Isis enacted privately in crypts to small groups. Festivals now became entertainment and spectacle.

THE FESTIVAL OF THE SAILING OF THE SHIP

The sail was shining white linen, inscribed in large letters with the prayer for the Goddess's protection during the new sailing season.

APULEIUS, *The Golden Ass*

On 5 March, the Ploiaphesia, the Navigium Isides, was held to mark the start of the sailing season. The Festival of The Sailing of the Ship took place. A contemporary writer tells us that the Egyptians celebrated Isis in this way 'because by her nature she presides over the waters'. She was of course intimately connected with the rising of the Nile at the appearance of Sirius, as it was said that it was her tears which caused the Nile to rise. She is said to have invented the sail. The lighthouse on the island of Pharos was dedicated to Isis.

The boat and the Nile were both deeply meaningful images for the Egyptian mind. Practically every temple contained a sacred barque which was paraded and sometimes sailed on ceremonial occasions. Here, far away from the life-giving waters of the Nile, the ship of Isis was launched with great celebration in a new and quite different spirit. The Ship of Isis, which was unmanned and piled high with gifts, was released to the cry, 'the ship has been let go'.

We have a full and very lively account of this festival in *The Golden Ass*.

Presently the vanguard of the grand procession came into view. It was composed of a number of people in fancy dress of their own choosing; a man wearing a soldier's sword belt; another dressed as a huntsmen, a thick cloak caught up at his waist with a hunting knife and javelin; another wore gilt sandals, a wig, a silk dress and expensive jewellery and pretended to be a woman. . . . These fancy-dress comedians kept running in and out of the crowd, and behind them came the procession proper.

At the head walked women crowned with flowers, who pulled more flowers out of the folds of their beautiful white dresses and scattered them along the road; their joy in the Saviouress appeared in every gesture. Next came the women with polished mirrors tied to the backs of their heads which gave all who followed them the illusion of coming to meet the goddess rather than marching before her. Next, a party of women with ivory combs in their hands who made a pantomime of combing the Goddess's royal hair, and another party with bottles of perfume who sprinkled the road with balsam and other precious perfumes; and behind these a mixed company of woman and men who addressed the Goddess as, 'Daughter of the Stars', and propitiated her by carrying every sort of light - lamps, torches, wax candles and so forth.

Next came musicians with pipes and flutes, followed by a party of carefully chosen choir-boys singing a hymn in which an inspired poet had explained the origin of the procession. . . .

Then followed a great crowd of the Goddess's initiates, men and women of all classes and every age, their pure white linen clothes shining brightly. The women wore their hair tied up in glossy coils under gauze headdresses; the men's heads were completely shaven, representing the Goddess's bright earthly stars, and they carried rattles of brass, silver and even gold which kept up a shrill and ceaseless tinkling. . . .

Meanwhile the pageant moved slowly on and we approached the sea shore. . . . There the divine emblems were arranged in due order and there with solemn prayers, the chaste-lipped priest consecrated and dedicated to the Goddess a beautifully built ship, with Egyptian hieroglyphics painted over the entire hull; but first he carefully purified it with a lighted torch, an egg and sulphur. The sail was shining white linen, inscribed in large letters with a prayer for the Goddess's protection during the new sailing season. . . . When the ship was loaded with generous gifts and prayers for good fortune, they cut the anchor cable and she slipped across the bay with a serene breeze behind her that seemed to have sprung up for her sake alone.[19]

In Eretrea, a number of 'captains' who assisted at the launching of the ship are listed. This was obviously an important and public role. It was fulfilled by two men and a number of women: Isigena, Parthena, Isadora, Theopompis, Isias, Demetria, and Paedeusis. Much like the modern carnival, the day itself was exuberant but short-lived. The temple rites ended as the people kissed the feet of Isis on the temple steps.

The rise and fall of the Isian religion outside Egypt was intimately bound up with politics and the newly emergent

Christianity. It is interesting to speculate on what might have happened subsequently if the worship of Isis had not been eclipsed by Christianity.

GLOSSARY

Athlopore, priestesses of secondary rank who probably awarded prizes at civic festivals

Canephore, priestesses of secondary rank, basket bearers who carried ritual baskets in processions

Ephebes, a band of young men who served as processional guards during festivities

Hydreion, a long-spouted pitcher filled with Nile water

Isiaci, the name applied to devotees within the Isian religion

Isides sacrorum, the name applied to the lowest ranks of worshippers in the *Isiastai*, the cult association of Isis

Koinon, a Greek cult association

Prytaneis, city officials

Thiasos, Greek associations formed to serve individual deities

Chapter 6

CRETE - THE POWER HOLDERS

Out in the middle of the wine dark sea there is a land called Crete, rich and lovely land washed by the sea on every side; and in it are many peoples and ninety cities.

HOMER, *Odyssey*, BOOK 19

THE STRONG OR RULING GODDESS

There can be little doubt that Crete was the home of a female priesthood: the evidence for this is overwhelming. However, we need to probe beneath the surface. What do we know of this priesthood and its functions? How did it relate to Cretan social and political organisation? What was the nature of the sacred rites enacted by its functionaries? How may we relate a priesthood of women to the many Cretan myths and legends? We know far less than we would like. Crete fascinates – myth and legend, fact and speculation fuse into a heady brew.

Crete's location proved to be a significant historical factor: roughly equidistant from Europe, Asia and Africa, it was a stepping stone for peoples moving across the Aegean. It is the fifth largest island in the Mediterranean, offering sufficient size and enough fertile land to draw settlers. Crete is readily accessible from mainland Greece, Syria and Anatolia. Peoples from neighbouring lands were an important factor in the development of Cretan culture. There were various waves of significant immigration including groups from Asia, Libya and Anatolia. The Anatolian influence was so strong that Evans wrote, 'Neolithic

115

Crete may be regarded as an insular offshoot of an extensive Anatolian province.'[1] This singular influence may well have been crucial to the development of Goddess worship which predominated the Minoan civilisation. However, Crete's island position brought vulnerability as well as advantage, as migration and trade routes might easily become routes of invasion.

The earliest settlements appeared in the Neolithic period, probably towards the end of the seventh millennium. At least half a dozen sites were established during this period, and became the cities of the later Palatial period. Agriculture, including animal husbandry, cereal crops, olives and viticulture, was established. An important migration of people from western Anatolia took place around 2600 BC, extending to the Greek mainland and the Cyclades. This particular influx brought metal-working skills and inaugurated the Bronze Age in Crete.

The Minoan civilisation was rooted in an agricultural framework based upon a clan system of kinship and common ownership. Each clan drew its identity from a mythical ancestor symbolised by a clan totem, often in animal form, e.g. bull, goat, sow, snake and dove. Initiatory training drew the individual into full clan life and into adult status at puberty. These social units would have been matrilinear. Such traditions survived well into the historical period, especially at Gortnya. Women would have played a predominant part in the maintenance of the clan and household cults as overseers of cult life – priestesses in effect.

The name by which we now know Crete is derived from the Greek word *crateia*, meaning 'strong, or ruling, goddess'.[2] Here is an important key as we begin to unlock the hidden mysteries of Crete, island of the fabled Labyrinth.

Crete both past and present remains dominated by the building at Knossos. Yet the Labyrinth was relatively short lived, being constructed in about 1930 BC and abandoned c. 1380 BC. The history of Crete is not simply the history of Knossos. However, the Labyrinth is the single key with which to unlock the Minoan civilisation. Evans called it a palace, Wunderlich called it a necropolis. Rodney Castelden refutes both theories and categorically concludes that the 'Labyrinth functioned as a temple'.[3]

The conflict of opinion is indicative of our misunderstanding. Defining the function of this key site is critical to our understanding of Cretan life. Contemporary Cretans called the site both 'Knossos' and 'Labyrinthos': *ko-no-so* and *da-pu-ri-to-jo*.

THE LABYRINTH

When Theseus emerged from the Labyrinth, spotted with blood, Ariadne embraced him passionately.

ROBERT GRAVES, *The Greek Myths*

The first Labyrinth was raised in approximately 1930 BC on a site which had been in continuous habitation since 6100 BC. It was not the first building of its kind. In eastern Crete at Vasiliki there was an earlier building of a labyrinth type which was burned down 300 years before Knossos was begun. It included features which were to be repeated at Knossos, a large paved courtyard and suites of rectangular rooms. The walls at the Vasiliki site were of mud brick, the ceilings of clay-plastered reeds. Later buildings of this type had ground floors of stone and upper storeys of mud brick.

The building at Knossos is roughly square, measuring about 150 metres on each side. Knossos is truly labyrinthine. On the ground floor there were some 300 chambers. Including the upper floor, the building may once have contained 1000 chambers. Knossos is built around a central courtyard 58 metres long and 27 metres wide. This area coincides with the top of the hill levelled by the first settlers. The Knossos site was linked to a sanctuary at the top of Mount Juktas, remains of which have been found. This site predated Knossos by some 200 years. It had a massive precinct wall, 730 metres in circumference, 3 metres high and 4 metres thick. Two terraces and five small cult rooms marked off a sacred area at the edge of the steep west-facing cliff. Between the temple and the precipice there was a cave-cleft, an altar and a pyre site. This site, embellished with parapets, flag poles, horns and altars, is shown on the Zakro Rhyton, a drinking vessel.

Knossos itself shows few signs of being a palace, despite the best attempts of its excavator Sir Arthur Evans, who projected much palatial imagery onto the bare stones. The architecture is not palatial but secretive, mysterious, even subterranean. The so called 'Throne Room' is not only small but would have been dark. It contained a sunken area and a rough rectangular slab coloured red. The chamber is clearly not designed for the reception of visiting envoys or a royal function. The architecture, however, is highly suggestive of cult activity, a priestly function. It is less easy to dispense with the possibility that the Labyrinth was itself a temple. The huge number of artefacts discovered at the site, bull-headed rhytons, votive bells, horns and libation vessels, indicate a very powerful ritual component to all aspects of life. The labrys and horns were ever-present symbols throughout the site, carved on stone blocks, cut into stucco, painted on pottery, inscribed on seals and visible on the numerous altars.

The building incorporated workshops where votive objects were made, store rooms, sanctuaries, cult rooms, living quarters, robing rooms and processional corridors. The Labyrinth has a distinct maze-like quality due to frequent rebuilding and alteration, as it was often damaged by earth tremors. 'The end result was a bewilderingly elaborate building, cunningly designed to create all kinds of unexpected pictorial effects.'[4]

THE LADY OF THE LABYRINTH – LABURINTHOS POTNIA

> It was, perhaps more than any other single phenomenon, the worship of goddesses, that gave the Minoan civilisation its distinctive character.
>
> WILLETTS, *Cretan Cults and Festivals*

In the Labyrinth, the Great Goddess was called Potnia, Lady of the Labyrinth. Her symbols were the pillar, the axe and the snake. The double-bladed axe as a symbol of female sovereignty was never seen in male hands. Her title was still used in the classical period throughout the Mycenean world as an honorific title meaning 'my lady'.

> The Goddess is represented in a rich variety of associations: with animals, birds, and snakes; with the baetylic pillar and the sacred tree; with the poppy and the lily; with the sword and the double-

edged axe. She is huntress and a goddess of sports; she is armed and she presides over ritual dances; she has female and male attendants. She has dominion over mountain, earth, sky and sea; over life and death; she is household-goddess, vegetation goddess, Mother and Maid.[5]

Here were many individuated goddesses too. It is difficult to know whether they were conceived to be quite separate in identity or as aspects of the one goddess. Certainly as time passed various divinities assumed a separate independence. Many established Greek deities were born on Crete to be later transplanted and developed into maturity on the mainland. The well-established deities of the post- Minoan period originated in the earlier Minoan substratum. The diverse Goddesses of the later historical period may each reflect the development of a single aspect of the Goddess as the one and the many.

We find the Mother and the Maid were often indistinguishable one from the other. Both Demeter and Persephone were to be found on Crete. Moreover, in a myth comparable to that of Persephone, Briomartis, the 'sweet maiden', escaped the attentions of Minos by fleeing for nine months. Finally she threw herself into the sea where she was caught in the nets of fishermen. From then she was known as Diktynna. There is more than a hint of Persephone in this tale. The concept of the disappearing virgin is indicative of a girl's initiation. Briomartis flees for nine months, the time taken to transform a maiden into a mother. 'There are indications in the evidence that the relationship is the old familiar one of Mother and Maid and that Diktynna is to Demeter as Briomartis is to Persephone.'[6]

Briomartis was worshipped at peak sanctuaries where ritual pyres were lit. Both Briomartis and Diktynna were depicted in hunting dress with bow and quiver. They were both assimilated into Artemis. Artemis herself featured on coins from Axos dated between 300–67 BC. A single inscription indicates that Artemis also had a temple there. At Eleutherna, 450-300 BC, she is shown as a huntress with bow and hound. At Soulia in the west, the names of both men and women were cut into stones from her temple even in Imperial times.

Artemis is known by the epithets *soteira*, 'saviour', and *toxia*, 'the archer'. She was worshipped as bear goddess in a sacred bear cult in the Arkoudia, the Cave of the She Bear where a stalagmite in the shape of a bear was venerated.

The Cretan goddess of childbirth was Eleithyia. It is probable that the month, Eleusynios, and the Cretan city, Eleutherna, were named in connection with her. With the exception of a single votive inscription found in Apotera she belongs to the centre of the island. A hill and stream near Inatos were sacred to her.

Ariadne was connected with both fertility and the moon. She showed Theseus how to escape from the Labyrinth. As the 'very holy maid', she may have led a dance to celebrate the collective marriage.

Athene too was found on Crete. Her image was portrayed on coins. At Allaria her head appears on drachmas. Coins from Arcadia, 300–200 BC, show Athene standing. There were also statues of Athena, sometimes armed. She was the special deity of the city named Oleros. She was also called *poliokhos*, protecting the *polias*.

Aphrodite had a small cult in eastern Crete at Hiearpytna. At Knossos she was called Antheia, 'flower goddess'. At Phaistos she was called *skotia*, the patron of young men about to undergo initiation and marriage, the *skotioi*.

Europa, who did not go on to become one of the Olympian divinities, was well represented on Crete. Coins from Gortyna and Phaistos frequently depict Europa riding on a bull. A series of coins depicts the marriage of Zeus and Europa, showing Zeus through his epiphany, bull and eagle. Europa sits in her willow, the bull on the reverse of the coin licks his flank. Next we see Zeus as eagle perched beside her, while she lifts her veil. Finally, there is an embrace between Europa and the eagle. The willow comes to assume a special relevance as the epithet 'welkhanos'. The marriage of Zeus and Europa was said to have taken place beneath a plane or willow tree near a stream at Gortnya. Ancestors of the historical Gortynians were called 'Cow-men' or 'Cow-herds', a direct reference to the specific clan totems from which the sacred marriage may have sprung.

These many female divinities reflect the many facets of the

earlier Minoan Goddess. On Crete she was predominant but she was not alone.

CRETAN ZEUS

The Minoan male god was a secondary deity. He represents the element of discontinuity, of growth, decay and renewal in the vegetation cycle, as the goddess represents continuity. Because he shares in the mortality of the seed, he is the annually dying god.

WILLETTS, *Cretan Cults and Festivals*

There was no conception of a male anthropomorphic divinity in the Neolithic period. The male divinity appeared late on Crete affirming the overwhelming importance of the Goddess. However, it is quite untrue to suggest that we find no references to a male deity on Crete. In fact we find the full realisation of a classic theme, the undying goddess and her annually dying god.

There were several Cretan male deities who each followed the path of the dying god. The Cretan deity who took an Indo-European name from the Archeans who came to Crete, became known as Zeus. His original name was probably Zan.

It has been suggested that his earliest representation appears on the lid of a tomb at Foresta near Knossos. The principle figure carries an object consisting of three wavy verticals like a thunderbolt. He strides towards a tripod. Zeus appears in inscriptions and coins. He is mentioned in three inscriptions from central Crete. At Gortyna, Zeus Kratagenes is named among the deities in an oath appended to a treaty drawn up with the town of Sabryta. From western Crete, Zeus Zagretes appears in another treaty where he probably represents the Gortynians who played a prominent part in the negotiations. Inscriptions from the cities of Itanos, Praisos and Hierapytna refer to Zeus Diktaois, an epithet taken from mount Dikte where legend placed the birth of Zeus. Zeus also appears on coinage, wreathed in laurel from Aptera, 250-67 BC, with a thunderbolt, 300-67 BC, and as an eagle from Lyttos. Another coin shows Zeus on the front and a square labyrinth on the reverse.

A temple of Diktian Zeus on the town site of Palaikastro served a number of towns in eastern Crete in the third century BC. Votive offerings have been found on the site dating from the seventh century BC.

Zeus was also known by a large number of epithets attested in Cretan inscription. These include the epithets *agoraios*, 'of the market place', *alexikakos*, 'averter of evil', *brontaois*, 'of thunder', *epoposios*, 'overlooking', *hekatombaios*, 'the god to whom hekatombs were offered', *oratrios*, 'guardian and patron of treaties', and *soter*, 'saviour'. Perhaps the most significant epithet is *welkanhos*. Coins from Phaistos dated between 430–300 BC show Zeus welkanhos as a bearded youth sitting in a leafless tree. The reverse side shows a bull. A coin series from Gortyna shows Zeus welkanhos, Europa and an eagle. Willett concludes, 'Welkanhos was the male partner in a sacred marriage with the Minoan Mother-goddess.'[7]

Welkhanos, whose name may mean 'god of the willow tree', was leader of the Kouretes, the young men who had come of age. A sanctuary of the Kouretes was possibly situated on the north-eastern flank of Mount Dikte. Diodorus reported that the Kouretes 'used to dwell on the mountains, as in wooded places and glens and in general where there was a natural cover and shelter'. Three inscriptions from districts near Gortyna describe the Kouretes as 'guardians of kine', another reference to the original clan totems. Jane Harrison tells us, 'the Kouretes are Young Men who have been initiated themselves and will initiate others, will instruct them in tribal duties and tribal dances, will steal them away from their mothers, conceal them, make away with them by some pretended death and finally bring them back as new-born, grown, youths, full members of the tribe.'[8]

The hymn of the Kouretes to Zeus Diktaios dates from the third century AD . However, it was inscribed twice on the same stone indicating that the original was far older. The style and metre suit the end of the fourth or beginning of the third century BC. The evidence for the existence of a Cretan Zeus in the post-Palatial period is substantial. His presence late in that period indicates far earlier origins.

Zeus was not the only Cretan male god. There is sufficient evidence to suggest an evolving separate cult of a god we may identify as Dionysus. Coinage shows a male figure bearing the emblems that were undeniably associated with Dionysus. Coins from Kydonia, 200–67 BC, show a male head with horns, coins from Sybrita, 400–300 BC, show a bearded head with *kantharos* and *thyrsos*, also a head wreathed with ivy. Euripides and Firmicus identified this Cretan god originally with Zeus Zagretes, whose mystic followers attained communion with their god by eating the raw flesh of a bull.

BULLS AND GODS

The male god's principal epiphany was in the form of a bull.

MARIJA GIMBUTAS, *The Goddesses and Gods of Old Europe*

Aside from the labrys, the bull is the key symbol of the Labyrinth. Bull-headed rhytons, bull leaping, the bull-headed Minotaur and the bull sacrifice all point to the extraordinary significance attached to this image. The bull was the very epiphany of the god. The Labyrinth was imbued with the presence of the god as bull, as the dying victim ever waiting on death. The bull epiphany probably originated in the clan totems of the Neolithic period. Through evolution the bull became associated with the male participant in the sacred marriage, the god, and finally the consort, resulting in the identification of royal consort and bull. 'It seems likely that the final evolution of the male deity from a bull into the anthropomorphic Zeus who later became associated with Europa must have occurred in the Mycenean period.'[9] In this way, 'the bull became associated with Minoan kingship, which had an important function in relation to the calendar. Hence the bull becomes a symbol of the sun.'[10] We cannot fail to notice the identification between Zeus and the bull epiphany. Nor should we fail to notice the connection between Zeus and Minos, 'the boon companion of mighty Zeus'.[11] The bull stood as the dying god-king. 'The cult of Zeus was at least associated with, if it did not grow out of, an earlier cult of Minos; and . . . the common link continued to be an annual festival in celebration of a god like Adonis or Tammuz, at which this god was eaten in the form of a bull.'[12] The bull as epiphany of the god-male-consort was sacrificed and eaten usually raw in a mystic meal of communion.

Gods were undeniably represented on Crete. What was their function?

THE BULL-MAN, PRIESTESSES AND THE SACRED MARRIAGE

Where woman is the divine queen, the king must die.

ROSALIND MILES, *The Women's History of the World*

Evans, the archaeologist, excavator and rebuilder of Knossos, was convinced of the existence of a priest-king. He never found the proof that he so badly wanted. However, he did not invent the idea of the Cretan king. Homer wrote, 'there is Knossos, the great city, the place where Minos was king for nine year periods, and conversed with great Zeus.'[13] Plato tells us that Minos retired every nine years to a cave of Zeus. The term 'Minos' is probably not a name but a royal title. Robert Graves tells us, 'Minos seems to have been the royal title of an Hellenic dynasty . . . each king ritually marrying the Moon priestess and taking the title "Moon-being" from her.'[14]

Women were undoubtedly the power holders on Crete. The male priesthood occupied only a secondary role. The king is understated, never depicted in person, his individuality carried no significance. He is the Minos, the bull-man. His time is short. Homer's statement is highly significant, indicating that kingship here was neither divine nor hereditary but limited and dependent. This pattern is found elsewhere, especially when kingship is bestowed at the behest of the Feminine. The Mother goddess empowers her consort as year king. His reign is strictly limited, ending either literally through his ritualised death or symbolically as he steps down to be replaced by another chosen of the Goddess.

The limited kingship on Crete suggested by Homer poses an important question. If kingship was neither divine nor hereditary, how was the king chosen? 'It seems then that the Minoan priest-king was a young man whose tenure of office was dependent upon the sanction periodically granted of the Minoan goddess.'[15] If kingship was not hereditary but at the behest of the Goddess,

124

what process confirmed the choice of the king? Is it really too far-fetched to suggest that it was at the bull games that the king-to-be was chosen. It has long been realised that the Cretan bull games were far more than mere feats of acrobatic excellence and served an initiatory function. It is likely that the games served more than one function. They served as the initiation rites into adult life and were in all probability part of group marriage rites. It is also likely that there were both annual games and games of particular importance every ninth year. It was probably in the 'great year' that the new king was selected.

Here in the arena watched by spectators, youths danced and cavorted, leaping through the horns of consecration. Using skills of bravery, strength, courage and dexterity the bull leapers performed for the honour of being the chosen champion of the Goddess. Young men vied to become the victor. 'The time of his choosing becomes an occasion of ritual ordeal, the young try their strength against the bull from whom in turn that strength especially the strength of the priest-king derives.'[16] Graves suggests that contact with the bull's horn, a highly dangerous act, enabled the sacred king to fertilise the land in the name of the Moon-goddess by bringing rain always presaged by the bellowing sound of thunder.

The sacred marriage is inescapably indicated on Crete through myths and imagery. Accordingly, Demeter was embraced by Iason in a thrice ploughed field. Europa as cow was mated with Zeus as bull. Pasiphae, wife of the king, mated with a bull. Legend states that Minos was sent a bull in answer to a prayer. Instead of sacrificing it, Minos hid the beast and sacrificed another in its place. As a punishment his wife, Pasiphae, conceived a great lust for the bull. As a result of her liaison while she hid within the body of a cow created for her by Daidalos, she gave birth to the Minotaur.

Here are the elements of a ritual marriage between the cow and the bull. It has been suggested that women of the cow clan danced in this guise to promote the fertility of herds. It has also been suggested that Hera was originally a cow goddess. Her priestesses were women of the cow clan. Pasiphae clearly has lunar connections. Her name means 'she who shines on all'.

The sacred marriage may have evolved from simple fertility rites between representatives of the cow and bull clans, to a time-based rite with solar-lunar overtones. Further adaptation resulted in a ritualised union between the goddess through her representative and the consort, the bull-man. Finally, this sacred marriage led to the personalised marriage between Hera and Zeus on mainland Greece. The sacred marriage took place every nine years. Sun and moon, priest and priestess, masked as cow and bull enacted the archetypal union of opposites, ushering in the new reign of the goddess and consort.

The ninth year was especially important in the Minoan calendar. The discrepancy between the lunar and solar calendar was recognised at an early stage in the evolution of time reckoning. In Egypt it was the custom to add an extra month in nine out of each twenty five years. In Mesopotamia an extra month was added in seven years out of every nineteen. In Crete the problem was solved by adding a thirteenth month in three years out of every eight, giving an octennial cycle known as *okateris*. The ninth year, the *ennaeteris*, was regarded as the beginning of a new cycle. The culmination of the cycle was the ninth year, the great year which marks both the end of the old cycle and the start of the new. It was the time to choose a new king and confer kingship upon him through the sacred marriage and ritual testing.

Homer refers to the nine-year king as *enneoros*. Literally translated it means, 'for nine years'. However, literally *enneoros* means 'at intervals of eight years'. *Ennaeteris*, though meaning a nine-year period, defines the octennium or eight-year cycle. But Greek reckoning includes both terms separated by the interval, whereas we include only one. *Enneoros* more accurately means 'at intervals of eight years'. 'Ennaeteris', though meaning a nine-year period, defines the octennium or eight-year cycle. We should remind ourselves here that the legendary Athenian tribute of seven maids and seven youths was payable every eight years!

What happened to the nine-year king at the end of his reign? 'Did the male partner, the original of the priest king die, if only a mimic death, at the end of his annual tenure?'[17] Plutarch suggests a more literal ending to his reign. He spent considerable time on Crete and mentions a festival of extraordinary celebration at which an image of a man without a head was exhibited. 'The Cretan goddesses and the youthful Cretan god are involved in the same essential pattern of oriental ritual which gave rise to the myths of Ishtar and Tammuz, Osiris and Isis, Venus and Adonis.'[18] This is the myth of the undying goddess and the dying god. In time-honoured tradition might the old king have met his end at the hands of the new king? Did the old bull-man face the new bull-man, victor of the bull court in the darkness of the labyrinth in a pre-ordained dance of death. Graves tells us, 'the combat with a bull or a man in bull's disguise was one of the ritual tasks imposed on the candidate for kingship.'[19] What of the defeated bull-man? Was his body as the once-living bull, epiphany of man-god-consort, devoured in a sacramental meal as if it were the raw flesh of the bull itself?

Evans was convinced that he had found the priest-king in the fresco depicting a young man, hair loose and long, clad in the loin cloth of a bull leaper. He called him the 'Priest King', or 'The Prince of the Lilies'. Evans failed to realise as he searched so diligently that he was surrounded by images of the priest-king as the sacrificial bull.

If the presence of the Goddess can be inferred through her animal epiphanies, bear, dove or serpent, we have to accord the god the same privilege of being represented by his epiphany. The bull games exemplified the bull as epiphany of the god and initiator of young men. At the bull games, 'the collective marriage produces also a sacred marriage of the chosen pair, later perhaps these are chosen from a pre-selected group of specially privileged persons. Marriage collective and sacred is combined with initiation.'[20] Social organisation also reflected the importance of the bull as living metaphor. Young men were organised into herds, the *agela*. Emergence from the herd was in all probability marked by initiation through the contest in the courtyard. Strabo tells us that it was the custom for all those emerging from the herd in a given year to marry at the same time.

OFFERINGS, AXES AND EPIPHANY

As far as the labyrinth was concerned, the priestesses were pre-
eminent.

CASTLEDEN, *The Knossos Labyrinth*

It is impossible to think of the Labyrinth without at the same
moment thinking of the priestesses who lived there. Yet this alone
tells us very little. What functions were performed by this
priesthood? What form did religious observance take? How was
daily life organised? What seasonal rituals were observed? Who
joined the priesthood? How was the priesthood organised? Many
questions spring to mind. We do not have all the answers, but we
have some clues.

The Agia Triadha sarcophagus shows priestesses involved in the
sacrifice of a bull. The Isopata ring shows four priestesses with
raised arms in ecstatic dance. Might the poppy, a distinctive
Cretan symbol, have any relationship to cults of ecstasy and
altered perception?

Another seal impression shows a priestess carrying a double axe
and an elaborately flounced dress. 'It may be that she is about to
wear the dress herself, or alternatively drape it over a wooden cult
image.'[21] The many votive offerings found in the shrines include
model robes. 'It is probable that by putting on these special
clothes and performing certain rituals a priestess was believed to
turn into an Epiphany of the goddess.'[22]

In the East Hall Evans discovered bronze fittings from a statue
of the goddess which probably stood about three metres high.
The Greeks attributed the invention of large wooden effigies,
xoana, to the people of Minoan Crete. It may have been customary
to drape robes over such effigies as a means of vivifying the cult
image. It is also possible that we see such a *xoana* depicted on the
Agia Triadha sarcophagus and not in fact an image of the
deceased. Sets of feet modelled in clay have been found. These
probably supported the wooden *xoana* which was then dressed
accordingly.

Sacred rite was obviously not confined to the Labyrinth.
Priestesses were also involved in rituals connected with sacred

128

Figure 6 The Agia Triadha sarcophagus shows a bull sacrifice, possibly on behalf of the deceased within the tomb.

trees. Boughs are quite often shown decorating altars, sometimes planted in shafts, sometimes laid horizontally. There was an actual uprooting of a tree accompanied by lamentation. This act probably presaged the fall of the yearling god.

It is likely that there were periodic processions from Knossos to the summit of the sacred mountain. Mount Juktas had an importance for the Minoan priesthood which is difficult to quantify. Mount Juktas possesses a unique quality: it strongly resembles a human head lying on its side. As sunlight and cloud moves across the sky casting shadows and different lights, the mountain head comes to life, opening its eyes like a sleeper just awakening. The Labyrinth lived in the foreground of this massive being.

In the 'Throne Room', the throne itself is mountain-like, symbolic of the mountain top itself. The griffins which peer from the frescoed walls like guardian beasts were Evans' own contribution. The original scene depicted a landscape and stream against a background of hills. This chamber was never a throne room. The stone benches flanking the throne were not actual seats but settings for offerings as was the custom throughout the Labyrinth. The chamber was part of a complex of small rooms, sixteen in all, designed as a self-contained unit within the temple. 'The intention of the Throne Sanctuary as we might call it, was to honour the same deity or deities that were honoured in the peak sanctuary by a symbolic re-creation of the peak setting.'[23] Are we able to reconstruct the cult activities of this chamber? We know that offerings were placed here though we do not know how often this took place nor do we know what form these offerings took. It is highly likely that the sunken area was used for ritual lustration, although we do not know why this was performed and who took part. The red rectangular slab is indicative of sacrifice, either real or symbolic, but we do not know the meaning of this. 'We cannot be sure whether a priest or priestess sat on the gypsum throne but it seems likely that it was a priestess mysteriously transformed by ritual into an epiphany of the deity.'[24]

We can never know the words that were intoned here. This room has kept its secrets.

The Labyrinth fell several times, wrecked by violent earthquake. In 1700 BC, in a particularly destructive outburst, a youth was laid across an altar, trussed like a bull and offered to the angry earth.[25] It changed nothing. The Labyrinth fell, to rise again and take a stance on the unsteady earth, the bellowing bull. The Labyrinth was finally abandoned in about 1380. Crete continued. A dramatic and extraordinary episode was over.

GLOSSARY

Agela, a term meaning 'herd', but applied to a social grouping of young men

Crateia, name meaning 'strong or ruling goddess'

Ennaeteris, a term meaning 'a period of nine years'

Kantharos, a high-stemmed cup usually filled with holy water

Okateris, the octennial cycle

Thyrsos, a staff tipped with ornament, a token of the worshippers
   of Dionysus
Xoana, a wooden effigy of a divinity

Chapter 7

GREECE – THE CULT OFFICIALS

The Greek priest or priestess, then, is one who is charged with specific religious functions or ritual acts, directed godwards, in the due performance of which the state, either as a whole or through its organic groups is vitally interested.

W.J. WOODHOUSE, *Priest, Priesthood, Greek*

PRIESTHOODS AND CULT DUTIES

Native Greek religion was derived from the land and the need for fertility. Cult activity was deeply embedded in agricultural rhythm, archaic fertility rites and sympathetic magic. The wine and grain harvests were embodied in the beings of Dionysus and Demeter. The twelve divinities of the Olympian family were rooted in Cretan soil despite the lofty symbolic tone. The Hellenes personalised these deities of land and sea, wine and grain, sun and moon, giving them distinctly human qualities and attributes.

Religion was an eminently practical matter, a slightly nervous love affair with the powers beyond human comprehension. The supernatural powers could disrupt the fabric of ordinary life if not correctly treated. Natural calamity, military failure or poor harvest were signs that correct observance had not been paid. Only correct ritual observance could maintain the proper balance between humankind and the forces of nature. It was the duty of humankind to hold the balance between the gods on the one hand and social structures on the other. The deities had to be respected

132

through correct sacrifice and rite. The state and the gods both had to be paid their due. The state was ever present at religious function, represented by the cult official and the state's sacrificial portion. It was the task of the priesthood, whether male or female, to carry out the correct procedures and offer the stated sacrifice.

The priesthood was responsible for the upkeep of sacred property and its precinct. They were also responsible for the behaviour of visitors including the observance of any special regulations. The priesthood of Athens was even audited at the end of the year. Women were included as cult personnel from the earliest times, although they were excluded from the cult of Heracles which was exclusively for men. The Greek priesthood developed none of the arcane overtones implicit in the priesthoods of Egypt or Babylon. They were not a separate class set apart either by temple wall or life-long vocation. Priesthood lay more in the nature of a civil duty, often prestigious and well rewarded. Cult personnel were neither moral advisers nor expounders of esoteric philosophy. They were simply officials charged with the fulfilment of a specified duty.

The state paid its priesthood. Salary as both payment and perquisite was written into the founding contracts of the later elective priesthoods. There is less evidence to show payment by the state in the earlier genos priesthoods. However, the priestess of Demeter of the genos Eumolpidai was paid an *apometra* of one hundred drachmas, a considerable sum when a day's labour for a workman was only one drachma.[1]

There were no educational or vocational requirements for the office of priest or priestess. Candidates had to be healthy, unmaimed and of good reputation. No special training was given or required. Each sanctuary had a fixed ritual, the celebrant simply followed the rubric. Greek religious practice was varied. Cities and districts developed their own ways of celebrating the patron deity. The cult official, whether male or female, 'was always a servant of a particular deity at that particular shrine and at none other'.[2] The priesthood, whether male or female, was employed and regulated by the state. As a state employee, the cult official had social and political obligations which far outweighed any spiritual or religious dimension of the post.

The Greek priesthood emerged from the tribal framework of the powerful family clan, the genos. The king was gone but memories of kingship were reflected in the office of *basileus*, the tribal head. Within Athens the office of Archon Basileus retained religious and priestly function, vestigial kingship. The office of *phylobasileus* of the Ionian tribes also retained a priestly function, yet another element of vestigial kingship. However, the early introduction of the *polis* as a basic political unit resulted in the diminution and final disappearance of royal power. The power of the king was eclipsed by the council and assembly of adult males. Divine kingship, elsewhere so significant to political and religious life, was never more than latent. Tribal structure diffused power, providing forces which prevented the emergence of centralisation and kingship. This background produced a priesthood characterised by regional sacerdotal officers who both represented and served the genos and its deities.

Different priesthoods were firmly in the hands of established and influential family clans. Certain families had the right to provide cult officials at particular sanctuaries. At Eleusis the Eumolpidai family provided the hierophant while the position of *dadouchos* was filled by a member of the Kerykes family. The Philaidai family provided priestesses for the priesthood of Demeter who presided at the Haloa. The Salaminoi family clan controlled four priesthoods. They provided priests of Herakles at Porthmos and for Eurysakes. They also provided priestesses for Athena Skiras, and for the priesthood of Auglauros, Pandrosos and Kourotrophos. The priesthood of Athena Polias was controlled by the clan Eteoboutadai who provided high-ranking priestesses of Athena in the Acropolis. Priestesses for the sanctuary of Artemis Brauronia were almost certainly drawn from a genos too.

Within the Philaidai clan the office of priestess was assigned. It was not strictly hereditary. The post did not pass from mother to daughter. Within the Salaminioi clan every member was eligible as the office was chosen by lot. Within the Kerykes the office of priesthood was confined to one house. In the priesthood of Poseidon, it was decided which family member would take up the priestly role.

The reforms introduced by Cleisthenes replaced the original

four tribes with ten. This further reduced any political power inherent within the system. These new tribes were assigned mythical founders. Cleisthenes suggested the names of 100 attic heroes, ten were then chosen by the Delphic Oracle. New priesthoods were created to serve these mythical hero-founders. These tribal priesthoods were annual in tenure and chosen by lot, representing an important development in the democratisation of Greek society. For the first time the names of individual members of the priesthood appear. Hitherto, the office had outweighed the office holder. Selection by lot was to become the regular means of appointing officials both secular and sacred. Plato favoured the lot as a means of decision-making. In the Laws he wrote:

> . . . as far as priesthoods are concerned, we must allow God to effect his own good pleasure by just leaving appointments to the inspired decision of the lot, but every man on whom the lot may fall must be subjected to scrutiny, first as to his freedom from blemishes and legitimate birth, next as to his provenance from houses pure of all pollution, and the cleanliness of his own life, and likewise of those of his father and mother from blood-guiltiness and all such offences against religion.[3]

Typically a priesthood was created in 430 BC. The Great Plague in the summer had made people dispirited and fearful. National crisis indicated a breach in religious observance. The Athenians decided to create a public festival for Bendis who had been previously worshipped by a small Thracian group. A priestess was to be selected. The stone is unfortunately fragmented but indicates that either the wife of a priest or a choice by lot from 'all the Athenians' was considered. The choice was submitted to the oracle at Dodona and it seems likely that the final choice was made by lot as was becoming the custom.

The individual states evolved comprehensive laws which governed and regulated the activities of its sacred civil servants. The state specified its requirements for candidates to the office of priestess. At Harlicarnassus the priestess of Artemis Pergaia was required to hold full citizen pedigree for at least three generations.

The law also covered other aspects of cult activity. Regulations proscribed behaviour on the Acropolis, 'sacrificers' were not to 'set up pots' or 'to kindle fires'. It was prohibited to throw dung or to slaughter in defined areas. Laity might be fined up to three obols, but priestesses could be fined 100 drachma, that is 200 times as much.[4]

The constitution of a new priesthood for Athena Nike 448/7 BC or perhaps 449 BC specified a salary of 50 drachmas a year with an additional perquisite of the leg of any sacrificed animal, though the skin was to go to the state. The salary proposed at the height of Athenian affluence fell into arrears during the straitened circumstances of the Archidamian war. A second decree from 433/2 BC records the decision to pay the priestess the 50 drachmas owing to her.[5]

Certain priesthoods, most notably the Eleusinian, enjoyed prestige and wealth. The Eleusinian functionaries were all paid for each initiation. The priestess of Demeter received one obol. Half an obol went to the *hieropoios* although this was not strictly a priestly office. Half an obol was also paid to other officers, the 'altar priest', the *phaiduntes*, and the 'all-holy priests'. A fund of 1,600 drachmas was used to pay expenses. It would have taken 3,000 initiates to contribute this amount. Numbers probably exceeded this each year. A stiff fine of 1,000 drachmas was imposable if the Eleusinian priesthood attempted to initiate en masse. As initiation did take place with large numbers presumably this was an attempt to legally ensure some individual attention.

The law covered all aspects of cult practice. Priestesses were often required to remain chaste. In many temples the priesthood was held by a girl until her marriage. However, married priestesses were not uncommon. The priestess of Demeter and Kore and the *hierophantides* at Eleusis were normally married. The priestess of Nemesis at Rhamnus was also permitted to be a mother. The role of priestess of Demeter Thesmophorous was also held by a married woman. The honoured priestess, Lysimache, who served as the priestess of Athena Polias for 64 years, was married with four children. She was honoured by the erection of a statue on the Acropolis.

Regulations and laws preserved the ritual purity of both cult officials and worshippers. An inscription in the temple of Aesclepius at Epidaurus stated, 'He who goes inside the sweet smelling temple must be pure'. Endless regulations defined purity and laid down the ritual prescription in the event of a breach of the code.

> Whoever wishes to visit the temple of the goddess (Athene Nikephoros), whether a resident of the city or anyone else, must refrain from intercourse with his wife (or her husband) that day, from intercourse with another than his wife (or her husband) for the preceding two days, and must complete the required lustrations. The same applies to contact with the dead and with the delivery of a woman in childbirth. But if he has come from the funeral rites or from the burial, he shall purify himself and enter by the door where the holy water stoups are, and he shall be clean the same day.

The rules for the purity of the priestess of Demeter Olympia at Cos were as follows:

> The priestess must be pure from the following: She must in no wise come into contact with anything filthy; she must not participate in a hero meal; she must not touch a grave, she must not enter a house where a woman has given birth to a child whether a live birth or a still one during the preceding three days, nor during the three days following a burial shall she enter the house in which someone has died and she must not eat the carrion meat of any animal that has perished or been suffocated. [6]

PRIESTESSES AND CIVIC HONOUR

Priests and priestesses alike throughout the Greek world enjoyed considerable social and civic distinction, which tends to increase rather than diminish as Greek civilisation develops.

W.J. WOODHOUSE, *Priest, Priesthood, Greek*

Priestesses were part of the religious fabric of Greek society. Quite simply, there were gods and goddesses, there were priests and priestesses. It is important to evaluate the role played by priestesses in relation to the contemporary social and political structure. We cannot assume that the role of the priestess

137

automatically carried a degree of freedom not given to other women. Women in Greek society had few freedoms. The Athenian law defined the status of women as that of a 'perpetual minor'. Roles for Greek women were clearly proscribed by law and custom. The appearance of freedom can be deceptively convincing, indeed the perfect illusion, when created by power holders who give only those freedoms which maintain the structure.

The status of women serving as priestesses appears unusually high. A fragment reveals an instance when a priestess was enabled to sign a report. In *Against Aristogeiton Dinarchus* the orator reminds the jury that Aristogeiton had previously filed a suit against the priestess of Artemis Brauronia and had so perjured himself that he had been fined five talents. Archias the hierophant was convicted on two breaches of sacred law. He had sacrificed on a day not permitted for sacrifice. Moreover the right to offer this particular sacrifice belonged to the priestess of Demeter. Archias was found guilty of impiety and offering sacrifice contrary to ancestral custom.

Priestesses were sometimes honoured for their service. An inscription from Delphi in the second century BC reveals the honours and privileges bestowed on a priestess of Athena after a procession to Pythian Apollo.

> Greetings. Whereas the people of Athens led a Pythian procession to Pythian Apollo in a grand manner worthy of the god and their particular excellence: the priestess of Athena, Chrysis daughter of Nicetes, also was present with the procession; she made the journey out and return well, appropriately, and worthily of the people of Athens and of our city. With good fortune, it was voted by the city of Delphi to praise Chrysis, daughter of Nicetes, and to crown her with the god's crown that is customary among the Delphinians. It was voted also to give proxenia to her and to her descendants from the city, and the right to consult the oracle, priority of trial, safe conduct, freedom, from taxes, and a front seat at all the contests held by the city, the right to own land and a house and all the other city honours for proxenoi and benefactors of the city.[7]

The priestess of Hera, Tata Aphrodisia is remembered in another second century inscription.

> The council and people and the senate honour with first-rank honours Tata, daughter of Diodorus son of Diodorus son of Leon, reverend priestess of Hera for life, mother of the city, who became and remained wife of Attalus son of Pytheas the stephanephorus, herself a member of an illustrious family of the first rank, who as priestess of the imperial cult a second time twice supplied athletes in hand-bottles, filled most lavishly from basins for the better part of the night as well (as in the day), who became a stephanephorus, offered sacrifices throughout the year for the health of the imperial family, who held banquets for the people many times with couches provided for the public who herself, for dances and plays, imported the foremost performers in Asia and displayed them in her native city (and the neighbouring cities could also come to the display of the performance), a woman who spared no expense, who loved honour, glorious in virtue and chastity. [8]

The priestess Berenice was honoured by the city of Syros for her unstinting public service in the second century. The resolution of the prytaneis was approved by the council and the people.

> Whereas Berenice, daughter of Nicomachus, wife of Aristocles, son of Isidorus, has conducted herself well and appropriately on all occasions, and after she was made a magistrate, unsparingly celebrated rites at her own expense for gods and men on behalf of her native city, and after she was made a priestess of the heavenly gods and the holy goddesses Demeter and Kore and celebrated their rites in a holy and worthy manner, has given up her life – meanwhile she had also raised her own children. Voted to commend the span of this woman's life-time, to crown her with a gold wreath which in our fatherland is customarily used to crown good women. Let the man who proposed this resolution announce at her burial, 'The people of Syros crown Berenice daughter of Nicomachus with a gold crown in recognition of her virtue and her good will towards them.' [9]

Another inscription from Thasos in the fourth century records the honours paid to Flavia.

With good fortune. The senate honours Flavia Vibia Sabina, most noteworthy high priestess, and because of her ancestors uniquely mother of the council: she is the only woman, first in all time to have honours equal to those of the senators.[10]

THE ATTIC CALENDAR

The Greek year was punctuated by a great number of public festivals of varying importance. The festivals which were invariably public holidays were an excuse for civic pride. Cities vied with each other in lavish celebration, costly sacrifice and elaborate processions. Envoys went out to summon other cities often bearing the cost themselves. Temples were decorated and hung with garlands. The statue of the patron deity was often paraded, given the annual wash and a new set of robes. Prestigious families were publicly honoured by being chosen to carry sacred objects in the procession. Major festivals were alive with music and dance and exuberant display. Hymns were sung, poems were recited. There was oratory, drama, athletic contest, friendly competition with neighbouring cities, acrobatics and mime. The festival spirit drew crowds and trade.

Priestesses played a part in these civic celebrations. In addition they were solely responsible for the management of the women's festivals.

The Panathenaia
The first month of the attic year was Hecatombaion, July–August. It began with the new moon before the summer solstice. The Greeks did not mark the new year. The *Panathenaia* was the major Athenian festival. Every fourth year the Great Panathenaia was held. Originally these celebrations marked the presentation of Athena's new robe as a birthday gift. Later in 566, civic games were added by the magistrate Hippocleides. The festival became a major event.

There were athletic and musical contests, a regatta and a horse race. Prizewinning singers received gilded crowns of wild olive and money. Crews raced for a purse of money. Athletes raced for prestigious jars of olive oil made from the sacred olive trees, supposedly descended from the original tree created by Athena in a battle for sovereignty with Poseidon. There was a huge sacrifice on the Acropolis. As time passed the presentation of the peplos became increasingly grandiose. Once life size, by the fifth century it had become the size of a ship's sail. The new robe was taken to the Acropolis upon a model of a ship mounted on wheels crewed by priests and priestesses.

The weaving of the peplos was surrounded by ritual and symbolic activity. It was begun some nine months earlier. The warp was set on the loom by the priestess of Athena on the first day of the month of Pynanepsion at the festival of *Chalkeia*, the festival of metal workers who were also under the protection of Athena. Two young girls, the *arrephoroi*, assisted at the start of the work. They were dedicated each year to Athena. The peplos was then completed by the *ergastinai*, 'workers' from aristocratic families. These workers were publicly honoured when they walked at the head of the presentation procession. The robe was decorated with mythic scenes. A part of the Parthenon frieze depicts the presentation of the peplos. A panel shows five figures in which two young girls approach the figure of an older dignified woman, a priestess of Athena Polias. They carry a four-legged stool with a pin cushion. On the right, back to back with the priestess, a bearded man holds the edges of a piece of rectangular cloth. A boy holds the opposite side and helps to fold it.

The two girls who helped with the work of commencing the peplos of Athena were among four *arrephoria* between the ages of seven and eleven chosen annually by the *basileus*. These girls followed a custom which was 'probably derived from the little girls of the royal family of the Mycenan period performing the private ritual of the palace goddess'.[11]

Two maidens have a residence not far from the temple of Athena Polias and are called the 'carriers of unspoken things' by the Athenians, they spend a certain time living beside the goddess and when the feast comes round by night they do as follows, they put on their heads what the priestess of Athena gives them to carry but neither she who gives them knows what she gives nor do those who carry it understand. There is an enclosure on the Acropolis dedicated to Aphrodite called Her in the Gardens and there is a natural underground way down to it.[12]

The girls wore white robes and gold ornaments when performing this service. We do not know for certain when this took place. Jane Harrison describes the *arrephoria* as 'the Thesmophoria of the unmarried girl', observing a similarity in the theme of descent into the earth in both rites.

The Eleusinian Mysteries

The Greater Mysteries took place in the month of Boedromion, September. On the 13th day, an escort of young men, the *epheboi*, left Athens to travel to Eleusis. On the following day they acted as escort to the Eleusinian priestesses who travelled in procession bearing 'holy things' in round boxes tied with purple ribbons. They rode in covered wagons. On arrival in Athens, a minor official known as The Cleaner of the Two Goddesses went to the priestess of Athena to report the arrival of the Holy Things and the escort. On the 15th day the Mysteries were ready to be opened. These Greater Mysteries were the culminating ceremonies for the Lesser Mysteries which took place in the month of Anthesterion some seven months earlier.

The Thesmophoria

The autumn brought the month of Pyanepsion. It was filled with agricultural celebrations, mainly minor, and the major women's festival, the *Thesmophoria*, and the men's festival, *Apaturia*.

The *proerosia*, which signifies a preliminary to the ploughing, represented the offerings of first fruits to Demeter. According to legend, when Greece was struck by plague, the Delphic Oracle recommended that the Athenians were to sacrifice to Demeter on behalf of all. In return for this, tithes of crops were to be sent from the rest of Greece to Athens. This was not a popular public festival. From the sixth century farmers were to set aside a six-hundredth of their barley crop and a twelve-hundredth of their wheat crop to be delivered to Eleusis.

Other ceremonies included *pyanepsia*, a feast of boiled seeds, *eiresione*, the carrying of a decorated bough of olive from house to house by singing boys, and *oschophoria*, the carrying of vine branches from the shrine of Dionysus to the shrine of Athena Skiras.

By contrast the three-day *Thesmophoria* was popular and widely celebrated. Two women were elected each year to act as officials. The celebrants of the *Thesmophoria* were called bees. Women met together to descend into the earth in an ancient fertilising rite.

The Haloa

In the month of Poseidon, December, the *Haloa* was celebrated, probably at Eleusis. This too was a festival of agricultural origins, deriving its name from the *halos*, the threshing floor. It was held for both Demeter and Dionysus. A banquet was held for women only. All kinds of food were served except that also tabooed at the Mysteries. This was however no polite dinner party. Women carried models of male and female sexual organs. The table was decorated with cakes in the shape of sexual organs. Here was a clear fertility ritual designed to create an atmosphere which would stimulate the new crop. The lives of Greek women were restrained and strictly ordered through social custom. This brief moment of unchaperoned freedom outside the social niceties in all female company was an exceptional event, another remainder from archaic times, a piece of sympathetic magic.

Anthesteria

The springtime *Anthesteria* originated as a festival for the placation of ghosts. It had become overlaid with Dionysiac revels and the symbols of springtime renewal. The three-day festival began on the 11th day of the month. On the first day, 'the jar opening', new wine was tasted. Samples were carried out to the shrine of Dionysus in the Marshes. However it seems unlikely that the shrine was opened until the 12th day. Wine mixed with water was drunk and prayers were offered. Once the new wine was sampled the rest of the day was probably given over to drinking and revels.

On the following day, 'the day of wine jugs', children were presented with miniature wine vessels made from pottery. There was also a drinking contest, presided over by the Archon Basileus. Winning drinkers deposited the wreaths into the keeping of the priestess of the sanctuary. The second day featured the main events, including a procession of Dionysus on a wheel-mounted ship and the wedding of the Basilinna to Dionysus which took place in the sanctuary to Dionysus in the Marshes.

On the third day, 'the day of pots', the mood changed sharply. The revels were over, the drinking was done. A meal of boiled vegetables was prepared for the dead. The sanctuaries of Athens were closed against the spirits of the dead. Doorways were smeared with pitch to prevent ghosts from entering.

Dionysia

Originally the month of Elaphebolion was named after a festival of Artemis at which stags were sacrificed. Later, moulded cakes were offered instead. The original festival to Artemis was superseded by a festival of Dionysus, in the city Dionysia. This featured a procession and a bull sacrifice. There were revels and singing by torchlight. Dramatic performance became an especially important feature of this celebration.

Munichia

This month was named after a festival of Artemis. On the 6th day there was a procession of the maidens of Athens to the Delphinion, the shrine on the banks of the Ilissos where both Apollo and Artemis were worshipped. The girls carried boughs of sacred olive bound with white wool. The festival probably sought the protection of Artemis.

On the 16th day of the month special cakes called *amphiphontes*, 'shining all round', were carried in procession and offered privately to the goddess. These cakes carried a lighted candle in the centre. In the comedy *The Girl from Rhodes* by Philemon a young woman prays, 'Artemis, dear mistress, to you I carry, lady, this cake shining all around.'

Skiraphoria

This festival remains the most confused; even contemporary writers were uncertain about its origins. It was probably connected to the *Thesmophoria*. Indeed Jane Harrison describes it as a 'summer Thesmophoria' which lasted for just one day. At this festival women also observed ritual chastity and ate garlic to keep demanding husbands at bay. It was undoubtedly a women's festival dedicated to either Athene or Demeter. Piglets were probably sacrificed to be recovered at the *Thesmophoria* later in the year. The word *skira* means 'hard, white earth', probably gypsum. Images made of gypsum and flour paste were probably a part of this festival, revealing another connection to the autumn *Thesmophoria*.

Attic festivals were boisterous and exuberant, practical communal enactments of mythic themes. These festivals provided social cohesion and civic identity.

ROME – THE STATE REPRESENTATIVES

He instituted also a Nunnerie as it were, of religious Vestal Virgins.

LIVY, 1.20

The Vestal Virgins are possibly the most famous group of priestesses of the ancient world. Yet ironically this college symbolises probably the lowest point for any female priesthood. This priesthood was quite removed from any sense of autonomous empowerment; they were priestesses in name only. The Vestals were powerless in their own right, only existing to fulfil a symbolic role in the Roman psyche. The Greek idea of ritual purity and sacred state functionary combined in the person of the Vestal.

The second king Numa founded the cult of the Vestals in Rome. Plutarch recorded this fact in *Numa IX*.

Numa, a man curious in his researches into nature, and on account of his wisdom supposed to have conversed with the Muses, consecrated this fire and ordered it to be perpetually kept up, as an image of that Eternal Power which preserves and actuates the universe. Others say, that according to the usage of the Greeks, the fire is kept ever burning before the Holy Places, as an emblem of purity; but here are other things in the most secret part of the Atrium, kept from the sight of all but those Virgins whom they call Vestals.

The post was clearly a mark of social prestige, not spiritual calling. Originally the post was offered to daughters of highest families, though in time the social qualifications were lowered. Candidates had to be between six and ten. Both parents had to be alive at the time. The candidates were selected by the Pontifex Maximus. Upon selection, the child was called *amata*, and the traditional formula was pronounced. The new Vestal was taken ceremonially by the Pontifex Maximus in the *capito* which resembled the abduction of the bride during a Roman wedding. She passed out of her father's control. Her property passed to the state, her new husband. She was given an amount of money, often substantial, the equivalent of a dowry. The Vestals perpetually wore the costume and hairstyle appropriate to a bride. The wedding day was captured, frozen in time for a thousand years.

The Vestals individually played out their role for 30 years each, the allotted time span.

> They are under a necessity of continuing unmarried during the space of thirty years; which they employ in offering sacrifices, and performing other rites, ordained by the law. During the first ten years, their duty was to learn their functions; in the second ten years to perform them; and during the remainder of their term, to instruct the younger ones. [13]

Their function was severed from any initiatory or mediating purpose. Here were cult personnel without a deity, serving only the state. Here were wives of the Roman state tending the fire, preparing the sacrificial cake, the *mola salsa*, cleaning the *aedes vestae*. The household tasks were raised to the level of sacrament to uphold the Roman nation. The Vestals attended religious rites, were in charge of certain religious relics and offered public prayers.

These wives of the state, unlike the Egyptian wives of the god, enjoyed no mythological identification of their own. They could not dispense divine blessing, speak in the name of the goddess, or represent the divine feminine. The Vestals were raised to a symbolic but not divine level, representing only the dutiful Roman *matronalia*. This position was essentially passive and

Figure 7 The High Vestal Flavia Publicia, from AD 257.

powerless. Breaking the primal requirement of faithfulness to the state brought death. This was the only logical outcome permissible within the male-defined, static, structural identification. Unlike Hera the Goddess of marriage, whose role encompassed cyclic movement and even separation, these divine wives were permitted only to be faithful.

Minor disciplinary offences were punished by the Pontifex Maximus. Twenty Vestal Virgins were punished by death for breaking their vows. Eighteen Vestals were put to death by being buried alive. Two Vestals committed suicide. The Vestal Virgin Rubria was seduced by Nero and escaped punishment, another was married for a short time to the Emperor Heliogabalus in a calculated act of sacrilege on his part.

A lapse in duty or morality by a Vestal was believed to put the state in danger. The sacred fire went out during the second punic war which resulted in panic in Rome. The offending Vestal was thoroughly scourged.

As wife of the state the Vestal received certain privileges. They attended the state festivals. They were often entrusted with wills and other legal documents and did not have to take an oath in court. They alone of all priesthoods had a right to burial inside the city. They were given special seats at the gladiatorial games, contrary to the norm when Roman women were given the uppermost and poorest seats. They were also entitled to the best seats at the theatre. The Vestals were attended by a lictor carrying the fasces whenever they travelled outside the temple. Even consuls and praetors made way for them, lowering the fasces in salute. A condemned criminal on the way to execution would be pardoned if he accidentally encountered a Vestal Virgin. Conversely, anyone who passed under the litter of a Vestal was automatically punished with death.

These outer signs of respect and power were in reality only empty gestures, a deference not to womanhood, certainly not to the goddess, but to Rome's own idea of a wife.

Times began to change. Constantine was converted to Christianity in AD 313. The law began to move against pagan temples. It was just a question of time before the sacred fire was extinguished. Rome was dying. The Vestal Virgin Coelia Conordia resigned and became a Christian. When Gratian became Emperor in AD 375 he refused to accept the honorary office of Pontifex Maximus. In 382 he abolished the college of virgins, withheld privileges, ended state support and closed the Temple of Vesta. Symachus, in a time-honoured tradition, attributed public calamity to the removal of the Vestals. An extraordinary formal debate took place between Ambrose Archbishop of Milan and Symachus before Gratian's successor Valentinian II. The Emperor Theodosius finally suppressed the ceremonies in 394. History provides one footnote however. In 400, after the Vestals had officially been closed for some time,

Serena the niece of the emperor Theodosius happened upon a temple of Cybele served by a single Vestal. The statue of the goddess was adorned with jewellery which she took for herself while being lambasted all the while by the solitary priestess. This was a bad time for acts of violation. Alaric was already at the gates of Rome, Serena was charged with treachery. The entire senate were unanimous in their decision – Serena was strangled.

The disappearance of the Vestal Virgins marked the closing of an era. The ancient world was changing. Christianity was settling in. Its star was in the ascendant.

Chapter 8

JAPAN AND OKINAWA –
THE SHAMANS

The shamanic crisis, when properly fostered, yields an adult not only of superior intelligence and refinement, but also of greater physical stamina and vitality of spirit than is normal to members of the group. The crisis, consequently has the value of a superior threshold initiation: superior in the first place because spontaneous, not tribally enforced, and in the second place, because the shift of reference of the psychologically potent symbols has not been from the family to the tribe but from the family to the universe.

JOSEPH CAMPBELL, *The Masks of God*

SHAMANS, ANCIENT AND MODERN

In the East a long tradition of female shamanism has remained undisturbed even into this century. In Japan and the island complex of Okinawa, it was usual for women to exercise spiritual office. This situation is now being eroded, more by twentieth century materialism than any attack on female power.

The shamanic tradition is perhaps the most ancient magical path emerging from the Paleolithic caves and the tribal hunting cultures. Unlike the functionary in any other system the individual is empowered directly from the invisible worlds, chosen by spiritual beings rather than elected or entitled to office. The individual is marked out by physical and psychological symptoms which are often extreme, bordering on insanity or critical illness.

These conditions are finally transformed through a powerful rebirth crisis. The individual is awakened to the spirit world and to the nature of his or her true vocation. This violent interior experience marks the end of the old life and the birth of the new. The individual often experiences a frightening vision of his or her own death and rebirth. Henceforth the shaman is empowered and serves the community through the ability to communicate with spiritual beings in deep visionary trance; travels to the other world in spirit journey, and is assisted by a company of spirit helpers.

DAUGHTERS OF THE GODS

Pure in heaven and pure in earth. Pure within and pure without. Pure in all six roots. . . . You who draw near, loosen now the reigns of your grey horse as you gallop to me over the long beach.

TRADITIONAL SUMMONING SPELL, *The Catalpa Bow*

Japan has a long history of female shamans. Women holding priestly functions were called in various ways, *itako, okamin,* or *kuchiyose.* Kuchiyose means 'to hear the words of gods or spirits', 'to consult the oracle', or 'women themselves who play an intermediary role'.[1] The kuchiyose were independent from any particular shrine and travelled where they chose. Collectively these women were called *miko,* 'the daughters of the gods'. Miko women served in shrines throughout the land as far back as the late prehistoric period. It was customary for the Emperor to be advised by miko women. The *kannagi* were 'the propitiators of the gods'. They were very often attached to high-ranking shrines.

These shamanic priestesses were quite unlike the sacred women of the ancient world. They were apprenticed directly to the supramundane powers and mediated directly between the deities, the deceased and the living. Their lives contain bizarre and even frightening episodes of possession. These women experienced the deities not as role model or psychological principle but as a possessing presence.

The shamanic tradition survived unbroken despite various legal prohibitions. Haniwa pottery figures from fifth- and sixth-century tombs show shamanic regalia. Pottery figures wear the flat hat like an oblong board, strings of beads around neck, ankles and wrists, and, from a sash around the waist, a round mirror with five bells and a bow. Each item carried a magical significance. The copper mirror was traditionally part of the costume of Tunguistic shamans of northern Manchuria. It was a receptacle for the dead person's spirit, a place to see the soul, and a receptacle in which the *kami*, the possessing deity might dwell. The bow, which emitted a resonating note, was used as a magical tool for attracting the deity. It also acted as a conductor, through which the deity might enter the body. The *magatama* beads, also found in Korea, were used to ritually summon the deities. When attired and empowered by full ritual regalia, the miko would prepare to enter the trance state in the sand-garden, the *saniwa*, a sanctified temenos serving as a magic circle. The miko would be accompanied by a musician who played magical tunes to soothe the deity and an interrogator who would address the deity. Questions might be asked about the harvest, fortunes for the coming year, the likelihood of robbery, sickness or fire in the village. Proper procedures had to be followed to ensure the safety of the medium and the smooth appearance and departure of the deity.

In the remote villages the miko acted as the link between the ordinary people and the tutelary village deities. Many miko women lived in enclaves affiliated to large shrines known as *miko-mura*, miko villages. They set out at specific seasons on long peripatetic journeys, delivering prophecies, messages from the dead, and offering consultation.

The different titles conferred on these women point to a rich and varied tradition. Women known as *kumano-bikuni* were based at the Jippoin temple at Nachi and were venerated as oracles all over the country. In the Edo district the women called *ichiko* were reported to travel great distances to make seasonal calls. Near Osaka women called *shinano-miko* were still visiting in the last half of the nineteenth century. The institution of the miko was widespread throughout Japan. They were part of both court and village tradition until the time of the Meji restoration.

Shamanic practice was not confined to commoners. Emperors took advice from miko women speaking as the mouthpiece for the deity. The *Wei Chronicles* include a description of a shamanic queen, Himako or Pimako by name, who lived alone in a heavily-guarded palace attended by a single man who transmitted her words. The consort of an Emperor, later to become the Empress Jingo, was herself a miko. Descriptions remain of a rite in which she acted as a medium. In this rite the Emperor and the chief minister took the other traditional roles of musician, who soothed the deity, and interrogator, who questioned the deity. The Emperor wanted to know whether to attack the Kumaso people. The deity advised an expedition to a rich land full of gold and silver which would be delivered into the Emperor's hands. The Emperor, instead of thanking the deity in the proper manner, committed the crime of 'raising words' in opposition to the deity. He laid aside the zither he had been playing and declared, 'it is a lying deity however high you may climb, you can see no such land in the west. There is nothing but sea.'

The enraged deity pronounced a curse: 'Go straight in one direction.' When the lights went up the Emperor was found to be dead. A second rite was conducted seven days later with the same interrogator and the consort again acting as medium.

'What are the god's instructions?'

'The land in the west is to be ruled by a child in the Empress's womb.'

'What child is this who is in her womb?'

'It is a boy.'

'What is your name?'

'This is the will of Amaterasu-omikami and of the three great deities Sokozutsu-no-o, Nakazutsu-no-o, and Uwazutsu-no-o. If you wish to find the rich land, then make offerings to the deities of heaven, earth, mountains, rivers and seas. Make a shrine for our spirit at the top of the ship, put wood and ashes into a gourd. Make many chopsticks and flat dishes and cast them on to the sea.'

With these words the account ends. We are left wondering what happened to the Empress. Did she have the son who ruled the lands of the west?[2]

Miko activities were suppressed in 1873 when the government

decreed that miko were all deluded and forbidden to practise. Many miko continued to practise in secret. In theory this prohibition lasted until 1945 when General MacArthur's legislation ended restrictions. There have been three outbursts of shamanic cultic activity in recent history each related to the Japanese legal and political situation. The first rash of new sects appeared in the middle of the last century at the time of the collapse of the feudal system. Of these, thirteen groups survived, misleadingly known as 'the 13 sects of Shinto'. A second period occurred in the 1920s and 1930s, at a time of economic depression and increasing militarianism. The third burst took place after 1945 with the liberalisation brought about by MacArthur. In 1964, 378 cults were still registered. The life histories of the cult founders share similar patterns and reveal strong shamanic overtones.

MEDIUMS AND MEDIATORS

Certain special human beings, however, may acquire a power which enables them to transcend the barrier between the two worlds.

CARMEN BLACKER, *The Catalpa Bow*

The life of Nakayama Miki, who founded 'Tendrikyo', follows the pattern typically seen in shamanic individuals. Her early life was marked with personal disaster and unhappiness. She survived the dreadful famine of the 1830s to be married at thirteen to a man she hated. When a neighbour's son fell ill while under her care she petitioned the local deity to take the lives of her two daughters in return for the life of the boy. In due course the boy recovered, her girls died. In 1837 her surviving son Shuji was afflicted with agonising leg pains. The local yamabushi, Ichibei, was called in to perform exorcism. One night Miki acted as medium for Ichibei as his assistant could not come. According to the story, the spirit causing the affliction possessed her and she fell into violent trance.

'I am Ten-no Shogun', came the voice.

'What manner of god might Ten-no-Shogun be?'

'The original god who has descended from heaven to save

mankind', answered the deity.

Miki was possessed for three days sitting upright, transmitting the words of the deity. The possession only ended when her husband agreed to follow instructions implicitly. She began to behave in excessive ways, giving away the family property, even having the family house pulled down. After a long period of total destitution she was blessed with the power of granting painless childbirth. Her fame spread. In 1869 she started to write an Ofudesaki, a long divinely-inspired poem. It took her another fifteen years to complete the work. She died in 1887 aged 90. Her teachings remain encapsulated in one of thirteen Shinto sects.

The foundress of the Omoto sect was Deguchi Nao. She was born in 1837. At eleven she was sent out to work due to the extreme poverty of her family. She was soon married to a drunken and spendthrift husband with whom she had eleven children. Of these three died in infancy, one disappeared, another was killed in the Sino-Japanese war. Two of her grown daughters later died after becoming insane. In January 1892, following the death of one of her daughters, she had a vivid dream in which she was wandering in the spirit world. A day or two later she fell into a violent state of possession, leaping up and down with pain. In this state a voice spoke, conversing with her own, announcing itself to be Ushitora-no-Konjin, come to restore the hideous state of the world to paradise. During the next year she often fell into trance, wandering around the town roaring wildly. She was arrested on suspicion of arson and confined to a room in her house. Here she began to write an Ofudeska, scratching characters with a nail on the pillar of her room. This work was to fill the next 27 years of her life. On her release from confinement she discovered that she had the powers to heal through prayer.

Another foundress in the shamanic tradition was Kitamura Sayo, who established *Tensho Kotai Jingukyo*, the Dancing Religion. She was called, 'Ogamisama', meaning great goddess. She too suffered an impoverished and miserable childhood. She became the sixth wife to a weak and mean man, procured by his mother, to be used as cheap harvest labour, dispensed with and divorced at the end the season. Half starved and treated cruelly by her in-laws she took up ascetic practice as an escape. In 1944 she became aware of the god Tobyo who began to speak through her, giving her sound advice on a wide range of matters. She underwent a complete change of personality, delivered sermons and extempore song. Her language however became so coarse and unconventional that she chose to wear men's clothing while speaking. She taught the 'Selfless Dance' to her followers. In 1964 she accomplished a world tour, visiting 36 countries giving three sermons a day. She continued to be worshipped after her death. In her life she was credited with healing miracles, diverting the course of streams, and arresting the spread of fires. Even today she is worshipped as a living goddess. 'The presence of the deity inside her has transsubstantiated her into a divine person.'[3]

These women who became the inspirational founders of popular cults, each experienced suffering and deprivation in early life, loneliness and even cruelty in close relationships, the untimely death of children and rejection by the social group as a whole. It is this alchemical process which gives birth to shamanic qualities, powers and inspiration. The true shaman only comes to birth after much personal suffering and misery; the cost is high.

The path of mediumship, is less extreme. It used to be an occupation reserved for the blind. This type of mediumship shows strong shamanic overtones but lacks the spontaneous crisis which gives birth to the visionary powers. It is replaced instead with a traditional training. The young blind girl was apprenticed at about twelve years of age, before the onset of menstruation, to an older *itako*, a blind medium. She lived with her teacher for several years. Her training was strict and lengthy and included an ascetic regime, learning sutras, chants and invocations. Finally, she was deemed ready to take initiation and prepared for the ceremony through severe ascetic practice. This included sleep deprivation, food taboos – neither cereals nor salt – and a regime of cold water over each shoulder daily. She had to keep away from all sources of heat.

At her initiation ritual she was wedded to her tutelary deity. The deity came to take possession of her. The initiation included a wedding feast at which she wore a bridal gown. Finally, at the transmission of power, she was presented with her own magical instruments, the bow or one-stringed lute, a rosary, a fan-shaped drum, a mysterious box and a pair of puppets. Once initiated she was expected to summon ghosts, call the *kami*, deliver inspired utterances, serve as an oracle and speak with the dead.

Carmen Blacker asks, 'if shamanism was so widespread in prehistoric Japan, if an inspired woman could be discovered to serve in virtually every shrine in the land, how is it that today these natural shamans are so rare? She concludes that 'they manifest themselves only in times of crisis, anxiety, and the collapse of tradition. Were the conditions of modern secular life more propitious to the display of such powers, it is likely that many more women would exhibit them in Japan today than might be suspected. Many women appear neurotic, or even half-wittted merely because these powers are repressed or disguised within them.'[4]

OKINAWA - VILLAGE AND ROYAL PRIESTESSES

Women seldom play a leading role in Japanese folk religion, while their place in Okinawa is conspicuously important.

KAMATA HISAKO, *Shaman Priestesses*

Okinawa is an island group with three main cultural divisions: Okinawa, Miyako and the Yaeyama archipelago. Okinawa's geography has produced surprising variations from island to island. Women have held a particularly significant role throughout Okinawa. 'It is women that are privileged to hold priestly rights in the rituals of the village or kinship group.'[5] The significance of women in the priestly role is reflected in the traditional folklore of the region. Ifa Fuyu summarises the mythological themes: 'According to Okinawa mythology, the first son becomes the king; the second the *anji*, (local governor) the third the farmer; the eldest daughter, the *kimi-gimi* (the royal priestess); and the second, first *noro* (village priestess).'[6]

The Okinawa people held a mixed concept of divinity, believing in both the ancestral gods and those of the elements. When the Sho family became the rulers of the Okinawa complex, their ancestral gods became the ruling gods of all the islands. The king's sister became the royal priestess, *kikeo ogimi*. In later days this position was assumed by the queen instead. This office holder represented the entire people before the divine presence of the ancestral gods.

In the villages there were priestesses called *norokumoi* meaning 'a person who prays'. In the days of the Sho dynasty, the village priestesses, also called *noro*, were appointed by the royal government and were under the control of the royal priestess. Shimabukuro Gen'ichiro, who was born on Okinawa, provides an insight into the succession of the noro:

> In the old days a noro was succeeded by her daughter, and as it was a matrilineal succession, the family name of the noro changed with each generation. But as the social customs changed and male-line succession became more dominant, with a strong consciousness of family name, the daughter of the noro became deprived of her right to succession and instead it became a practice to make her niece (her brother's daughter) the next noro, thus making it possible to retain the position of the noro within patrilineal relatives. In more recent times the position is succeeded by the son's wife, as in the case of the noro of the Itoman village, so that the position is succeeded constantly along a given line. [7]

Each of the three islands of Okinawa had its own practices and organisations. Hirara city in the centre of the Miyako Island was once the branch office of the court. A divine priestess, *o-amo*, used to be attached to this office. She was appointed by the court. In 1865 the o-amo requested that her post might pass to her son as she had neither daughter nor granddaughter, indicating that the legitimate line of succession was matrilinear.

Villages continued to enjoy independent organisation despite the court's appointee, and followed their own traditions. In some villages any woman of a certain age might act as cult official. In the Ikema island divine posts were selected from village-born women over 43. Tenure was held for three years. The women of Oura village in the northern part of Miyako island were eligible for office at 49. In other villages the post was reserved for women in special families. Still other villages preferred to select from those women with an unusual physical condition, taking this as a special sign.

On Miyako island, the supreme priestess was called *upu-zukasa* (*upu* means 'great one'). Once appointed she served for life and was not encouraged to leave the island even for short journeys. She was selected by ritual lottery, though it is said that the choice was known to the incumbent through dream premonition.

Miyako island had a unique religious organisation called *uyagami*. Its members performed just one ritual a year. The wives of certain families who had reached the age of 50 were qualified to serve. The office was inherited from mother-in-law to daughter-in-law. Between June and October the uyagami women met for a week each month in the bush, which was extensive on the island.

The festival which they performed was especially important to the whole island. Islanders returned home especially to attend. The women represented the group lineage both past and present of the island. The uyagami were called the ancestor gods. They wore huge crowns a meter in diameter made from vines. During the festival these women were perceived as being deities by both themselves and others. In the 1960s there were fourteen uyagami on Ogami island.

On the Izu island those who wished to become miko had to show psychic abilities including sensitivity and the ability to have significant dreams. These signs were called miko inclinations. Women here might become miko only after the menopause. Women showing obvious signs were examined by the existing miko. In order to be formally recognised, the miko had to pass a final trial called *kami-sode*, 'the descent of the god'. The prospective candidate had to prepare for seven days, bathing every morning in the sea when the sun rose, pouring sea water upon her head seven times. She carried a branch of a sacred tree and a fan. At the end of the seven days she was recognised ceremonially in a special hut or hall. She sat with the fan and branch amidst drumming and music. Other miko danced around her, encouraging trance and awaiting her possession. The new miko was expected to become frenzied, shrieking with convulsions as the power descended. Her motions were thought to become especially intense when the correct name of her deity was spoken. When the descent was completed, she was divinely possessed. The frenzy passed. She joined the dancing miko.

The miko officiated at public rituals and assisted with every aspect of village life, giving advice, consultation and prophecy to help the general welfare of the villagers.

This way of life is now fading. The ubiquitous television and western cultural values have spread like a plague into even the most remote places of the world, bringing the all-knowing eye and the deities of the technological age.

GLOSSARY

Ichiko, a shamanic medium

Itako, a local name for a female shaman

Kannagi, mediums serving high-ranking shrines

Kami, spiritual beings

Kimi gimi, a royal priestess

Kuchiyose, 'to hear the words of gods or spirits', women who play an intermediary role delivering messages while in trance

Kumano-bikuni, a buddhist nun with the powers of prophesy and divination.

Miko, 'daughters of the gods', shamanic mediums

Ofudesaki, the revelations of a founder of a new religion, usually written through automatic writing in poetry form

Saniwa, 'the sand garden', the temenos especially purified for a ritual

Chapter 9

TEMENOS –
THE SACRED ENCLOSURE

Any society shapes and is shaped by certain rites which enact the myth of the community.

M.J. HATCHETT, *Sanctifying Life Time and Space*

THE SACRED SPACE

The sacred space has a long history. Symbolic acts which are neither practical nor rational, but nevertheless highly meaningful, appear at the dawn of time. The recognition and articulation of needs which are not survival based is a unique human expression. Humanity, unlike other animals, is driven to make sense of life's experiences, to abstract a symbolic code from the concrete actuality of life and death, to explain the mysteries and the paradoxes of the human life experience. This in essence is at the root of all religious expression.

Sacred acts are those which evolve in the attempt to convey something of the meaning of life as distinct from those acts which make up the mundane experience of life itself. At its simplest level those acts which are deemed to be of special significance by the group for its own well-being take on a special status. In a social context, human transitions, physical maturation and especially death call attention to themselves. Rites of passage and cults of the dead universally acquire a sacred status. Human contact with the deities, whether to seek blessing, make offering, or seek guidance demands a particular procedure. The contact is potentially dangerous for the deities are always associated with supra-mundane powers. Humankind has little intrinsic power to exert in this equation. Celebration is less fraught with risk, the whole group or those who come to represent the group may safely meet to honour the shared relationship between deity and group. The sacred acts evolved by the group eventually become concentrated into a sacred place; the temenos, the sacred enclosure is born. It is not difficult to understand the evolution of the sacred site as a place set apart, for the life events commemorated and sanctified are those charged with both mystery and fear. The sacred and the feared are inextricably linked. Transition is a time of danger and instability. Contact with the deities is potentially fraught.

The temenos becomes a symbolic container for all the unresolved mysteries within life which ever present themselves as contradictions and oppositions, birth and death, appearance and disappearance, success and failure, weakness and strength. It is the place of offering and appeasement, the meeting place between the worlds of humans and deities. It also becomes the place of witness, where the deities are summoned to attend and legitimate power in the world of humans.

The sacred place, once defined through ritual consecration, becomes a place set apart surrounded by taboos, the invisible walls which maintain and reinforce the air of mystery attached to the site. It is looked after by those who have themselves been sanctified, especially chosen either by the group or by unseen powers. The temenos is forbidden to those not themselves sanctified unless they are under the protection of sacerdotal figures at communal events. The creation of sacred buildings followed naturally in time as society generally moved into created structures. The building enshrines the beliefs and special collective symbols in its arrangement and architecture. The spiritual philosophy of the group is stated in stone and line, space and enclosure, revealing the spiritual stance of the people as clearly as a sacred book. The relationship between the temenos, its personnel and those acts which are deemed sacred, represents the tangible expression of the group's spiritual philosophy. From the whole land, to the specialised landscape, from the natural land to the artificial construction, from the empty land to the sacred building, the temenos moves and changes like a chameleon responsive to fluctuating social, political and philosophical forces.

THE LIVING EARTH

We live because the Earth is an immense repository of organised life-fields within which our own life-fields are contained.

MARY SCOTT, *Kundalini in the Physical World*

The whole land was once experienced as a living entity. It was the primal sacred space. Outstanding or unusually-shaped landmarks in the likeness of a divine image naturally presented themselves as places of special significance. Openings into the earth were likened to the orifices of the feminine body, sacralised and revered as places close the heartbeat of the mother. Streams, wells, hot springs and caves took on a special significance, becoming places for ceremony and sacrifice. When the hunt was significant, dark places represented the hidden depths where animals began or were renewed. People too were renewed in such places, both young men and young women passed through initiatory rites in the darkness of the Earth's womb.

When the hunt was succeeded by the harvest, the land took on an even greater significance. The land was alive, constantly changing, constantly renewing itself. Rising mounds and rolling hills were clearly the body of the Earth Mother.

The land itself offered its own symbolic code. Running water, lush pastures, copses of trees and vegetation signified growth. Dry plains and thin soil spoke of want. Different colours, subtle textures, shapes and land formations spoke to the psyche open to symbolic experience.

Later, the symbolic language was extracted from the landscape so that elements could be artificially manipulated and combined to create a highly-charged setting rich in symbolic overtones. Landscape elements were incorporated into natural ceremonial theatres, constructed from the earth. Sacred landscapes with all the appearance of natural forms were created, mimicking the shapes and forms of nature. Artificial mounds were built up, ditches were dug out, banks were created. Natural features, rivers, woods, vistas and horizons were incorporated into a living pattern of season and ceremonial activity. The sacred site merged into the land like a seamless garment. Sacred landscape was grafted so invisibly into the already existing framework that in many cases time has erased the join.

Such sites represented the social cohesion and intent of settled people who perceived nature's processes in feminine form. The land and the year presented the framework against which life took place. Communal life and activity was modelled upon the rhythms perceived in nature. The life cycle of the Great Goddess was also the life cycle of the people.

Land-based peoples invariably developed a sensitivity to the repeating patterns which create the seasons. Close proximity to the changing rhythms of day and night, summer and winter, autumn and spring, brought a heightened awareness of the presence of light and dark, the balance of warmth and cold, the interplay of sun and moon, the power of water and wind. The elemental forces of nature revealed themselves as both powerful and subtle to people who lived alongside the ice of winter, the thaw of spring. The changing seasons marked by equinox and solstice points carried a vital and practical significance; the cosmic clock regulated activity. Human drama was united to the cosmic drama, experienced through the life of the Divine Feminine.

The religious practices of both Paleolithic and Neolithic peoples were eminently practical. Group ceremonies served as markers of changing rhythms heralding a different phase of communal activity. Social order was aligned to cosmic order. The sacred site was the cosmic clock, a place of initiation social and biological, a communal expression of a communal life.

THE COSMIC DRAMA – THE HUMAN DRAMA

Symbols activated by rites told the community's master story, the narrative which embraced all others, the Myth Cycle.

MICHAEL DAMES, *The Avebury Cycle*

European Neolithic people were acutely aware of cyclic change.

Each season was aligned to a different aspect of the current mythology. People partook of the essential nature of each phase by witnessing, enacting and symbolically experiencing its key themes. The year was punctuated by the solstice and equinox points and further subdivided by midway markers at May, August, November and February. These latter points provided the ritual calendar. The story of the year, the people and the Goddess was probably enacted throughout the length and breadth of Europe. The sacred sites of our distant forebears have merged invisibly into the land from which they were originally built.

In Wiltshire, however, one huge site at least remains, straggling across an expanse of landscape. 'The overall purpose of the entire ensemble was to celebrate the annual cycle of the great goddess, at temples which were her seasonal portraits.'[1] The entire Wiltshire site includes the Sanctuary Temple, Silbury Hill, the Avebury henge and West Kennet barrow. 'The worshippers moved around this extended gallery of symbolic architecture in time with the changing seasons, and the farming year, synchronised with the comparable events in the lives of the human community, namely birth, puberty, marriage and death.'[2] Human life is marked out through transitions, puberty, childbirth, and the final transition into death itself. This is the process of endless becoming, mirrored in the passage of the year and undoubtedly told in the stories of the Goddess herself.

This vast temple site provided the setting for group participation in mysteries both human and divine. The four sites are part of a whole, each complete by itself, each related to other sites through symbols and subtle nuances resonating in the land.

THE SANCTUARY - THE END OF GIRLHOOD

In almost every primitive society, the passage from childhood to maturity is marked by a long periods of instruction, accompanied by physical tests.

MICHAEL DAMES, *The Avebury Cycle*

A small circular temple hut with a wattle and daub fence was built on Overton Hill. It was still known as the Sanctuary when Stukely made a visit in 1719. By 1724 it had been destroyed by two farmers. It was not rediscovered until 1930.

The Sanctuary was some 65 feet in diameter with a conical roof. At the summit an opening permitted sunlight and moonlight to penetrate. Like a great eye high on the hill the Sanctuary looked towards the future, its open iris at the centre.

It served as 'Silbury's Candlemas beginning', the preparation site for what was to follow at Silbury. Its relationship to Silbury was clearly indicated through its construction. The wattle wall of the Sanctuary was mirrored by an exact replica, a circular wattle fence with the same circumference built into Silbury Hill, hidden deep in the great mound. The potential of the Sanctuary was realised and integrated in the hill. Silbury Hill multiplies the Sanctuary's diameter by eight, a significant number in a year marked by eight landmarks, the solstices, equinoxes and halfway points. The Lammas full moon rose over the Sanctuary and the hill at the same time, flooding them both with silver light. The Sanctuary was further aligned with Silbury: twenty pieces of lava were buried beneath the post marking the axis at 250° of the harvest moonset at Silbury. Burying symbolic significant items as markers of some kind was a common Neolithic practice.

A piece of haematite iron ore which gives a blood-red powder was buried beneath one post in the Sanctuary. A red deer antler was buried beneath another. The red nature of these items give us a clue to the function of this place, to initiate girls into the significance of their own redness, the menstrual blood. It is very likely that girls were taken here at menarche in the company of older women who prepared them for future womanhood. 'By their sojourn in the sanctuary, the girls died to an outworn childhood and were born to the prospect of fruitfulness.'[3] We cannot know what transpired here. We may speculate that such initiation rites included instruction, awakening and rebirth into adult status through celebration, seclusion in the company of women and dramatic enactment employing current symbols. The Sanctuary site was an integral part of the whole pattern laid out in the landscape. It was aligned to Silbury Hill, symbolic of birth but also to the temple of death at West Kennet. An adolescent male and a young ox had been sacrificed and buried only six feet beyond one of the posts on an axis connecting the two sites. All was connected, nothing was separate. The Neolithic mind delighted in such interconnections, understanding the inner messages interwoven by the complex of symbols.

AVEBURY - THE RITUAL MATING

The henge was the Goddess of Love.

MICHAEL DAMES, *The Avebury Cycle*

The construction of Silbury Hill preceded the Avebury site by some 2,000 years. Silbury is dated at about 4500 BC, Avebury henge is dated approximately 2600 BC. The monument to the act of birth preceded that to sexual reproduction. The henge was the site in which male and female participants played their part in the cosmic life of the Great Mother. The temple architecture is the living land itself. To a mind sensitised to the symbolism of landscape, the site itself presents living symbols. Two streams meet to conceive a new entity, just as male and female will come together to create a third. The Horslip and the Winterbourne waters meet in the Swallowhead spring which rises to create the River Kennet. Furthermore, due to the particular geological structure, new water appears every spring in the Swallowhead only to dry out in the autumn. Here was the living proof, should proof be needed, of seasonal renewal.

The Avebury henge was built to contain male and female energies, to release human sexuality and offer it as a sacrament. The site was built to 'provide a communal May festival wedding ring shaped as a living image of the goddess as Bride pictured in union with her male consort.'[4]

The henge itself is a three-dimensional symbol system, sited at the confluence of two streams, and takes its dimensions from the proportions of the Swallowhead and the Waden, the living waters. The Avebury site symbolised the head in relation to female anatomy of the land as defined by the waters. But also represented is the womb awaiting seeding. The inner circles of the henge stood for the two eyes of the goddess and as sun and moon, male and female symbols united in the same space. The Neolithic mind delighted in double meanings and the wealth of association created as symbol piled upon symbol.

The henge was designed to be big enough to be occupied by a large assembly, the whole community was involved. It was reached by two serpentine processional ways defined by one hundred pairs of standing stones. The Beckampton avenue is undeniably male in nature; phallic symbols were buried beneath the processional way. The female West Kennet avenue ended in an open snake mouth ready to swallow the male in mouth-womb symbolism. On May Day a double column of young men poured across the west causeway, extended its male head into the female jaws. They made their way to an obelisk, the primal May Pole for the first ritual penetration. The sexual energy now running high was released through the ritualised love-making which took place under the shadow of another obelisk in a group of four pits filled with dark brown soil. This is unlikely to have been the romantic love of young couples but the communal rut of tribal youth. Neolithic society was concerned to renew itself in the image of nature herself. Individual life was lived through the community. Children conceived at the May ceremonies would be born before Candlemas after the midwinter. It is unlikely that paternity was individuated, the child belonged first to its mother and secondly to the group.

The appearance of life at the season of death was yet another living paradox. Oppositions were resolved through the life cycle of the Great Goddess.

SILBURY – THE TEMPLE OF BIRTH

As an image of the great Goddess, Silbury is probably the largest surviving version of the subject in Europe.

MICHAEL DAMES, *The Silbury Treasure*

Silbury Hill is an extraordinary site built to reveal a great mystery, the birth of the harvest from the womb of the Great Goddess. Here the great cosmic drama of the Lammas birth was played out on a sanctified landscape. Silbury Hill remains an extraordinary feat of construction, a testament to the spiritual drive and commitment of its builders. The planning and foresight required to unite land and sky in a single dramatic moment reveals a high level of astronomical knowledge, the physical labour needed to establish the great mound reveals group endurance and determination.

Silbury Hill is the Great Goddess herself in the Neolithic birth position, squatting. Her form is built into the land. Her womb is the hill itself, 520 feet in diameter, 130 feet high. Her thighs are water, her head and neck are water, her breasts and back are water now overlaid with a 15-foot deposit of silt masking the original intention. Her head extends towards the west, her back faces north, her breasts and knees point south.

The features of the landscape both constructed and natural combined to represent symbols and themes readily understood by the Neolithic observer. Michael Dames outlines twelve themes which are symbolised through the site. These are:

1 The pregnant seated goddess
2 The goddess half buried in the ground
3 The eye-goddess – supreme intelligence
4 The white mountain in the primordial water
5 The cosmic egg
6 The sickle, grain and cornstook
7 The throne
8 The stag
9 The umbilical snake
10 Mother and child
11 Woman with phallus-androgyny
12 The spinning and weaving goddess[5]

These themes were significant to the Neolithic psyche quite independently one from another. The site at Silbury is unique. It drew together all the major themes of Neolithic spirituality. 'At Silbury they appear together to form a symbol of awesome comprehensiveness.'[6]

The size of the site was determined by astronomical factors. The scale of the mother was crucial. It had to be broad enough to absorb all known variations of Lammas full moon behaviour.

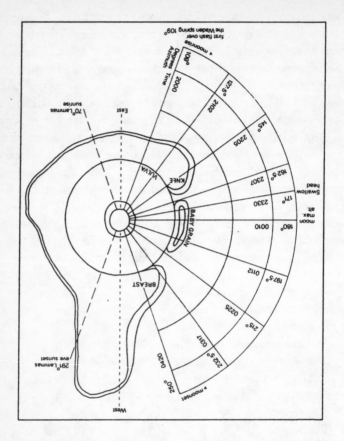

Figure 8 The Lammas Eve nativity sequence created by the
interplay between the moon and Silbury Hill.

In some years the celebrations would be shifted backwards or
forwards by as much as fourteen days to find a full moon bringing
appreciable variations in the length of the night. The site at
Silbury was designed to accommodate both extremes. The
imagery of the birth was still clear.

In an ideal year, the full moon coincided with the halfway stage
between summer solstice and autumn equinox. This gave a
sufficient balance between darkness and light, and a sufficient
time lapse between the moments of sunset, moonrise and the
following sunrise. In such a year on Lammas Eve, we can imagine

an assembly of peoples gathered and waiting in anticipation. The stage was built, all was made ready for the cosmic drama to begin.

The following cosmic scenario unfolds. The sun disappears in the northwest shortly after 7.30pm. Even this event is included in the drama for the dying sun is aligned with a pronounced curve in the otherwise straight moat edge. The orange light touches the land to create the fleeting illusion of a plait of hair. There is now a pause of about 30 minutes. The observers move to the southeast edge of the terrace to await moonrise. They do not have long to wait. At 8pm the moon's edge shows itself, appearing directly over Waden Hill spring. This conjunction was probably planned so that the moon was seen to be born from Waden and Silbury water simultaneously. The Lammas moon appears at the Silbury moat, in reflection, over Waden spring and over the silhouetted sanctuary temple on nearby Overton Hill.

At 110° the full disc occupies the Silbury moat, its light falling across the thigh indicating the vulva which joins Avebury to Swallowhead spring. For the next few hours the moon climbs into the sky, travelling to the south. By 10pm the reflection falls on the left knee. True darkness comes at 10.45pm, when the moon is hanging over a narrow gap between knee and child. The gap is the eastern causeway. The child waiting to be defined is the intercauseway moat. At 11.30pm the infant's head appears as a full round lunar reflection on the intercauseway moat. At the same moment it is seen suspended over the Swallowhead. Another birth is proclaimed, that of Swallowhead-Silbury, matching the first display of Waden and Silbury. Silbury Hill Mother and River Mother share the child-making, affirming the bisexuality of the creator, the phallus clearly seen as the ditch. At midnight the moon is at the highest altitude, lying 180° due south. It is now aligned with the part of the mound where the navel cord might be. This was the moment to cut the cord, perhaps the time to cut the green corn possibly growing on the summit. The moon indicates the nipples at 3.17am. The breasts swell with light. Sunrise comes at 4.35am. The child is born. Harvest has come. The cosmic drama has been witnessed for another year.

WEST KENNET – THE TEMPLE OF DEATH

In Stone Age imagery and belief, the long goddess grew from and
returned to the squatting goddess.

MICHAEL DAMES, *The Avebury Cycle*

The Neolithic mind was acutely aware of the reality of death,
human life was ever fragile, reliant on weather, the harvest and
other forces outside human control. Death was ever present.
Disease, sickness and accident were realities liable to bring
tragedy to a community. It would have been impossible to
celebrate the high moment of birth without also acknowledging
the presence of death in life.

The fruitful goddess now appeared as the withered hag, life
energy spent, withdrawing from the landscape into the dark earth.
Her rounded womb once full with child was now empty. The
hollow womb of the Long Hag awaited the coming of new life.
The West Kennet long barrow was the Temple of Death. It
contained 46 skeletons in a small tomb which occupied one eighth
of the total area. The barrow was built over running water, as
confirmed by recent water diviners. The arrangement of the
interior dry stone walling resembled the underground stream as
a symbol of life hidden but latent. The chalk of the site like the
whitened bones of the long dead, spoke effortlessly of the
reabsorption of the deceased into the womb-tomb of the earth.
Additionally, the barrow contained a five-fold chamber, the
squatting birth goddess slept ready to play her role in the coming
season.

The barrow is dated at approximately 3250 BC. A bulky stone
formation, ox-like in shape, was added at the entrance in
approximately 2600 BC. It was also about this time that the
barrow was filled with rubble and organic matter in layers,
resembling the soil of Silbury doubtless for symbolic reasons. The
ox was an important Neolithic image. It was a familiar figure at
the everyday level as the provider of meat, hides and physical
strength. Its curving white horns marked it out as being especially
close to the Goddess. The ox took on the role of sacrificial victim
being dispatched to the Goddess in her winter barren aspect at

the entrance to the underworld. 'There is overwhelming evidence to support a November slaughter of oxen, with a persistent sacrificial quality. Thus the beast upon whose broad back the Neolithic queen of death rode in annual triumph may perhaps have been killed at the start of every winter at her West Kennet forecourt.'[7]

The cycle was complete. The year was complete. Human drama and cosmic drama united in a group participation of a myth which sustained a society. At Avebury we find no evidence of a specialised priesthood, either male or female, yet it is obvious that various sites were built with precision, knowledge and extraordinary astronomical accuracy which can only represent generations of observation and recording. We can safely deduce that the ceremonial events themselves were in the hands of tribal elders of both sexes who took on the priestly roles as initiators, sacrificers, and mediators between the Goddess and the people.

At Avebury male and female roles are balanced, indicating equality before the Great Goddess.

The balance evident in these rites of passage, however, diminished as shifts of power took place in society. Female initiation commonly fell into male hands constituting a true distortion of social power. Finally, marriage itself came to serve as the sexual initiation providing a biological and social transition. The temple was enshrined in the land, its message encoded in symbols obvious to the Neolithic psyche but often veiled from us. We have lost the art of synthesising symbols, our natural inclination is to dissect and separate. We see only the appearance of form, the Neolithic mind saw meaning in that same form.

The cycle so clearly laid out at Avebury resonates elsewhere in different forms, taking on other symbols relevant to other peoples. Nevertheless, symbolic language knows no boundaries and still speaks volumes across generations.

MALTA – THE SACRED BODY OF THE MOTHER

These buildings reproduce, in a fixed symbolic form, the body of the Great Mother; as medieval churches reproduce the cross of Christ.

ZUNTZ, *Persephone*

At Malta another fascinating Neolithic temple site beckons. The Maltese archipelago lies off Sicily and is less than two hundred miles from the coast of Africa. The island covers only some 314 square kilometres but hold a remarkable and unique series of temple sites at Tarxien, Kordin, Hagar Qim, Mnajdra, Ghain, Tuffieha, Mgarr, Skorba, Ggantija, and Santa Verna. These temples are in effect artificial caves, created by humankind, modelled from nature to express a very precise theological view.

The sites at Malta raise as many questions as they answer for we remain woefully ignorant of the detailed purpose and functions assigned to these underground temples. Yet we cannot ignore them for their basic message is clear and unambiguous. We have little idea of the cultic calendar followed here. We cannot with any certainty point to the types of rituals undertaken here. We are not privy to any particular or unique mythic components. Such speculations remain beyond our reach, tantalising us with possibilities.

The sanctuaries here are based on a unique three-fold shape, a trefoil. This is in all probability a cultic representation of the being of the Mother. The first hall represented the breasts, the greater hall the womb and the rear bay represented the rest of her body, perhaps the head. The sanctuaries were designed as bays, apses, extending from a central court. Straight lines have been reduced to an absolute minimum. We can sense something akin to the West Kennet barrow here. This is the womb-tomb, where life and death unite. It is highly likely that incubatory sleep was practised at Hal Saflieni in the chamber now called the hypogeum. Oracles were probably given through an aperture from an adjoining chamber. It is tempting to wonder on what occasion and under what circumstances the oracle might have been consulted. It is also tempting to wonder how the oracular mouthpiece obtained an answer. Two statuettes of sleeping women were found here. In the hypogeum, the ritual was predominantly in the hands of women. Can we conclude that consultations were based primarily on women's questions? Incubatory sleep was often part of the initiation process as the candidate sought inner validation through an inspired dream.

Zuntz supports the idea that initiation took place here.

'Following the rite of entering, the ceremonies must have been performed in the interior of the sanctuaries. In the dark or dimly lit halls the neophyte must have been guided by a knowing priest (or priestess) and it is likely that successive stages of initiation were attained through various rites in different parts of the temple.'[8] In this instance, is Zuntz referring to initiation as social or mystical process? What form might such a process have taken?

A number of seated female figurines in long skirts have been found. These in all probability represent actual priestesses. It is also likely that men also played a priestly role. At Hal Tarxien, the priests seem to have prevailed. Perhaps this was used as a centre for male puberty rites. Underworld chambers are the classic setting for the drama of rebirth. We can imagine the individual being led after days of preparation into the darkness, to spent time incubating within the earth to emerge to a triumphant reception of elder and peers as the newly-born child of the Goddess. Boys-becoming-men would have entered into the underground chamber with a sense of heightened expectation as participants in a living drama. 'He who stepped over the divine symbol at the entrance . . . had mystically experienced death; at the same time having passed through the divine vulva, he had, in a realistic symbolism become the mate of the Goddess. It must have been a ritual act of profound solemnity and an experience of deep emotion and significance.'[9] The entry into the body of the mother like the ritual mating at Avebury provided a personal encounter between man and Goddess. Girls-becoming-women might experience the numinous power of the female nature, the Great Mother, as both womb and tomb.

Unfortunately we know too little of the ritual calendar and practically nothing of the ceremonies that took place here. Yet the basic symbolism is inescapable, it is undeniably female. 'She is the deep earth receiving in her womb the bodies of the dead; she is the power of birth which renews all life; she is the force of sex through which, miraculously and unceasingly, this renewal is brought about and therewith, the eternity of all life, in plant, animal and man. The dead entering her womb are themselves the seed of renewed life.'[10]

If the temples of Malta offer more speculation than certainty, we can look elsewhere for a more definite view into a temple of a Goddess.

THE SACRED BUILDING

Sacred and ceremonial buildings were planned in conformity with the heavenly prototype so that they might share its qualities of perfection.

W.R. LETHABY, *Architecture Nature and Magic*

As civilisation moved into permanent constructions, the urge to create the sacred building was inescapable. The temenos moved away from the land itself into an artificial construction placed upon the land. Yet the link between the land and the original temenos was not lost, for the building now incorporated symbols and even symbolic structures which highlighted the very same themes expressed previously through the land.

The ability to construct form and shape, height, width and depth gave unlimited scope for imitating and embellishing natural principles. Sacred symbols inform as well as decorate areas, encoding the language of the sacred in picture form. The arrangement of space is itself expressive of the fundamental approach to the deities; deep in the earth, or high on a tower, hidden in small chambers or open in vast courtyards, confined to the priesthood or shared by the people.

MESOPOTAMIA – THE HOUSE OF THE GODS

Like a human dwelling, the temple was the place where the owner could be found.

THORKILD JACOBSEN, *The Treasures of Darkness*

Silbury Hill was created in approximately 4500 BC. At about the same time a quite different religious trend was coming to birth elsewhere. The Mesopotamian landscape had little in common with the damp, green forests and rolling grass meadows of Europe. Here were mountains, rocky outcrops, a fierce wasting heat, date palms, reeds, goats and sheep. Here were dark brooding skies and sudden thunderstorms, violent winds and parched desert lands. The seasonal pattern was unlike the four-fold rhythm. The religious impulse here reflected the immediate environment.

Temple building appeared in a primitive form in the fourth millennium, consisting of little more than simple huts with walls of plaited wickerwork. A primitive shrine to Inanna was no more than a reed hut marked by her insignia, two reed bundles.

The Sumerian civilisation was from its earliest beginnings pantheistic, seeing a numinous quality within all phenomena, growing grain, the budding date and the stormy sky. The divine was immanent within its own particular manifestation. It was the power of the vegetation or stone to be itself. The gods were many as the numerous manifestations of nature.

The immanence of the divine powers could be transferred to a specialised location which through emblem, insignia and symbol represented the original home of the god. The divinity immanent in the natural manifestation was invited to reside in an artificial residence marked out to represent the original form. If the power of the deity was naturally to be found in the date cluster, the temple artificially created the 'house of the date cluster', Eanna, so that the 'Lady of the date cluster', Inanna, might reside there.

From the earliest time the temple was regarded as the house of the deity, an artificial substitute for the natural home. In Sumerian and Akkadian the word for temple and domestic dwelling are the same. This basic belief was to shape the function of both temples and temple personnel for millennia to come. Almost as soon as the natural powers were translated into an artificial dwelling, there began a tendency to personalise and individuate the indwelling divinity began.

By the end of the third millennium the simple hut had developed into a temple complex, a central court and a chamber housed the statue of the deity. Important temples had several courts surrounded by robing and store rooms. The goddess Bau in the time of king Urukagina, c. 2600 BC, had a staff of over 700. The divinity was treated as a living presence dwelling in the temple, immanent within the cult statue, its clearest personification. The deity, whether male or female, was served by cult personnel who dressed the image and offered food. The public had no rights to the temple except at festival time. The deity's house was called *e gal*, 'the great house'. The belief that the divinity lived in the temple inevitably cast the priesthood, both male and female, in the role of personal servants. The vast staff included administrators, singers, crafstmen, swordbearers, ecstatic prophets, castrated priests, hierodules, temple purifiers, scribes, diviners, astrologers and exorcists. The ziggurat, a unique Mesopotamian development, was the outstanding architectural feature of each temple. At its very top was a small chapel.

The Mesopotamian temple was the place of cult ritual, the sustaining force upholding society. Daily ritual ensured the well-being of the deities, seasonal ritual created the reciprocal relationship between humanity and divinity. The most important ceremonial events were the celebrations at the New Year and at the Sacred Marriage. Rites of passage appear to have been of little consequence, as none have been recorded. Mesopotamian religion did not revolve around the needs of individuals but around the perceived needs of the deities. Remarkably few concepts dealt with the nature of the human being or speculated on the after-death state. Instead, religious literature emphasised the duties incumbent upon the human condition.

The Mesopotamian civilisation in its successive Sumerian, Akkadian and Babylonian phases was long lived. Gods changed through the millennia, but the temples remained essentially the same, the dwelling place of the deities among the people. Religious beliefs evolved slowly in response to prevailing conditions and circumstances. It is not always possible to detect the factors which set a trend in motion from such a distance in time. However, particular developments like events in a chain impose a certain shape upon the future. Once the deities were contained with the temple walls it was logical to approach them for favours, blessings, justification and divine sanction in return for temple servants and propitiating daily rituals. This new relationship moved worship into the political sphere of contending rights. The temple became in effect a power base representing a patron deity and the local ruler together. Pantheistic religion was the perfect background for rivalry and internecine struggle. Religion and power became inextricably intertwined and have for the most part remained enmeshed one with another ever since.

EGYPT – THE LAND OF KHEM

The temple was not simply a building but a miniature image of the world, a kind of model representing symbolically the regions of the universe where the gods moved.

SAUNERON, *The Priests of Egypt*

The Egyptian civilisation inherited several themes from Mesopotamia. Here too temples were built to house the deity who was thought to be immanent within the cult statue. Here too the temenos was literally the sacred enclosure cut off from mundane life with high walls and gates. The temple took its inspiration from the landscape. Here are no rolling streams, mounds or green woods. This is the land of the burning sun where the horizon is sharp and clear. This is the land of hot sand and hard rock.

All Egyptian temples are remarkable as being entirely rectangular, both in plan and elevation; at no period was a curved structure used. This is perhaps due to the fact that the landscape is a landscape of lines, vertical, horizontal or diagonal; and, as the artist knew nothing else, his buildings conformed to their surroundings. Vertical columns, horizontal roofs and sloping pylons were the abiding forms of the Egyptian temple. [11]

This could not be more different from the climate and seasonal cycle of Europe. The cycle of the year was established upon the rise of the Nile, the tears of Isis.

The basic form of the temple was determined by an underlying mythology. Building texts were commonly inscribed on walls to summarise the history of the temple and explain the usage of the chambers. At the temple of Horus at Edfu, the mythological foundation for all temples is given: an island emerged from the waters which covered the face of the earth. This mound provided the landing place for the first divinity represented by a falcon.

Walls of reed were constructed around the stalk where the falcon had perched. The room containing the perch became the sanctuary, always placed at a slightly higher level than the rest. The ceiling depicted the sky above the island, plants carved at the base of the walls suggested vegetation. The enclosing mud brick wall was built in sections with wavy lines arranged in alternative concave and convex courses to suggest the primal waters. All temples mirrored the first island and commemorated the cosmic events of creation.

The temple was an artificial landscape, a retreat from the burning sun and brilliant light. Cool courtyards, shady corridors and darkened chambers provided a haven. Seth, the enemy of civilisation, personified the burning desert. The desert could kill, so fierce was its heat. The sacred enclosure was a world set apart. Here was an enclosed ritual theatre in which cosmic drama was enacted. Unlike their Mesopotamian predecessors who remained essentially the servants of the gods, it was thought possible for Egyptian temple personnel to participate in the cosmic drama alongside the divinities. Such drama was by definition not intended to be upon a human scale. Its aim was to elevate the human condition through the experience of the cosmic domain rather than stating the human condition before the deities.

Hathor was one of the most popular and indeed significant Egyptian goddesses. She was a goddess of the populace but also a goddess with strong royal connections. She was worshipped at several sites. Her temple at Denderah still stands today several thousand years after its construction.

HATHOR – MISTRESS OF DENDERAH

I am Hathor.
I have appeared as Hathor
Who descends from the primeval age
The mistress of the universe
Who lives by truth

COFFIN TEXT 331

Hathor's temple at Denderah is still well preserved. The sanctuary was not completed until Ptolemaic times, yet an inscription makes it clear that a temple of Hathor had stood here even during the time of Cheops in the fourth Dynasty. This setting provides a fascinating glimpse into Hathoric rituals.

In typical Egyptian tradition an encircling wall demarcates the temple from the outside world. An open courtyard leads into a vestibule. Here the roof is supported by six rows of four Hathor-headed columns. The ceiling is decorated with astronomical images of the firmament. Behind this vestibule is a smaller room with six pillars called The Hall of the Appearance where the goddess, probably represented by a cult statue, was carried in her boat during the great processions.

Small chambers leading from the Hall of the Appearance were used for the preparation of incense, perfume and ointments, flowers, garments and toilet for the statue. The Linen Room housed robes. The Silver Room housed treasures. Two further forecourts and rooms followed. The Hall of the Divine Ennead led to two other rooms. These included the Chamber of Purification where offerings were presented to be sanctified and the Hall of the Altar where sacrifices were made.

The heart of the temple was the sanctuary of the Great Place, a dark chamber where shrines and barques were accommodated. Behind this chamber, the Holy of Holies contained the principal statue of Hathor. This was the 'great house' open only to the pharaoh or his representative the high priest. Her shrine was called 'the dwelling place of the Golden One'. The sacred boat stood here along with her sacred image. This statue was regarded as the presence of Hathor herself. In the daily ritual her statue was gazed upon in adoration.

Temple life revolved around daily service and the annual festivals. There were three daily services which took place in the morning, afternoon and evening, the main service being held in the morning. The pharaoh represented by the high priest made offerings and gazed upon the sacred countenance. Scenes throughout the temple show the king offering both the sistrum and the menat to Hathor.

Eleven small rooms surrounded the Holy of Holies. These chambers bore mythological titles which denoted their use. In

The Flame Room, burnt offerings and incenses were proffered. In The Throne of Ra Hathor's relationship to Ra was told. Another chamber was called The Union of the Two Lands. The Room of Resurrection reflected a mystery play called the Rite of Denderah.

A staircase led to the roof where a Hathor chapel and a small shrine to Osiris were used at the New Year's Festival on 1st Thoth. The festival of Re was celebrated to coincide with the rising of the Nile. A statue of Hathor was carried to the roof so that 'Hathor might meet her father'. Led by the king, the priesthood followed bearing cultic objects. Sunlight fell upon her effigy. 'She unites her rays with those of her father in the horizon.' This meeting of lights was believed to establish harmony throughout the temple and to imbue her with vital life, probably because her essence was normally confined to the semi-darkness of the Holy of Holies.

Twelve crypts were built into the walls and foundations of the rear and side wall, 'whose content no stranger knows whose doors are concealed'.[12] The number of hidden and secret chambers in the temple of Denderah suggests a mystery cult. 'The secret chambers are more numerous here than elsewhere. They were constructed in the thickness of the walls and under the floors, and the entrances to them were by movable slabs, so that they were entirely hidden.' Some of the crypts were for the secret rites of the goddess. It is possible that these rites enacted the birth of Hathor. The birth of the divinities was a part of the cultic calendar but it was thought too sacred to depict. On the fourth intercalary day, the festival of the 'beautiful day of the night of the child in the cradle' was held to commemorate the birth of Isis herself.

Hathor's festivals included both public and private ceremonies. She was a popular and much-loved goddess. The ordinary populace rejoiced when she travelled out from her home. 'Fortunate the ones who have taken part in the festival of Hathor.' She voyaged from Denderah several times a year. She travelled to the temple of the seven Hathors at Beni Hassan between 21st and 30th Mechir. On 19th Tybi and 28th Tybi Hathor voyaged, possibly also on 1st Hathor. The most famous and best documented voyage was that to Edfu to celebrate her sacred marriage to Horus. Not all her voyages had such definite destinations and purposes. Sailing upon the Nile was itself of profound symbolic value to the people, a celebration of the life-giving powers of the waters by the Goddess of regeneration. Doubtless the banks were lined with rejoicing people hoping to be blessed by Hathor through her priestesses.

Other public festivals included the ceremony of plucking papyrus and the festival of the inebriety for Hathor. The natural and extremely ancient custom of plucking papyrus evolved into a ritualised event. A pleasant day in the papyrus groves ended with offerings to Hathor which might accompany a request, a prayer or a thanksgiving. On 20th Thoth, the wine festival commemorated Hathor as the sun-eye of Re sent to punish mankind. According to the myth, she ceased her chastisement only when intoxicated by red beer. The sacral drunkenness of this festival was likened to Hathor's ecstatic nature.

Denderah was regarded as her home. As she fulfilled her own cosmic pattern, she brought beauty and rejoicing to human life. Her birth may have been celebrated as a mystery along with the birth of Isis. Her marriage to Horus of Edfu was certainly re-enacted. She also had a son, Harsomtus, later identified with a form of Horus. Hathoric rites did not become models for human life. Neither maturation nor marriage took on an initiatory significance. The deities lived out cosmic themes in the midst of human society. Benefit was derived from being present at moments of transcendence, through sharing, not copying the lives of the gods. This was the house of Hathor where the goddess lived.

HERA – GODDESS OF WOMANHOOD

The Heraion was for centuries the sanctuary of the whole country, originally in the same way as the Temple of Jerusalem for instance, was a unique temple of Israel.

CARL KERENYI, *Zeus and Hera*

In our time a sacred building is a thing set apart, bearing no relationship to the exterior landscape. We have in fact lost sight of the sacred code enshrined in land itself. Mountain peak, cleft and plain once spoke to the observer in a language as clear as any. Siting a sacred house was once not a matter of convenience but of sacred dynamics taking the landscape as a whole into account. Different deities represented different qualities of being, each ruling particular kingdoms. Each different character demanded a specific location to reinforce, complement and make plain their nature.

When we look at the temples of Hera we find structure and land speaking with a single voice. The cult of Hera can be traced to Crete. It is likely that her cult evolved from the marriage between the Cretan cow and bull, the sun and moon. The sacred marriage continued to be the single outstanding theme in her cult activity. It has been suggested that the earliest priestesses of Hera came from the women of the cow clan.

Hera's cult was probably transported to mainland Greece where it was adopted and adapted through time. Hera became a goddess of womanhood. She was even made to play the part of the jealous wife to the ever-faithless Zeus. She became popular with women. In her aspect as Hera Elithyia she presided over childbirth. Huge temples testify to her popularity. Our best description of the temple of Hera comes from Pausanias:

> The Heraion is on the left about two miles from Mycenae. The stream called Eleutherion runs beside the road. The women of the holy place use it for purifications and the sacrifices which are not spoken of. The sanctuary itself is on the lower slopes of Euboia as they call this mountain. They say the river Asterion had three daughters Euboia, Prosymna and Akraia the nurses of Hera. The mountain opposite the Heraion is called after Akraia, the country below it Prosymna and the ground around it after Euboia. The Asterion runs into a chasm above the Heraion and disappears. A herb grows on his banks, and they call this herb asterion as well they carry it to Hera and twine garlands of its leaves.
>
> The statue of Hera is enthroned and very big, made of gold and ivory by Polykleitos. She wears a diadem worked with Graces and Seasons; in one hand she hold a sceptre, in the other a pomegranate. [13]

This straightforward description is deceptive, concealing the subtle way in which the whole landscape was made meaningful to contemporaries. Place, mythology and topography combined to create Hera's kingdom in her three phases. Even the river and its flowers were drawn into the mythological reality. The leaves and star-shaped flowers of the plant from the banks of the Asterion, River of Stars, were twined into garlands, stars for Hera as Queen of Heaven.

Her name was three-fold Pais, virgin, Telia, wife, perfected or fulfilled one and finally Chera, widow. Her countryside was divided into three areas, high, middle and low, each presided over by a mythical nursemaid, the daughters of the river god. The middle mountain was Euboia meaning, 'she who is rich in cattle', a subtle reference to horned cattle as epiphanies of the Goddess in her crescent moon phase. Cattle were once sacrificed to Hera who was also called by the name Euboia.

The area below the Heraion was named Prosymna, an epithet used to indicate a low-lying underworld place. Prosymnos was the name given to the guide of Dionysus who took him to the underworld from Lerna through the waters of a swamp and Prosymne was an epithet of Demeter in her underworld aspect. Hera as Prosymna, in the form of a wooden statue, was annually conducted to her bath, probably in the brook with the name 'freeing water' by a procession of women. It was the new moon which was celebrated here, heralded as it appeared from the underworld darkness, probably summoned by a chorus of women. Akraia is an inhospitable jagged mountain peak opposite the Heraion where Hera was called 'she of the mountain ledge'. Kerenyi suggests that 'Akraia means the same in topography as Teleia means in myth and in the sky during the full moon.'[14] Although this mountain top would have been an unsuitable site for cult ceremonial, it nevertheless symbolised the high point of the Goddess's epiphanies. It is likely that full moon marriage celebrations were held at Hermione on the coast which had both a low hill where Hera was worshipped as virgin and a higher temple upon Mount Cuckoo where she was worshipped as Hera Teleia. Greek weddings were traditionally held at the full moon to represent completion.

In this intermingling of myth and reality, the landscape itself took on a symbolic quality much as it had done for the community at Avebury. The story being enacted here was that of womanhood. The original temple which had occupied the top of the mountain was destroyed by fire in 423 BC. 'Chryseis, the priestess of Hera was once overcome by sleep while the lamp in front of the old wreaths and garlands was setting them alight.'[15]

A new temple was built on a slightly lower slope. The Heraion was carefully located, 'as if planted on a balcony'. Its situation 'consciously makes use of the landscape elements as integral parts of the overall architectural design and the elements chosen as pivotal are those which had always been the old potent symbols, the horns and the cone.'[16] Its terrace, 'an immense cult stage', and altar enjoyed an uninterrupted view across the open countryside and faced the vast sky with the ever-changing moon in clear view. Landscape was used in the same way elsewhere, to reinforce a symbolic message. Pausanias speaks of three temples at Stymphalos. It is likely that the temple to Hera Pais was in the town. The temple to Hera as Teleia was probably in the mountains and the temple to Hera Chera as widow near the lake. On the island of Samos, also called Parthenia, 'island of the virgin', or Anthemoussa, 'rich in flowers', Hera was honoured in all her aspects. Here lygos flowered in three colours. Lygos was especially significant in all the female mysteries. It dampened the sex drive but stimulated menstruation. The whole island was consecrated to Hera, perhaps simply because the lygos was wild and plentiful. The island was dominated by the Heraion which stood upon a site of great size. The temple was placed at the end of a long coastal plain at the point from which the whole landscape could be viewed. Its main focus was towards the east and it was orientated towards the strait between Samos and Mount Mykale on the mainland. Mykale itself is breast-shaped with a hard cone of rock at its summit. The temple is placed opposite the single spot where the hills to the north are cleft into a dramatic gorge, another female symbol.

The first temple on this site was built in 800 BC. It was an architectural triumph, innovative in its use of columns. According to the local mythology, Hera's statue was once stolen by pirates and later returned to its pedestal by the priestess Admete. This disappearance was annually re-enacted. The search for and discovery of the cult statue was led by a priestess with the title Euangelis, 'she who is the messenger of good tidings'. She proclaimed that the goddess had been found again and that her wedding could be celebrated. This priestess had to both hide and discover the statue, bind and release the goddess. The statue was to be found in the estuary where sacrificial cakes were offered before a ritual bath and triumphal return to the temple. This disappearance and return mirrored the moon which successively disappeared and returned in the sky and women who disappeared into the bush at menstruation to return later.

These paradoxical acts symbolised the pattern of a woman's life, disappearance like the dark moon waiting to be reborn, bound by lygos which symbolically and actually brought a state of withdrawal, release and appearance, triumphal return and ritual bathing. The rites on Samos served Hera in her three aspects. The River Imbrasos was also called Parthenios, no doubt because women bathed here after menstruation to be restored to a state of virginity like Hera herself. This mythic act was repeated wherever Hera was celebrated in her virgin aspect. Her statue was bathed annually in the Kathanos in Argos where women also bathed.

At Paestum, which derived its name from Pais, there was another vast site sacred to Hera, stretching some five miles from the city temples to those at the estuary of the Silaros River. Hera was worshipped here as Pais and Telai, virgin and wife. There were three large temples and a dozen smaller ones. The building is based on the number nine with nine Doric pillars at the front and eighteen at the sides. It contained two naves. A statue of Zeus was probably placed in one of them. The main temple in Paestum was called the Basilica. It is dated from 550 BC. The temple included a precinct for the underworld, with trenches for votive offerings. Like the West Kennet barrow this underworld was viewed as the place of regeneration not as empty death.

The Temenos of the Goddess has been enshrined in stone and soil, risen to the heavens, descended into the earth. The living temenos is woman herself.

Chapter 10

WOMEN'S MYSTERIES – THE LANGUAGE OF EMPOWERMENT

Individuation is the core process in analytical psychology. It is the goal of life and the way one becomes truly oneself – the person one was always intended to be.

DEMARRIS S. WEHR, *Jung and Feminism*

SEEKING

Ultimately the aim of every woman, indeed every person, is simply to discover and become the person you were always intended to be, to individuate in psychological terms.

Women today are in conscious search of their own womanhood. Women are simply seeking themselves. This would appear to be a modest enough request in an educated, democratic society with a high level of psychological knowledge, yet this basic urge has unleashed a radical, even violent tide against current values both spiritual and political. Women have discovered that the very symbols which empower have been removed, reviled and profaned. Individuation cannot take place when the symbols which give access to the dynamic processes have been repressed, destroyed and defiled.

Women's Mysteries disappeared long ago from the Western spiritual tradition. It is only recently that women have met again for themselves, not to make jam or quilts, not to pass the time of day or indulge in idle gossip, not to fund raise for worthy causes or promote the causes of others, but to find themselves and identify with the common sisterhood of women throughout the ages. This development marks a radical departure in Western society now fragmented into nuclear families and diverted by material goals. By simply seeking to be together, these groups echo the women's lodges of less developed societies. Modern women have discovered the value in such all-female gatherings.

Women have looked about them, and finding little of value in the present have turned to the past, to the ancient symbols which simply bypass the ravages of patriarchy and skip the pages of history which despoil the feminine.

Women have embarked upon a personal quest which has finally led them to the House of Women's Mysteries in the Temple of the Goddess. Here symbols of the Divine Feminine are recognised and exalted.

It is important not to underestimate the significance of cultural symbols. These cultural significators give value and attribute worth to individuals and groups. Conversely, cultural markers also have the power to devalue and convey a sense of worthlessness. We each find our place in a given society through the available avenues. These are represented and reinforced by cultural signs and symbols which act as a shorthand, either blocking our path or opening the way forward. Society at large needs to recognise the value of empowering women to be themselves. Personal alienation on a large scale reflects upon the whole group.

We are each surrounded by a continuous barrage of symbolic messages emanating primarily from the media in its many forms. Like subliminal propaganda these 'symbols and images operate pre-verbally and pre-rationally and find their way into the thought systems by which we live, including the ones society sometimes holds as the most rational. Because of their pre-verbal, pre-rational and often unrecognised character they have great force.'[1] We are most affected by this cultural conditioning before we have established a strong personal centre through self-knowledge.

These images are immensely powerful, representing as they do cultural authority, 'not only because of their pre-verbal, non-rational character but also because of their frequent alliance with religion'. Religion still epitomises cultural authority despite its recent diminution of power.[2]

Cultural and especially religious symbols serve as landmarks;

signposts to group expectation. Girls will become women. Their experience of the world and of themselves will be shaped by the subtle messages hidden deep in society's symbolic code. We recognise this in the field of education where we now find a developing sensitivity to stereotypical material. We recognise the same subtly-coded forces in the field of the workplace where policies of equal opportunity represent the attempt to counterbalance the existing imbalance. Yet at the level of ultimate authority, religious legitimacy, symbols of power are undeniably male. Feminist theologians have demonstrated that masculine symbols for the divine legitimate male power and authority in society.

> Vesting divine power in the masculine reinforces internalised oppression in women, giving it a sacred cast. As long as we live with masculine symbols for the Divine intact, we tend to avoid the discomfiture that feminine symbols of the Divine tend to evoke. If we allow ourselves to change our religious language to feminine language, and to fully experience all the ambivalent feelings that change elicits, we can begin to comprehend the ambivalence that we have towards the full power and authority of the female in general. [3]

Women widely feel a sense of loss and personal alienation which results in the divided self. Esther Harding correctly diagnosed the particular spiritual malaise befalling women and was indeed prophetic as to the remedy. 'Today, however, the ancient feminine principle is reasserting its power. Forced on by the suffering and unhappiness incurred through disregard of the Eros values, men and women are turning once again towards the Moon Mother.' [4]

Esther Harding sees Eros as 'a spiritual or psychological principle, or, in the older term, it is a divinity. To be related to this principle means to be orientated to that which transcends personal aims and ambitions, it means gaining a relation to a nonpersonal value.' [5] The sterility of this arid life can only be cured by the life-giving waters of Eros, of emotions which have been repressed.

The Waste Land of Elliot's poem gives a true picture of a large proportion of individuals as well as of the Western nation in general. The rational attitude to life, with its attempt to control nature in the fullness of her creation and destruction, has resulted in a one-sidedness which threatens to fall over into its opposite. The disregarded emotional factors have accumulated in the unconscious, while the conscious attitude has become dry and unsatisfactory on account of the absence of those very elements which have been strictly eliminated.[6]

This spiritual principle can be found in Feminine Divinity. The Goddess shows women how to be become women. She teaches through symbolic image and ritual, the enactment and vivification of symbol. Her primary symbol is the moon. 'The ancient religions of the moon Goddess represent the education of the emotional life as taking place, not through a course of study, not even as the result of discipline, though both these things doubtless entered in but through initiation.'[7]

By contrast, traditional religion offers a male god mediated through a male figure. The first woman is created from the rib of the first man. She is to be a helpmate for him. In the paradisal state, Eve disobeys God by tempting Adam to eat from the Tree of the Knowledge of Good and Evil. The pair are exiled from the Garden of Eden. The original sin has been committed.

This mythological tale has justified and produced the vilest persecutions against the Daughters of Eve; the temptress must be tamed, the disobedient child must be punished, the wayward daughter must follow the rules of the father, unto each succeeding generation.

Every society lives by its own stories, whether consciously or unconsciously. In the past the mythos of the group was ritually and ceremonially enacted to empower and connect each generation to its spiritual source. This particular myth has been enacted through the generations, usually unconsciously through the lives of men, the archetypal Adam, the first son, and Eve the first woman, helpmate, reviled temptress and cursed daughter.

This myth is seen by many women as the foundation stone of their own imprisonment. It is not the only story.

Goddesses too have their own stories, symbolic tales of creation, initiation and rebirth. We should not forget that the Eleusinian Mysteries were built upon the search undertaken by Demeter, the Isian Mysteries were built upon the search undertaken by Isis. These myths of female divinities sustained and spiritually nourished countless generations.

In the many tales from all countries and societies we find feminine images, symbols and themes to which women may relate in their ordinary lives. Goddesses can appear as mothers and lovers, bearers of wisdom, workers of magic, saviours and initiators. The rediscovery of these timeless images has served as a source of inspiration and brought about a restoration of lost dignity through the renewal of pride in exalted womanhood.

It is possible to relate to these images of feminine divinity at many levels and in many ways. Initially, women may experience sheer delight, relief and satisfaction at the personal discovery of the divinised feminine. Goddesses can serve as role models, instructors, and ideals for women more effectively than images of male deities who do not share or represent the female experience. Beyond this, women can enter into a personal relationship with the Goddess, offering Her worship and devotion, making a space in the heart for the deity to enter.

THE STOLEN MYSTERIES

> But really we have been stealing what belongs to them, for it is mostly all women's business; and since it concerns them it belongs to them.
>
> ABORIGINAL SPEAKER

Women's transformations are naturally marked by blood, menarche, loss at the breaking of the hymen, the blood of childbirth and finally the cessation of bleeding with menopause. Men have collectively reacted to this with transmuted violence, institutionalised jealousy, fear and loathing. Men took control of women's rites of passage. The first transition at menarche was frequently accompanied by seclusion from normal life. It was a common practice to shut young girls away, often in semi-darkness.

Return to society at large was marked by the imposition of taboos which represented men's projected fear. The young woman grew up to believe she was potentially dangerous, the bearer of contamination. This insidious brainwashing, generation after generation, eventually produces women who not only come to believe the lie but even come to participate in the supporting psychological framework which upholds the lie. In a closed value system there is after all no alternative belief. Power resides in the hands of men alone, for the first rite of passage is but a part of a network of related controlling mechanisms which ultimately enslave women.

We can sadly see the same process at work in the lives of battered women who are disempowered by psychological and physical violence. In a classic pattern of sexual violence and psychological terror the woman is reduced to a position of total powerlessness. 'In an abused woman's perception her partner is all powerful.'[8]

Historically, we find the same processes writ large. They are less obvious through being institutionalised and less exceptional through being normalised. The suffering endured by the individual abused women is multiplied million-fold as women en masse suffer the loss of self-determination and personal freedom.

When all women perceive all men as being all powerful anything is possible, mothers can no longer protect their daughters but instead comply with mutilation, murder and enslavement. Genital mutilation, now illegal but still practised, is carried out by women on women-to-be in the belief that this act will secure a husband and a safe future. The women who, generation after generation, both receive and inflict the wound that alienates women from womanhood are themselves the victims of institutionalised abuse. They have been rendered powerless. It is a vicious circle.

Female infanticide still exists in countries where the male has a higher status. Currently Chen Munhua, one of China's most influential and powerful women, believes that literally millions of baby girls have been murdered by the families into which they have been born. In China only males can worship the ancestors, only sons support elderly parents. The daughter enters the husband's family. Imagine the terror of a pregnancy haunted by the fear that a female baby must die, probably at the hands of the father or the father-in-law. Worse still a male child is a prize every father must have. The hapless wife must conceive again, carrying a child for the husband-murderer until a boy is born.[9]

Yet another ancient and pernicious custom still survives in the modern world in the form of the child bride. Hyderabad is now known as Urus al Balad, the City of Brides, where impoverished families sell their daughters for less than the price of a TV set. Here, 8,000 girls were sold in a decade.[10]

These enslaving practices all derive from the single belief that women's natural biological functions belong to men.

The vicious circle of indoctrination and disempowerment begins the moment a girl crosses the threshold from childhood into womanhood at menarche. Menarche belongs to women and to women alone. The current reclamation of this first rite of passage breaks the cycle. An empowered woman will not sell her own daughter into slavery, prostitution or marriage.

THE BARTERED BRIDE

Patriarchy values virginity. It is the prize worth taking. The virgin bride has been and in many places still is the patriarchal ideal. Virginity ensures ownership. It ensures that a girl belongs solely to her father before marriage and her husband after marriage. Western women have only recently escaped the built-in hypocrisy of this trap through modern contraception and new values. Many millions of women around the world are not so fortunate. Virginity is still the only passport to marriage in a society that provides no avenues of opportunity outside marriage. Unlike menstrual blood which cannot be controlled, the hymenal blood is easily controlled, spilt on demand as proof of purchase. The act of ritual defloration is a statement which defines power-holding between the sexes. The girl-woman has no power, she does not even own her body. All power is invested in the authority of the male. The customary showing of virginal blood upon the wedding sheets revealed the nature of the marriage covenant.

This is the pattern where men have usurped women's rites of passage.

THE WOUNDED WOMB

Patriarchy values mothering. Mothering may produce sons. Birth is a true female initiation, it remains a mystery. Even this natural biological event has fallen prey to social manipulation, turning women into victims. In the devil-filled delirium of the Middle Ages, when patriarchy assumed its most terrifying and monstrous form, it was seriously feared that midwives were in league with the devil. Birth was surrounded by taboos and fear. It had passed from a mystery to a taboo; it had become a time of great fear when the soul of the child was more important than the agony of the mother. Birth itself was polluting. Women had to be ritually re-admitted into the pure life of the church thirty days after the birth of a boy child and some sixty days after the birth of a girl child. How bizarre that the natural, extraordinary and wonderful event of birth should have become so twisted, feared and perverted.

In our own times the process of birth has again become distorted. Trends in medical practice have produced a sense of alienation among women who have felt themselves dehumanised and robbed of autonomy by a faceless system. In recent years the handling of pregnancy and childbirth has become the focal point for feminist politics with good effect.

THE HIDEOUS HAG

When virginity and mothering have long passed, patriarchy turns its back. The post-menopausal woman is cast in the role of the hideous hag, ugly and often vindictive. Post-menopausal women are permitted to become grandmothers of course, this is another form of mothering after all. Menopause is still anticipated with a certain dread. It beckons like an abyss. Until recently the problems associated with women's changing physical state were dismissed and trivialised, contributing to a sense of misery and isolation. Women generally are beginning to reclaim this period of life, to emerge from a set of externally imposed values. The main tasks of mothering are done. The woman is now free to be herself if she has earlier discovered her own personhood.

Today, society finds itself in the wasteland. Thankfully, gross initiatory rites by men have gone. However, the stain of insecurity remains as an indelible imprint upon the female psyche. Women's rituals have not touched society as a whole yet. Women find themselves in a period of redefinition, the classic initiatory situation. The initiation has been begun, it is not yet complete.

THE RESTORATION OF RITES

The return to the Goddess, for renewal in a feminine source-ground and spirit is a vitally important aspect of modern woman's quest for wholeness.

SYLVIA BRINTON PERERA, *Descent to The Goddess*

It is highly significant that the women's movement is currently reclaiming those rites which serve as the foundation for a woman's whole life and sense of her own value, namely rites of physical initiation. It is when these rites are usurped that women are disempowered, imprisoned at the very emergence from childhood.

History presents an unremitting and indeed continuing horror story of crimes against women, masquerading as the socialisation process. A woman's life is marked by a series of transformations which are both physical and psychological. These natural boundaries provide obvious periods of transitional status. The way in which these transitions are marked and interpreted is absolutely critical, stating where power lies in the domestic situation and in society at large. These key moments serve to carry the individual from one state to another, from the past into the future with a clear idea of a new role with both its responsibilities and possibilities. When Women's Mysteries are presided over by the archetypal Feminine, the individual is welcomed, celebrated and honoured as she changes from one state of being to another. Where Women's Mysteries have been usurped and have fallen into the hands of male initiators, the individual comes to identify fear at the recognition of her own womanhood and experiences continuous loss of self.

The potential power of such rites is clear, the subsequent disempowerment suffered by women is historically demonstrated.

It is no surprise to find women returning to the Goddess as the rightful guardian of Women's Mysteries.

JOURNEYING

The heroine's journey is an individuation quest.

JEAN SHINODA BOLEN, *Goddesses in Everywoman*

In *A Cross Cultural Study of Female Initiation Rites*, Judith Brown correlated the incidence and type of initiation rite with patterns of child rearing, patterns of residence and the contribution of women to society. She found that rites of passage for women occur more often when marriage itself does not bring a change of location. Rites involving pain were more likely to occur when patterns of childrearing created a conflict of sexual identity between boys and girls. In societies where women did not contribute to subsistence activities no rites were celebrated. 'In societies where women have real importance in the subsistence activities of their society female initiation rites will be celebrated, under such circumstances it is necessary both to assure the girl and those around her of her competence to fulfil her future obligations.'[11] Brown's study does not evaluate the symbols used to initiate. The deepest message is invariably embedded in the symbols used to enact the rite of passage. The theme of the descent into the underworld is common to initiatory myths: it is the place of death-in-life, the in-between world where the initiate has no status. The initiate has left one set of identities behind and awaits the bestowal of the new identity. Kore-Persephone was abducted to the underworld, that is to say she herself did not initiate the process.

In the Descent of Inanna we again see the motif of the personal journey. However, Inanna takes the decision to go to the underworld willingly. In other words she is ready to begin the process of self-initiation; she is prepared to plumb the depths of her own being to face her dark sister. Esther Harding reminds us of the need to undertake this journey. 'To find the limits or boundaries of one nature however and to come to know the impersonal depths which really rule in the depths of the psyche necessitates exploring one's own capacities to their uttermost.'[12] Inanna journeys to witness the funeral rites of the great bull of heaven. The underworld ruler, Ereshkigal, 'Lady of the Great Place Below', is sister to Inanna. She is reminiscent of the Black Isis raw and unrefined, the underlying energy of the psyche itself. At her behest Inanna is stripped of the symbols of the upper world which denote her status and power. Inanna is rendered naked.

At Ereshkigal's instructions Inanna is judged and found guilty, killed and nailed upon a hook. She remains pinned upon the hook but sends Ninshibur, 'Queen of the East', back to the above to bring in a higher agency. 'Psychologically, she seems to embody that small part of us that stays above the ground while the soul descends, the still conscious and functioning aspect of the psyche which can witness the events below and above and feel concern for the fate of the soul.'[13]

Finally Enki the God of Wisdom, who represents super-consciousness, creates two figures from the dirt beneath his fingernail. They slip into the underworld unnoticed bearing food and life-giving waters. Ereshkigal is deep in the pangs of labour, a presage of Inanna's own second birth. The initiate must be reborn while still gripped by the unconscious. Even a particle of wisdom with its life-giving and nourishing qualities brings freedom and release. Ereshkigal, appeased by the empathy revealed to her by the figures, asks them what they would like. They ask for the corpse of Inanna. She is then restored to life. Inanna is free to make her way back by the ascending path into the upper world again, but is reminded that she must send a substitute in her place. Equilibrium must be restored. Inanna chooses Dumuzi, her husband who has failed to lament her death in the proper fashion. Dumuzi, unlike Inanna, is unwilling to make the journey and flees. 'The story presents a model for health and for healing the split between above and below, between the collective ideal and the powerful bipolar, transformative, processual reality underlying the feminine wholeness pattern.'[14]

We all need to make the journey to the great below, so that we may return to the above complete.

THE THESMOPHORIA

They fast in honour of Demeter.

CORNUTUS

The motif of the descent and ascent characteristic of the initiatory scenario was actualised in the Thesmophoria, the Greek women's festival. This took place throughout Greece over three days from the 11th to 13th days in the month of Pynepsion.

The first day of the festival was called *kathodos*, 'going down', and *anodos*, 'return'. On this day a small number of women, authorised to act as priestesses, went down into caverns to recover the remains of pigs sacrificed earlier in the year. On the second day, *nestia*, the women fasted seated on the ground in memory of Demeter's mourning on the 'Stone of No Laughter'. All the things that had been drawn up from the ground were displayed. On the third day, *kallingeneia*, 'the fair born', seed corn was mixed with the remains which were then scattered onto the fields by women who had experienced no death in their families. The festival ended with music-making and general celebration.

This festival contained significant agricultural elements culminating in the distribution of seed corn on the fields. Women both married and unmarried could attend. Those acting in an official capacity observed certain restrictions. They remained chaste for three days, avoided iron implements and the eating of pomegranate seeds. The pomegranate is usually regarded as a symbol of fertility. However, *kykos*, the word for the pomegranate seed, conveyed a double entendre, representing the seat of the male seed. Kerenyi tells us that the Thesmophoria was 'nothing but the periods of Greek women elevated to an annual festival'.[15] The Thesmophoria may well have originated in a menstrual-agricultural gathering when menstrual blood was used to fertilise plants and seeds.

The women took *lygos*, a derivative from a type of fir tree. Lygos suppresses the sex drive but promotes both menstruation and lactation. According to Shuttle and Redgrove it brought about a 'highly archaic experience'. Lygos was the female medication par excellence. The *Peri Gynaikeion*, a contemporary medical textbook,

199

recommended lygos as an astringent in a severe flux, to encourage conception, to bring on birth after a long labour, and to expel the afterbirth. It was clearly identified with women's special needs. Branches were made into bowers for the festival and strewn on couches. It was an extremely versatile plant. Its strength and flexibility made it ideal for bonds, thongs and ropes. It was widely used for wickerwork, perfumes, medicines and ritual purposes. Artemis has the epithet, *lygodesma*, meaning 'bound with lygos'. Lygos was also connected with the rites of Hera. Detienne researched the use of lygos during the Thesmophoria. He concluded that quite apart from its medicinal function it also symbolised the image of the ideal Greek woman – that is to say, faithful but fruitful, yet bound.

The Thesmophoria embodied a journey into the earth. It enacted the descent by which women and the earth were together renewed as seedbearers.

THE BEARS OF ARTEMIS

I was a bear at Brauronia.

ARISTOPHANES, *Lysistrata*

Greek society initiated its young men and women in a system which clearly and unequivocally prepared them for prescribed roles in adult society. Young men were prepared for war, young women were prepared for marriage.

Maturation rites took place at two major sanctuaries, Brauron and Mounichia. At Brauron excavations have revealed a fifth-century temple of Artemis, a stoa with dining rooms, a small classical temple and the legendary tomb of Iphigenia. This sanctuary was important enough to be placed under the control of the board of the ten Hieropoioi, 'the performers of sacred acts'. The sanctuary at Mounichia was set on a hilly outcrop. This site was also involved in male initiation rites.

Both sites were linked by two remarkably similar mythological stories. According to the legend, Artemis was angered when a she-bear was killed. In the Mounichia version, Artemis sent a plague as a punishment. In the Brauron version, she sent a famine. In the

Mounichia story, Artemis demanded the sacrifice of a daughter. In the story from Brauronia, the oracle decreed that the maidens must perform the Bear ritual as a penance. In the Mounichia version, one Embaros dressed a goat in his daughter's clothes and sacrificed it in her place. The sacrifice found in both myths points to the sacrifice of daughterhood which must take place to permit the birth of womanhood.

Girls became 'Bears of Artemis'. Service to Artemis as a bear commenced when girls were not younger than five and not older than ten. It began with the Brauronia, a four-yearly festival, and ended with the Arkteia, a ceremony of graduation. The optimal age for completion of this was ten. The actual period of service was probably a year. The physical attendance of all eligible girls in any year would have been highly impractical in terms of numbers. Those who did not take up full service probably purchased a pot depicting the Bears, made a libation and ceremoniously dashed it to the ground. The obligation was thereby discharged. Many such pots have been found. Serving *arktoi* were seen as a tithe, a representative of the whole age group. The girls wore a simple tunic for everyday activities and a *krokotos*, a yellow tunic for any formal events. The girls tended the shrine, ran races, joined in ritual hunting and were permitted and indeed encouraged to be wild. This behaviour was a complete contrast to that expected of them in later life. This period of permitted wildness was intended as a necessary exorcism for the future socialised women. The Greeks believed that wildness was part of the female nature. It had to be purged early in life. At the *arktiea*, the completion of their service, the bears raced, shedding the krokotos as they ran towards the altar. The first signpost to womanhood was passed.

This age rite did not mark menarche itself but the transitional period between childhood and puberty when physical changes presaged menstruation. According to the Greek outlook, menarche itself signified ripeness for marriage. The girls emerged at the age of ten into the transitional period of maturation which culminated and ended with menarche. This was followed by betrothal, marriage and child-bearing. A woman was seen to have completed her path to maturity only with the birth of the

Figure 9 A 'Bear of Artemis' from Brauronia, the centre for girls'
maturation rites

first child. The Greeks observed a specific path to womanhood,
commencing with daughterhood, the maiden *kore*, followed by
parthenoi, with the girl not yet married, and finally completed with
the first birth to the married woman, the *gyne*.

At each stage of her journey towards the goal of womanhood,
sexual status was clearly defined. It was outwardly symbolised by
the wearing of a girdle, first worn at puberty. It was later dedicated
to Artemis as part of the marriage process. The same girdle tied
with a ritual knot was worn on the wedding night and untied by
the spouse. It was also untied for labour. After the birth the girdle

was dedicated to Artemis as protector of childbirth. The process was complete. In Greek eyes the girl had reached womanhood.

The passage from child to woman was regulated and signposted, outwardly marked and inwardly observed.

> A girl's life until she reached maturity was perceived as a series of gradual transitions based on the culturally mediated perception of biological events. Thus the most important transition from parthenos to gyne begins with menarche and ends with the first lochia, the completion of the arketeia marked the entrance into the transitional period of maturation which culminated and ended with menarche.[16]

Each stage took place under the aegis of Artemis and her cult representatives at the sanctuary sites.

Let us make no mistake: the goal of the process was the ideal marriageable gyne, faithful but fruitful. The status of women was regulated and formalised within clearly defined boundaries. These rites represented the first step towards 'the Greek cultural ideal, marriage, which was under close male control, [and] was closely connected with the less controllable changes in a woman's life.'[17] Quite simply the Greeks realised that the onset of menarche was itself beyond control, so they chose instead to substitute the pre-menarche period.

Should we be tempted to think that these rites represented a force for independent female power, we should remind ourselves that the sanctuaries themselves were controlled and organised by an official civic board as bureaucratic and hidebound as any. Nevertheless, this process was graduated and gradual. Although Bear service ultimately served a deeply male-orientated society, it was in the hands of women, under the aegis of Artemis, the protector of young girls.

The image of the bear appears often in stories of Artemis. The nymph Callisto having been seduced by Zeus was changed into a bear. An older version of the story however states Artemis herself was seduced by Zeus, although she first changed herself into a bear to escape. Perhaps this is the real clue to the meaning of Bear service. It replaced the more primitive initiatory pattern, namely rape, ritual defloration.

KORE-PERSEPHONE

Demeter of the beauteous hair, goddess divine, I sing,
She and the slender-ankled maid, her daughter, whom the king
Aidoneus seized, by Zeus' decree, he found her, as she played
Far from her mother's side, who reaps the corn with golden blade.

HOMERIC HYMN TO DEMETER

The story of Persephone may well represent an archaic account of women's initiation at the hands of male initiators. It was Jeanmaire who originally connected the term *kouros*, meaning a young boy at the moment of initiation to adult status, and the feminine form of the same word *koure* or *kore*.

The Homeric Hymn tells us that while Kore was gathering flowers with her playmates she was snatched away by Hades and dragged to the underworld. Hades is Demeter's brother and Persephone's uncle, a classic figure as sexual initiator. When Demeter learns of her daughter's fate she laments and, grieving, searches high and low. Here again we find the classic image of the underworld as a place of transition. While in the underworld Kore suffers a loss of virginity, 'but along with my virginity, the sky is taken from me'. She also undergoes a change of state represented by a change of name. She is no longer Kore, the young woman of initiatory age but Persephone. 'She has in effect been initiated by rape, a pattern found in a number of male-centred, misogynist inclined cultures, and strongly suggested in numerous Greek myths.'[18]

Meanwhile the crops fail as Demeter grieves. Zeus sends Hermes the guide of souls to the underworld. It is Zeus who exercises control. He both instigates and ends Persephone's stay in the underworld. Hades is still loathe to give her up. She has eaten from the pomegranate, a contemporary euphemism for the male seed, representative of the 'irresistible power of reproduction'. She now becomes a new person, 'whole, mature, fertile, and infinitely more complex than before'.[19] Childhood is done. Kore has become Persephone. The daughter has become a woman.

The text introduces another initiatory episode. Demeter stays at the court of Keleos and Metaneira in Eleusis. She prepares the royal child Demephon for initiation by anointing him by day with ambrosia and laying him in the fire by night to burn away his mortality. Interrupted by the Queen, Demeter reveals her true nature but the child dies. In her anger at the failure Demeter demands that Metaneira builds a temple on the site at Eleusis. The Eleusinian Mysteries were born. These Mysteries serve to initiate both men and women at a spiritual level.

FINDING

The Goddesses are patterns of representations of what women are like - with more power and diversity of behaviour than women have historically been allowed to exercise.

JEAN SHINODA BOLEN, *Goddesses in Everywoman*

The many goddess images reveal different aspects of the feminine nature freely expressed. These images have the power to enable ordinary women to restructure themselves and their lives. The therapist and writer Jean Shinoda Bolen has combined her Jungian background with her feminist perspective to create a meaningful tool for working with women. She uses the Greek goddesses as blueprints for the female nature. These goddesses and their stories still have the power to bring insight into individual problems, life crises and deeply hidden needs.

She divides the Greek pantheon into the virgin goddesses, Artemis, Athena, Hestia, the vulnerable goddesses Hera, Demeter, Persephone and in a class of her own the alchemical goddess Aphrodite. Her work brings these Goddesses into the nitty-gritty of women's daily lives. Women relate to these different archetypes at different phases of life and in different situations. 'Moreover there are many "Goddesses" in an individual woman. The more complicated the woman, the more likely that many are active within her.'[20] Identifying personal behaviour by relating it to an archetypal pattern not only brings unconscious behaviour into consciousness but also opens the possibility of modification.

Artemis expresses a fierce independence. She is the protector of young girls and women. Today she might be the patroness of rape clinics, self-protection classes and shelters for women. Athena is the business administrator, the tactician, the diplomat. She combines a sharp intelligence with skill and success in power games. Hestia by contrast is the wise woman inwardly focused with no need to compete in the world. Hera is the loyal and faithful wife who finds deep fulfilment in a relationship. Demeter is the nurturing mother, the teacher, nurse, carer and home maker. Persephone, passive and chameleon-like, visits and guides others to the underworld. She is the medium, the psychic, the therapist, the unorthodox artist. Lastly comes Aphrodite, the bringer of sensual delights, the awakener. Here are role models for women now. Esther Harding describes the wilderness many women have found themselves in as a result of the spiritual straitjacket imposed on them through external rules and rationality: 'Perhaps if more attention were directed to reinstating the Goddess in the individual life, through psychological experiences, the modern equivalent of the moon Goddess, a way out of this impasse might open before us.'[21]

Jean Shinoda Bolen shows women how to do just this, to reinstate the Goddess in the individual life, and shows women how to cultivate the energy of the archetype in daily life. She helps women to become more aware of the feminine archetypes within themselves, and employs a range of psychological techniques to discover the guiding representative of the feminine force within. There is no doubt that wisdom, power and inspiration in feminine form can be discovered and contacted through meditation, creative visualisation and ritual which is enacted symbolism.

Individual women whose lives have been repressed, distorted and robbed of meaning have been liberated, revitalised and restored through the Divine Feminine.

There is no doubt whatsoever that at a psychological level these archetypes bring a transformative and creative dimension to life. The mechanism for understanding this process is not difficult to understand: self-esteem is derived from external images. If women have only been exposed to weak, dependent and inadequate images then a new set of positive symbols will doubtless be refreshing and strengthening. Is the Goddess only a role model?

Carole Christ expresses this basic question. 'If the simplest meaning of the Goddess symbol is an affirmation of the legitimacy and beneficence of female power, then a question immediately arises, "Is the Goddess simply female power writ large, and if so why bother with the symbol of the Goddess at all? Or does the symbol refer to a Goddess 'out there' who is not reducible to human potential?"' [22] For many women the Goddess remains a role model encountered through psychological techniques, experienced within. She remains, as Carole Christ says, 'female power writ large'. However, there is also no doubt that many women also experience the Goddess as being external to themselves, as a glorious, compassionate and radiant being in her own right.

THE GODDESS OF THE MOON

The moon goddesses are many; yet as soon as we begin to study their attributes and characteristics and the stories of their lives we cannot fail to recognise that they are in reality all one and the same.

ESTHER HARDING, *Women's Mysteries*

It is no coincidence that Goddess figures from quite different cultures are invariably associated with the moon, the ultimate symbol of the feminine nature. Every woman carries her own lunar image inside her own body: at the top of the vaginal passage is the cervix – 'Looking through a speculum one sees a cone with the tip missing and an aperture like the pupil of an eye. This cone is contained in the rounded vaginal passage, on which it rests, making the shape of a globe resting in a crescent like moon.' [23] This is the moon ark, an ancient and mysterious symbol seen as a full moon riding in a crescent boat. It is extraordinary to realise that the lunar crown worn by many a Goddess reveals so deep a secret.

The moon became associated with women so early in the history of the human race that the correspondence is deeply embedded in the collective psyche. It was the brightest light in the sky. The people who lived beneath the sky would have naturally become aware of the changing pattern of the moon. The full moon would have been especially welcome, the bright light permitting additional activities. Women change shape during pregnancy just like the moon which fattens and decreases. Women follow a monthly cycle as does the moon. The moon was thought to cause pregnancy and menstruation. The words 'menstruation' and 'moon' are derived from the same root, 'mens', to measure. The moon's growing and diminishing was thought to have the power to make other things grow. The moon of course does have a direct physical effect upon the physical world. It draws up the tides and affects the flow of fluids. The light of the moon directly affects the activity of both plants and animals. It is not surprising that our ancestors related growth and fertility to the moon. They saw the effects of the moon on the world about them. Bamboo knots at the full moon. Herrings, eels and the now-famous palolo worms swarm at the full moon. Women too had the power to make things grow. Men did not have this mysterious power. Women were like the moon, men were not.

The different phases of the lunar cycle were easily likened to the different stages of a woman's life. The new crescent moon symbolised the young woman looking towards fullness. The full moon represented the mothering woman. The waning moon represented the post-mothering woman.

The lunar correspondence has the power to instruct a woman about herself and her nature. Both woman and moon pass through a monthly cycle of change, yet each are complete in themselves. A woman's life is changed continuously according to a cyclic pattern. This correspondence is known by women all over the world. Yet it can come as an important revelation to a woman who has been separated from this ancient knowledge by cultural conditioning. By tradition the Goddess, by whatever name she is called, is crowned by the moon. She is in effect bearing the sacred emblem of all women for all times. She implicitly states that the moon symbolises the key to the feminine nature. When the lunar symbol is upheld women may freely acknowledge themselves in its cycle, when it is reviled women themselves repress their own nature. Esther Harding notes that 'the recent development of the masculine side of a woman's nature which has been a marked feature of recent years . . . has caused profound changes in her relation to herself and to others'. [24]

In the attempt to compete with men, especially in the world of work, women have possibly been tempted to override or ignore their deepest patterns. She suggests this approach to the feminine nature is just as unhealthy as that imposed upon women by men. Women should not destroy the feminine within but acknowledge, liberate and exalt it. The ancient Goddess images embody the awe-inspiring and life-giving qualities that the realised feminine can bring. The Moon is possibly the most ancient of feminine symbols. When the moon was honoured so were other symbols which were in themselves reminiscent of the moon in some way. By correspondence these images rose to prominence and became epiphanies in their own right. The curving horns of the bull, like the curving horns of the moon, took on a symbolic value which extended to all horned beasts. Crescent shapes, reminiscent of the moon, became female symbols. The curved axe became a sign of the goddess, a horseshoe became a lucky charm. Water and fire were both connected with the moon, water because of its life giving and fertilising qualities, fire as the bringer of light in the darkness. The tending of water and fire passed into the hands of women: 'it is significant that everywhere the moon is served by women. These women have charge of the magical practices intended to foster the fertilising powers of the moon. The most important of these functions are the care of the water supply and the tending of a sacred flame or sacred fire representing the moon.' [25]

As Esther Harding reminds us, the moon and attendant symbols keep us in touch with natural rhythms. They remind us of our relationship to the natural world. 'The worship of the moon is the worship of the creative and fecund powers of nature and of wisdom that lies inherent in instinct and in the at-one-ness with natural law.' [26]

It was only when nature became despised that the symbolism of the moon was pushed from grace and along with it fell the sacrality of women and the realm of the goddesses.

We cannot ignore the fact that modern poetry and art and the dreams and phantasies of many people agree with the myths and religious teachings of the past. The symbols which appear today, and their development beneath the surface of consciousness, show that a movement is taking place beneath the threshold of consciousness which resembles in a fundamental way the movements which have been immortalised in the teachings of the past. They tell of a path for renewal which is new in our day but old in actual fact, a path of redemption through the things that are lowest, which is the fundamental teaching of the moon religions, and of the worship of the feminine principle.[27]

THE TRIPLE GODDESS

The triple Goddess allows the Witch to envision herself as a regal, valuable being.

NAOMI GOLDENBERG, *Feminist Witchcraft*

The Triple Goddess, maiden, mother and crone represents the natural stages of a woman's life. The maiden goddess symbolised by the crescent moon, represents the post-pubescent emerging woman. The mother goddess symbolised by the full moon, represents woman as life giver. The crone goddess symbolised by the waning moon, represents the post-menopausal woman. Each phase of life is represented through mythological tales, symbols and epiphanies of the goddess. Every woman regardless of her age can identify with these archetypal images.

The three aspects are each faces of the Eternal Feminine. Together they represent the continuous process of endless becoming. The virgin becomes the mother. The mother becomes the crone.

When the various stages of a human life are aligned to sacred images, the personal life is raised to the level of the sacred, giving a sense of individual worth and wholeness. The Triple Goddess empowers by representing the feminine life processes through positive, indeed glorious images which combine beauty with power, sexuality with the sacred and life itself with mystery. The Three-in-One Goddess is whole in herself. The Virgin, the

Mother and the Wise Old Woman are all facets of the one. The Triune Goddess represents both the totality of female life and expresses the initiatory transformations which nature herself holds for the individual.

The twentieth-century emerging woman consciously searching for identity might well look to the triple Goddess as a source of empowerment.

The Virgin Goddess belongs to herself, not her father or lover. Virginity denotes completeness and self-worth and independence. Virginity is a state of self-containment which is dependent on no man for completion. Physical virginity is given, neither taken nor demanded. It is a woman's right to give her virginity at the time of her own choice. It remains her decision. When she has crossed this threshold, she is not diminished but fulfilled in her own right. She retains her own independence and suffers no loss of status.

Many women in the spirit of freedom and choice actively decide not to have children. Many women do become mothers. The experience of birth has in some measure been reclaimed by women. Motherhood has its own lessons to teach in womanhood. The year of the crone at fifty-six marks a new beginning. The Goddess as Crone empowers women by showing the third face of womanhood. Here we see the face of Knowledge and Wisdom culled from the experience of life itself. In mythology and fairytale we frequently find the Old Woman sitting by the cave pool or well. Her advice, when sought, is often cryptic. She may set a task or a series of tasks, assuming the role of the initiator. She may also be in charge of the cauldron or the cup offering a secret brew which brings transformation. Only the Crone may offer the initiation into wisdom.

Hera's third face was that of Hera Chera, widowhood or separation. Widowhood of course does have its literal interpretation. However, the separation from the marriage partner implies a return to individual interests and needs. It has to be said that marriage alone may not fulfil a woman's need to be herself. When the children are gone, many women discover a gaping hole in the relationship. This yawning abyss can only be filled as the woman sets out to meet her own needs. In effect she has been widowed, the marriage is over. Now is the time for a woman to be true to herself.

When we look into the past, we find symbols and symbolic enactments which either empowered or robbed the potential for complete womanhood. When we look at the present, we find that the Women's Movement is currently re-establishing symbolic enactment as a means of returning power to women. Society as a whole, however, has lost touch with the function and value of initiation. The girls of today are destined to be the women of tomorrow. The women of today have a significant role to play in their future.

THE POOL OF LIFE

You may experience the Goddess in her triple aspect through the following guided visualisation. Prepare yourself by becoming centred for a few moments, then allow the scenes to build in your mind.

Find yourself standing upon a path in a large garden. Feel the gravel beneath your feet. Look about. You see well-tended flower beds. There are green lawns and trees. You continue walking along the path. As you walk notice that the scenery seems to be changing. The flower beds have been replaced by rough ground. There are more trees and fewer open spaces.

Ahead of you in the distance at the end of the path is a wrought iron gate. You walk a little quicker in order to reach it. Now you stand before the gate. When you are ready push it open and leave the garden.

Now you find yourself in a wood. The way ahead is clear. A track has been established by others who have come this way. The ground is rough and stony. You walk on. Trees grow close to the path. Sunlight filters through the leaves. You continue on your way, moving deeper into the wood enjoying the peace and quiet of this place. In the silence you unexpectedly hear the sound of a young girl laughing. The path turns suddenly and you see the figure of a young woman. She wears a long white robe. Her hair is loose and long. She wears a garland of flowers decorated with ribbons. She dances for her own pleasure. She sees you approaching and stops her dance. She smiles at you as you draw close. You may exchange words . . . . . .

She bends down and picks up the posy of spring flowers that she was gathering for herself. She gives them to you. You would like to give her something in exchange and though you have come unprepared you find something to give her. She accepts your gift. You continue on your way.

The trees seem to be getting thicker and it now seems darker. The path has become quite stony and overgrown. You pick your way with care. The trees now rise above you forming a green arch overhead. The path swings unexpectedly.

There seated on a throne beneath a canopy of living green is a red-robed woman. You approach her quietly. She is preoccupied. In her arms, enfolded in her robes is a new born child. She croons softly in gentle tones. You draw closer and now she sees you. She looks up, smiles and motions for you to come closer. She uncovers the face of the child for you. You step forward and gaze upon the face of the child. This is her gift to you.

You may exchange words . . . . . . You would like to give something. You find that there is something you may bestow. She accepts your gift and you leave. You continue on your way. The wood now appears to be thinning. You emerge from the trees and find yourself on the top of a hillside. The path has now disappeared. Make your way down the hill, stepping carefully over the stones. The land ahead of you is dry and treeless. At the bottom of the hill the landscape changes again, the ground is strewn with great boulders. In the silence of this place a piercing voice calls your name. A woman stands before you. She is robed in black. Her face is hidden by a long black veil.

She reaches deep into her robe and brings out a small box which she hands to you. Your name is inscribed on the lid. If you have not come of Crone age the box will be locked, though you may still take it. If you have already achieved Cronehood, you may open it and you may find something inside. She smiles.

You may exchange words . . . . . . You would like to give her something in return for her gift. You find that you have something for her.

She turns and you follow. She leads you to a wall of rock, a cliff face hung with creeping greenery. She pulls aside a curtain of green to reveal an opening, a narrow tunnel. You enter alone, stooping as you walk. A curious light fills the place. Each mineral seems to offer up a different light. Now you hear the sound of running water trickling upon rock. You walk on following the sound of the water. The tunnel opens out into a vast cavern. In the centre of the cavern is a pool fed by running streams. Step down from your vantage point and make your way to the water. Reach down and put your hands into the water. It is warm, the temperature of life blood. The water is crystal clear. The pool seems to summon you. You take off any outer clothing and then step into the warm waters.

Immerse yourself. This is the Pool of Life. Bathe yourself here for as long as you wish. A palpable power surrounds you. You feel enveloped by a living presence. Now is the time to speak your heart's desire. Speak and say what is in your heart.

A voice intones in your head.

> *I am she who ere the earth was formed was Rhea, Binah, Ge.*
> *I am that soundless, boundless, bitter sea*
> *Out of whose deeps life wells eternally.*
> *Astarte, Aphrodite, Astoreth*
> *Giver of life and bringer-in of death*
> *Hera in heaven, on earth Persephone*
> *Diana of the ways and Hecate*
> *All of these am I and they are seen in me.*
> *The hour of the high full moon draws near*
> *Shaddai al Chai and Rhea Binah Ge*
> *I come unto the one who calleth me*

When you are ready withdraw from this place and return slowly to normal consciousness. Perhaps you have been blessed by an experience of the Goddess in this place.

Chapter 11

TRANSCENDENT MYSTERIES –
THINGS SACRED AND GLORIOUS

Do not reveal what you have seen in the Mysteries.

FROM THE TEMPLE OF HORUS AT EDFU

SACRED DRAMA – THE TRANSCENDENT MYSTERIES

In popular fiction the priestess has come to assume an archetypal
role as the holder of arcane knowledge. Elizabeth Haich's novel
Initiation, set in both the present and the past, offers a typical
portrayal of the work of the Egyptian priestess.

> The priestesses in the temple have different tasks corresponding
> to their different abilities. Some teach the temple dancers. Some
> help the restless souls of the departed dead who wander aimlessly
> in the earth's atmosphere. In holy sleep, the priestesses help them
> on their path towards further spiritual development . . .There are
> priestesses who work towards developing healthier, more beautiful
> and more spiritual young people through initiating them in the
> mysteries of physical love. They teach young men to transmute
> their physical urge through the power of the spirit and to aim for
> a higher spiritual union – a sacrament . . .Lastly, certain
> priestesses perform the same tasks as the priests. They teach
> groups of neophytes, give instructions for exercises in
> concentration, and receive people who need advice regarding
> special problems.[1]

The fictional image with its clear arcane overtones persists as part
of the Egyptian legacy; fascinating, mysterious and shrouded by

silence. Contemporaries were just as fascinated by the hint of a secret wisdom and the possibility of arcane encounter. We are not the first to speculate on the occult tendencies of the Egyptian priesthood, whether male or female. Separating fact from fiction will not be straightforward.

Every social group lives by a story, whether it is the lives of the ancestors or the first animals, stories of the gods or parables from the teacher. These form the frame of reference for the group. The enactment of the group's mythology becomes the sacred rite through which individuals are fully admitted into sacred life. Sacred drama has a long and universal history. We underestimate its potency if we cheapen the concept with twentieth-century usage. Sacred drama was never theatre to be observed, it was the enactment and conscious realisation of the group's sacred myth by the participants. Its key players were those who impersonated the gods, priests and priestesses.

Impersonating the gods is both awesome and dangerous, fraught with liability unless contained by a code of conduct. Masks, ritual garments and specific roles serve to demarcate the boundaries between the human and the divine, to differentiate the human being from the mediating functionary.

Sacred enactment took place in the Paleolithic caves, continued through the Neolithic settlements, survived the birth of the city state and emerged into the dynastic civilisations. These mythic dramas were the lifeblood of Egypt. Unlike the mystery plays of medieval Europe which functioned to both entertain and educate, the mystery plays, the sacred rites of the ancients served to empower and initiate.

There were two types of mystery enactment in Egypt. The first type was that performed for and by the priesthood. These were referred to as *seshtaou* and *akhout*, 'things sacred or glorious'.[2] The second type was that performed by the priesthood for the public. The twentieth-century metaphysician Colonel Seymour concurs with this distinction. He says that there was a difference between 'the ordinary priesthood whose members performed the exoteric rituals, and the initiated priests, selected from the ranks of the ordinary priesthood who were taught to work both the exoteric and esoteric rites.'[3] The difference between the esoteric and exoteric traditions is one of mediation. It is through human mediation that the presence of the divinities is made real.

The Egyptian Mysteries were mythic enactments, sacred dramas in which both priests and priestesses took the role of the deities accordingly. On the surface this does not appear to be a cause for secrecy especially if we continue to think of this process in terms of simply 'acting', a concept quite unimaginable to the Egyptian mind. However, deeper psychological and spiritual dynamics are at work here. We must cease thinking in our terms. Those who impersonated the gods and goddesses were treated as the gods themselves. Impersonating the deities, a switch of identity still referred to as the assumption of the god-form (goddess-form), was not a task lightly given or accepted. The deities were represented by priests and priestesses of a particular class, those with a specialised vocational calling and psychic disposition. Even today metaphysicians rarely comment openly upon this particular operation. Seymour did, however, write briefly about the assumption of the god-form and stated that 'it is difficult to explain to anyone who has no experience of this'. Nevertheless, 'the whole of the magical rituals and rites derived their effectiveness from the ability of the officiating priest (or priestess) to identify himself (herself) with the god (or goddess) being personified.'[4]

An entry from the House of Life refers to a 'royal scribe and lector priest (who functions) as Horus'.[5] This lector priest was clearly identified as Horus. He undoubtedly took the part of Horus in the relevant dramas, that is, he made the presence of Horus palpably real. The House of Life was known among other functions for its esoteric training and magical traditions.

We can conclude that such ability required training, probably through studying the relevant mythology and what we would now call meditation. As an actor must study and prepare for a role, so a priest or priestess acting as a deity must also prepare.

The experience of these Mysteries is not to be confused with initiatory rites of passage which mark the emergence into adult life. Women's Mysteries initiate into womanhood. Men's Mysteries initiate into manhood. The Mysteries initiate into Life Transcendent.

The contemporary term 'mysteries' derives from the Greek language. The word, *mysteria* was used to designate festivals in Mycenean as well as the later Greek. Additionally, the Greek word *myein* means to close, with reference to the eyes or mouth. It conveys the idea of keeping a silence. The verb *myeo* means to receive initiation. The Egyptians had their own vocabulary for such events. The word *st* (sheta) had both a secular and a sacred meaning. In daily life it meant concealed, hidden, difficult, unprecedented or curious. In a religious context, it was used mainly in funeral texts where it denoted the participation in a secret rite which actualised a mythic idea. The verb *bs* means to usher in or to introduce several times. In a religious context it meant to initiate into a mystery, into hidden knowledge. It is used in this way in the *Coffin Texts* and the *Book of the Dead*. Furthermore, the same word is used for the introduction of the king and the priest to sacred office and also on the occasion of introduction to special knowledge connected with a cult, especially the netherworld cult of Osiris. As a noun it simply meant 'mystery'.

The notion of 'mystery' played an important part in the structure of Egyptian temples. Inner chambers were darkened, light was admitted only through narrow slits to highlight statues and create the sense of another dimension. Plutarch even likened the subterranean rooms to caves and graves. Certain chambers were always forbidden to those not privy to the mysteries enacted there. The function of the crypts in Denderah still remains unknown to us. All the facts, however, suggest that these chambers were reserved for the enactment of a mystery to a very small group. The Holy of Holies was the 'pure place'. All intrusions were kept at bay, including music, drumming, singing, harping, fluting, shooting of birds, catching of fish, and speech, 'during the holy times that Isis was dwelling there'. Such rules were designed to maintain the atmosphere of reverence and spiritual presence.

Certain cultic rituals were regarded as being so holy that no depiction of the ceremony was ever permitted. At the festival of Min, we find representation of two phases of the drama only. The culminating act of the ceremony, the elevation of Min on his staircase is conspicuous by its absence.

The Egyptian mythological foundation is rich with goddesses –
Isis, Hathor and Nephthys among many others. We know that
these goddesses were represented by priestesses for ceremonial
and ritual purposes. Two young women played the role of Isis and
Nephthys in the play of the succession. Priestesses also took the
part of Isis and Nephthys in the Mysteries of Osiris. They
prepared themselves through seven days of ritual purification.
The text states, 'Ah I have washed my mouth, I have chewed
natron, I have fumigated myself with burning incense. I am pure
clean and censed with natron that has come from El-Kab, with
incense that has come from punt, the sweet perfume that has
come from the eye of Horus.'[6]

On the first day of every dekad, Isis, we are told, went from
Philae to Bigah to make libation to Osiris in a sacred grove. 'This
rite would surely have been performed by a female officiant
impersonating Isis.'[7] Priestesses were totally identified with the
deities of the cult in which they served. Priestesses of Hathor were
often called Hathors themselves. The priestesses enacted and
actualised the functions of the deities as described in the
mythological texts. In effect the roles were written and partially
scripted in the stories of the gods, the Osirian cycle especially.

Impersonating the gods was a sacred act. The deities were
deemed to be present through the intermediary mediators,
whether male or female. Sacred ceremonial formed the backbone
of Egyptian and indeed Mesopotamian culture. Myth was brought
to life as an empowering force. Wherever we find female deities
in major mythology so we correspondingly find priestesses
portraying the role.

THE DRAMA OF OSIRIS

In this lake they perform by night the representation of that
person's adventures, which they call mysteries. On these matters,
though thoroughly accurately acquainted with the particulars of
them, I must observe a discreet silence.

HERODOTUS, *The Histories*

The Mysteries of Isis and Osiris were intertwined, being the enactment of their shared mythos. According to the story, Osiris was murdered by their jealous brother, Set. Osiris was tricked into laying inside a chest which was then closed and cast out to sea. The distraught Isis as the devoted and loyal wife searched for the body which had been dismembered. She found all the pieces except the phallus which had been devoured by a Nile fish. She conceived her son Horus magically. Horus was brought up to be the avenger of his father and the inheritor of his throne.

The eternal themes of life, death and resurrection were woven into this foundation. Osiris came to represent the cyclic pattern of the seasons. His resurrection symbolised the birth of the new year.

The drama of the death of Osiris was celebrated on the first of the month of Pachons. The pharaoh took the part of Osiris. Two separate sets of rites were enacted, the public rites described the life of Osiris, the cultic rites carried out in private enacted the death and resurrection of the god. The secret drama consisted of 24 scenes, one for each hour of the day and night. The rites were inscribed on the architrave of the *pronaos* of the tiny Osirian temple on the island of Philae. It was inaccessible to all but temple personnel.

The scene showed Osiris enveloped in a funeral shroud upon a bier surrounded by ritual regalia, crowns, sceptres, vases containing myrrh and other fumigations. The Osirian family were present. Shou, Geb, Horus, Anubis, Isis and Nephthys, each represented by a member of the priesthood. Officiating priests recited a cult formula in chorus. The body was guarded day and night. A new guard changed at each hour. The rite commenced on the first hour of the night at 6pm and concluded at the same time the next day.

At the beginning of each hour the guardian god of the hour entered with his train and enacted the appropriate rite. Isis and Nephthys lamented. The two papyri which document the lamentations were discovered in Luxor. The chants of Isis were found inside a statue of Osiris. These are the very words intoned over the body of Osiris by the two priestesses.

Behold now, Isis speaketh -
Come to thy temple, come to thy temple, oh An!
Come to thy temple, for thine enemies are not!
Behold the excellent sistrum bearer - come to thy temple!
Lo I thy sister, love thee - do not thou depart from me!
Behold Hunnu, the beautiful one!
Come to thy temple immediately - come to thy
temple immediately! Behold my heart,
which grieveth for thee;
Behold me seeking for thee - I am searching for thee to behold thee!
Lo I am prevented from beholding thee, oh An
It is blessed to behold thee - come to the one who loveth thee!

Behold now, Nephthys speaketh -
Behold the excellent sistrum bearer! Come to thy temple!
Cause thy heart to rejoice, for thy enemies are not!
All thy sister-goddesses are at thy side and behind thy couch,
Calling upon thee with weeping - yet thou art
prostrate upon thy bed!
Hearken unto the beautiful words uttered by us
and by every noble one among us!
Subdue thou every sorrow which is in the hearts of us thy sisters,
Oh thou strong one among the gods - strong
among men who behold thee!
We come before thee, Oh prince our lord;
Live before us, desiring to behold thee;
Turn not thou away thy face before us;
Sweeten our hearts when we behold thee, oh prince!
Beautify our hearts when we behold thee!
I, Nephthys, thy sister, I love thee. [8]

The gods then entered the 'pure place' where Osiris lay dead.
They carried magical instruments, vases of fresh water, incenses
and unguents. The resurrection commenced with the skeleton,
then the flesh and finally the reuniting of the separate members.
Lastly Isis and Horus made magnetic passes to recall the soul. The
god was brought back to life, each organ revived with the touch
of a magical instrument.

An inscription preserved on the stela of Ikhernofret now in the Berlin Museum describes how Ikhernofret, chief treasurer in the reign of Sesostris III, not only replenished the temple furnishings at Abydos but also took part in the mystery play. Pilgrims known as The Followers of Thoth came from miles around to observe the public aspect of the rites.

INITIATION – ENTERING THE MYSTERIES

By initiation nothing can be gained but that which has to be gained.

LEWIS SPENCE, *The Mysteries of Egypt*

Initiation as a spiritual rite of passage is quite different from the maturation rites which primarily serve a social function.

> The primary object of 'initiation ceremonies' is to effect rebirth by means of a mimic death and resurrection. This is done in order that the individual may take his proper place and part in society both sacred and profane, may fulfil his functions as a consecrated person in a holy estate, and finally attain to the hope of everlasting life – whether this be when the mortal body puts on immortality, or when the soul is united with a divine mystery. [9]

Many societies have evolved and used initiation rites as part of the process of spiritual awakening. Initiation in the form of ceremonial enactment introduces the candidate to a mythological scenario. The symbolic truths presented in dramatic form ideally precipitate the birth of a new level of awareness and understanding. The inclusion in the sacred drama legitimates entry into the cult. The individual is empowered by the cult symbols and ultimately by the cult deity. We have no records for the induction of a priestess. But we have a fragmentary record for the ceremonial installation of a God's Wife at Thebes. The text states that she

> . . .went into the house of Amonrasonther, the prophets, the we'eb priests, lectors, the temple staff of Amun following her, the

222

great courtiers in front. She did all that was customary at the
induction into the temple of a God's Adorer of Amun. The scribe
of the god's book and nine we'eb priests of this temple fastened
on for her the amulets and ornaments of a God's Wife, Adorer
or Amun.

She was then crowned with the double-plumed diadem and
appointed mistress of the whole circuit of the solar disk. We are
informed that 'all the customary things were done for her as they
were done for Tefenet (daughter of the sun god) in the first
instance.'[10] The Nubian King Apsalta assembled the chief officers
of state and the priests of Amun to inform them that he had
appointed his daughter to the office of High Priestess of Amunh
of Napata. At the installation a silver pail for libation was placed
in her right hand and a silver sistrum in her left.

We know little of the context in which these installations took
place. We do not know of any preparatory rites or of any spiritual
practices which might have preceded the ceremony. In both
instances the event is important, being witnessed by officials and
state representatives. The priestess is given those symbols which
empower her as the cult representative. We are reminded of the
priestesses of Hathor who received the menat and sistrum as signs
of their authority.

Seymour, who worked with both Dion Fortune and Christine
Hartley, brings the process to life for us:

> In the secret recesses of a mystery temple the method of initiation
> appears to have been something as follows – there was a long
> period of disciplinary preparation by teaching and fasting. The
> neophyte retired for a time from the world and took a chamber
> in the temple of the cult into which he sought initiation. We know
> that he (she) was taught the various stages of the science of
> meditation, and when the appropriate stage was mastered he was
> taught how to contemplate the sacred symbols and given their
> inner meaning. By daily attendance at the temple rituals he (she)
> learned the method of bringing the numinous power of the cultus
> into manifestation.[11]

In other words each cult practitioner learned how to mediate the
presence of their own deity, whether it was Hathor, Isis, Horus

or Anubis. 'As priests of a particular cultus they had for their own use a definite meditation technique and they were able to build up for others a definite life of religious experience by means of study, meditation and sacramental ritual.'[12]

Initiation itself takes place in consciousness. The outer theatre serves only to focus the mind. 'The priestly initiates of the Mysteries knew how to enter upon certain valid and potent states of consciousness by means of combination of ritual and meditation.'[13] By partaking in a sacred mystery the individual is transformed. The very moment that we attempt to analyse and dissect how consciousness takes on a quantum leap, we find ourselves floundering. We, like our predecessors, are at a loss to find the correct words to explain moments of personal transcendence. The initiate too kept a silence. The secret of the Mysteries was not being withheld, it simply could not be told in words. There never was a single 'secret'. The secret lay in the power of experience to turn the soul. Aristotle said that at the final stage of the mysteries there should be no more 'learning' (*mathein*) but experiencing (*pathein*) and a change in the state of mind (*diatethenai*). In this at least, he was correct.[14] The initiate underwent an experience which conveyed the essential meaning, the mystery of the presiding deity. Initiates of Isis experienced the presence of Isis mediated through her priestess. Initiates of Demeter and Persephone experienced the presence of these deities mediated through their representatives. In the following modern day ritual adapted by Dolores Ashcroft-Nowicki the priestess mediates the presence of Isis. The priest makes contact with the deity through the priestess. The ritual is adapted from a grade ritual of the priesthood of Isis. It is reproduced here in shortened form with the author's kind permission. The ritual can provide a glimpse and flavour of Egyptian rite. The emphasis is upon mental control and self-discipline. The Star Hall of Isis is not an initiation ritual but a ceremony in which the priestess has already developed the ability to mediate the presence of the deity. Both participants are working continuously at a high mental level throughout the rite.

Note that both participants should be in the East facing West. There should be a small table covered with a white cloth and a chair for the priestess to sit on if she is as tall as the priest, as she will need to be a head shorter. On the altar there should be a nightlight in a heat-resistant bowl serving as a chalice, three candles arranged around it, charcoal and incense, traditionally Kyphi.

THE STAR HALL OF ISIS

The priestess and priest stand in front of the altar. The priest adds incense to the charcoal. The priestess lights first the altar light and from it the three candles. She then places both hands on the altar, palms facing down. The priest standing behind her raises his palms outwards. They speak together saying:

THOU WHO ART THE MOTHER OF ALL THINGS, WHOSE SON IS THE SUN, COME FROM THY FAR OFF PLACE AND WALK AMONG US WHO ART THY CHILDREN. COME FROM THE HALLS OF ON AND BE OUR TEACHER AND OUR GUIDE. LOOK WITH FAVOUR UPON SHE WHO IS THY PRIESTESS AND MAKE HER THY GARMENT, AND UPON HE WHO WOULD BY THY PRIEST, AND OPEN THE STAR CENTRE OF ISIS WITHIN THE PRIESTESS TO HIM, THAT HE MAY KNOW THEE IN THE MIND.

The priest can now open the temple facing the Eastern gate. He should first raise both arms and then with outstretched forefinger visualise a point of intense light from which will grow concentric circles in a continuous stream. The priest speaks:

LIGHT OF RA, FILL ME WITH THY RADIANCE THAT I MAY OPEN THIS PLACE OF WORSHIP.

TO THE EAST I CALL HORUS THE HAWK OF THE SUN, TO GUARD AND GUIDE THIS PLACE OF WORKING.

Moving to the South keeping the forefinger outstretched:

TO THE SOUTH I CALL ANUBIS WHO WALKS IN BOTH THE LIGHT AND THE DARKNESS WITHOUT FEAR. MAY THE JACKAL OF THE DESERTS OF THE MIND, BRING TRUTH TO THIS PLACE OF WORKING.

Moving to the West:

TO THE WEST I CALL HATHOR LADY OF JOY AND BRINGER OF LIFE, TO MAKE THIS PLACE OF WORKING FRUITFUL IN ALL ITS ENDEAVOURS.

Moving to the North:

IN THE NORTH I CALL NEPHTHYS THE COMFORTER, THAT SHE MAY BRING STRENGTH TO THIS PLACE OF WORKING.

The priest should now take his place behind the priestess. If seated she should rise for her prayer and resume her seat at the end of it.

GREAT ISIS, BEHOLD THY HANDMAIDEN WAITS FOR THY PRESENCE. MAKE ME THY GARMENT FOR A SHORT SPACE OF TIME; A HALL WHERE GODDESS AND PRIEST MAY MEET MIND TO MIND. IT IS HIS WISH TO KNOW THE MIND OF THE MOTHER THAT CAN AWAKEN IN HIM THE KNOWLEDGE OF THY ETERNAL PRESENCE IN THE HEART OF EVERY MAN. MAKE HIM FREE OF THE STAR CENTRE THAT IS THE HOUSE OF ISIS IN EVERY PRIESTESS. FOR ME THY PRESENCE IS REWARD ENOUGH.

The priestess standing or seated should raise both hands palms outwards. The priest should place his hands on hers with his palms covering the backs of her hands. She should then cross her arms, the priest following so that his thumbs should be touching the pulse points on either side of her neck. He should become deeply conscious of those pulse beats.

During this time the priestess should go deep within herself drawing the Isis power to her from the Western gate through her throat and into the region of the pituitary gland. She should keep the head erect. The area to be energised is the Star Centre, sometimes called the Hall of Isis. The priestess should see it as a great hall within herself. This is where the garment of Isis meets with her Goddess. It is filled with a silvery light that emanates from all around.

When she feels the moment is right, she may indicate to the priest who may begin the entry. For his part the priest must now through his will extend a thread of light from the pineal centre down through the back of the priestess's head and into the hall prepared for his meeting with the goddess. When the thread of alignment has been established the second part of the exercise may be attempted. The consciousness of the priest must be sent along the thread until he is able to stand within the hall of the Star Centre . . . . . . The priest will know when it is time to withdraw, and should take care to withdraw slowly. Using the same road back the priest settles within his centre of awareness.

When the priestess is ready to return to herself and when both are ready to do so, they should prepare to close.

The priestess places both hands on the altar and speaks:

GREAT MOTHER, I THANK THEE FOR WHAT THOU HAS GRANTED TO ME THY HANDMAIDEN. IT IS MY DELIGHT TO BE THY GARMENT AND TO SERVE THEE IN THY PURPOSE. TO THEE MY PRAISE AND MY SERVICE.

The priest speaks:

FOR THE GIFT OF THIS MEETING WITH THEE, I GIVE THANKS TO GREAT ISIS. TO THEE MY PRAISE AND MY SERVICE.

Both priest and priestess should turn to the East and say together:

PRAISE BE TO THAT WHICH IS GIVEN TO ALL, THE LIGHT BY WHICH WE FOLLOW AND BE LED. PRAISE TO THAT LIGHT WHICH IS HELD IN THE HEARTS OF ALL AND BY WHICH WE COME TO THE HALLS OF OSIRIS RISEN.

The priest closes the temple at each quarter by offering thanks, seeing the deities depart, and visualising the doorways closing. [15]

THE MYSTERIES OF ISIS

Isis provides thee with life.

PYRAMID TEXT

It is not possible to separate entirely the Mysteries of Isis from those of Osiris. Lucius was initiated first into the Mysteries of Isis and then into the Mysteries of Osiris. The worship of Isis was ever concerned with relationships both human and divine. She was both wife and mother. Yet her worship transcended human limitations and conveyed a deep sense of mystical union with all creation. She was the divine saviour of her day. This aretalogy, the Praises of Isis, reveals her presence in both cosmic and human domains.

> I am the mistress of every land, and I was taught by Hermes and
>   with Hermes I devised letters, both the sacred and demotic, that
>   all things might not be written with the same letters.
> I gave and ordained laws for men, which no one is able to change.
> I am the eldest daughter of Kronos.
> I am wife and sister of King Osiris.
> I am she who findeth fruit for men.
> I am mother of King Horus.
> I am she that riseth in the Dog Star.

I am she that is called goddess by women.

For me was the city of Bubastis built.

I divided the earth from the heaven.

I showed the path of the stars.

I ordered the course of the sun and the moon.

I devised business in the sea.

I made strong the right.

I brought together woman and man.

I appointed to women to bring their infants to birth in the tenth month.

I ordained that parents should be loved by children.

I laid punishments upon those disposed without natural affection towards their parents.

I made with my brother Osiris an end to the eating of men.

I revealed mysteries unto men.

I taught men to honour images of the gods.

I consecrated the precincts of the gods.

I broke down the governments of tyrants.

I made an end to murders.

I compelled women to be loved by men.

I made the right to be stronger than gold or silver.

I ordered that the true should be thought good.

I devised marriage contracts.

I assigned to Greeks and barbarians their languages.

I made the beautiful and the shameful to be distinguished by nature.

I ordained that nothing should be more feared than an oath.

I have delivered the plotter of evil against other men into the hands of the one he plotted against.

I established penalties for those who practise injustice.

I decreed mercy to suppliants.

I protect righteous guards.

With me the right prevails.

I am the Queen of rivers and winds and sea.

No one is held in honour without my knowing it.

I am the Queen of war.

I am Queen of the thunderbolt.

I stir up the sea and I calm it.

I inspect the courses of the sun.

Whatever I please, this too shall come to an end.
With me everything is reasonable.
I set free those in bonds.
I am the Queen of seamanship.
I make the navigable unnavigable when it pleases me.
I created walls of cities.
I am called the Lawgiver.
I brought up islands out of the depths into the light.
I overcome fate.
Fate hearkens to me.
Hail, O Egypt, that nourished me. [16]

The Isian Mysteries were celebrated for several thousand years before contact was made with the outside world. We know relatively little about the worship of Isis in the early period. Egypt was in effect closed. It was not until classical writers and scholars, including Herodotus and Plutarch, went to Egypt as fascinated and intrepid travellers, that we can glimpse something of the Isian rites. Their records give us some idea of the current temples, religious practices and Egyptian beliefs. As a Greek, Herodotus saw Isis in Greek terms, 'Isis is in the Greek language called Demeter'. He wrote respectfully of the rites and observed his own discreet silence. Fortunately, we have one other account of the Mysteries of Isis in a novel form.

In the classical novel, *The Golden Ass*, we have a fascinating account of the progress of Lucius from an occult dabbler to an initiate of Isis. Lucius is at first turned into a donkey through the misuse of magic. Through the intervention of Isis, he is returned to human shape. The transformation metaphor points to the true impact of the Mysteries, the turning of the soul. When his animal adventures can sink no lower, he finally calls out to Isis, 'I beseech you, by whatever name, in whatever aspect, with whatever ceremonies you deign to be invoked, have mercy on me in my extreme distress.'[17] He is granted a vision.

I had scarcely closed my eyes before the apparition of a woman began to rise from the middle of the sea with so lovely a face that the gods themselves would have fallen down in adoration of it, first the head, then the whole shining body gradually emerged and stood before me poised on the surface of the waves. Yes, I will try to describe this transcendent vision, for though human speech is poor and limited, the Goddess herself will perhaps inspire me with poetic imagery sufficient to convey some slight inkling of what I saw.

Her long thick hair fell in tapering ringlets on her lovely neck, and was crowned with an intricate chaplet of flowers in which was woven every kind of flower. Just above her brow shone a round disc, like a mirror, or like the bright face of the moon, which told me who she was. Vipers rising from the left hand and right hand, partings of her hair supported this disc with ears of corn bristling beside them. Her many coloured robe was of the finest linen; part was glistening white, part crocus-yellow, part glowing red and along the entire hem a woven bordure of flowers and fruit clung swaying in the breeze. But what caught and held my eye more than anything else was the deep black lustre of her mantle. She wore it slung across her body from right hip to left shoulder where it was caught up with a great knot resembling the boss of a shield; but part of it hung in innumerable folds, the tasselled fringe quivering. It was embroidered with glittering stars on the hem and everywhere else, and in the middle beamed a full and fiery moon. In her right hand she held a bronze rattle of the sort used to frighten away the god of the Sirocco; its narrow rim was curved like a sword belt and three little rods, which sang shrilly when she shook the handle passed horizontally through it. A boat shaped gold dish hung from her left hand and along the upper surface of the handle writhed an asp with puffed throat. Upon her divine feet were slippers of palm decorated with palm leaves, the emblem of victory.

The Goddess Isis addresses Lucius:

You see me here, Lucius, in answer to your prayer. I am Nature, the Universal Mother, Mistress of all the Elements, Primordial Child of Time, sovereign of all things spiritual, Queen of the dead, Queen also of the immortals, the single manifestation of all gods and goddesses that are. . . . Though I am worshipped in many aspects known by countless names propitiated with all manner of rites, yet the whole earth venerates me. . . . The Egyptians who excel in ancient learning and worship, call me by my true name, Queen Isis.[18]

She tells Lucius what he must do to be returned to human shape; he must attend the ceremonial launching of the ship on the following day. Isis herself will instruct the high priest to carry a garland of roses. Lucius is told to 'pluck the roses with your mouth'. He does this and is returned to human shape, changed in every sense of the word. He now finds that his greatest pleasure in life is 'contemplation of the goddess'. He says, 'I managed to obtain the use of a room in the temple and took constant part in her services.' Furthermore, 'not a single night did pass without some new vision of her. She always ordered me to be initiated into her sacred mysteries.' Lucius finally dreams that he has been summoned to initiation by Isis and commences ten days of preparation. At the appointed time he is invested in a new linen garment and the ceremony begins.

Lucius clearly understands the curiosity surrounding the initiation. He says, 'curious reader, you are eager to know what happened when I entered. If I were allowed to tell you, and you were allowed to be told, you would soon hear everything'. His account is tantalising, it describes his experience without revealing the proceedings.

> I approached the very gates of death and set one foot on Proserpine's threshold, yet was permitted to return, rapt through all the elements. At midnight I saw the sun shining as if it were noon; I entered the presence of the gods of the underworld, and the gods of the upper world, stood near and worshipped them.
>
> Well, now you have heard what happened but I fear you are still none the wiser.[19]

His concluding remarks express the ever-present gulf between the experience of the initiate and the incomprehension of the hearer. The rites ended at dawn. Lucius emerged at dawn wearing twelve stoles, a chaplet of palm, carrying a lighted torch. He is now in the service of Isis.

His account contains the classic elements of an initiatory

experience – death, rebirth and personal resurrection. We cannot understand the precise manner in which this transformation was effected but we see the results clearly in the actions of Lucius himself. He is deeply changed, born again through Isis. The Mysteries are indeed aptly named for many things take place which can only be described as mysterious and truly wonderful.

The initiation of Isis is not confined to classical times but functions today in just as mysterious and powerful a fashion. The following report was submitted by a contemporary devotee of the Goddess:

I participated in a powerful ritual and played the part of a rather rebellious and totally disrespectful Earth. I was to stand before the gods who were to judge whether the Earth was ready to partake of a cosmic initiation. The most powerful part of this ritual occurred when Isis mediated through her priestess addressed me. It was as if Isis herself was talking personally to me, at that moment it seemed as no-one else existed in the room but us two.

The words of Isis, 'from now onwards until the very last day of your life you are dedicated to my service', struck deep inside me bringing me out in 'goose pimples'.

The following evening back at home, I had just gone to bed and I was relaxing prior to sleep when Isis in the form of her priestess appeared by my bed, leaned over and took my right hand in hers. I felt a distinct jolt. Her presence and physical contact left the most vivid impression. It was not a dream. I was clearly in my own room and the experience was real and intense.

Now I feel a deeper bonding with Isis. Also two women have come into my life who are bringing me healing. I feel strongly that this is the work of the goddess.[20]

THE MYSTERIES OF ELEUSIS

Greetings
Goddess!
Preserve,
this city and direct
this song.

THE SECOND HOMERIC HYMN TO DEMETER

Herodotus recognised a similarity between Isis and Demeter. The Mysteries of Isis are paralleled by the Mysteries of Eleusis. We find remarkably similar motifs in both mythologies. Isis searched for the body of Osiris her murdered husband, Demeter searched for her daughter, the abducted Kore. The quest for the beloved is instrumental in engaging the human emotions. Osiris is resurrected. Persephone is found. In both mythologies the goddess figures act as initiators to royal children, representatives of humanity who are placed in the flame of spiritual initiation. In both cases the initiation process was interrupted by mortal queens who failed to recognise the divine presence.

In the Mysteries of Isis, priestesses impersonated the goddess and assumed her cult functions. We have no reason to expect anything different in the Mysteries of Eleusis. We know that priestesses played an integral part in the Eleusinian Mysteries, the mysteries of mother and her daughter. Two priestesses, hierophantides, acted as assistants to the hierophant whose task it was to reveal the central epiphany. A hierophantide possibly named Kallisto speaks of herself as 'one who stood near the doors of Demeter and Kore as torchbearer'. She cherished the recollection of 'those nights lit by a fairer light than the day'. Another priestess set the crown upon the head of the emperor Marcus Aurelius when he was initiated.

These priestesses came from the traditional priestly clan, the Eumolpidai family. They held office for life but served for a year. They enjoyed certain privileges including the right to erect statues in the sanctuary area. The priestesses of Demeter lived at Eleusis in a dwelling called the House of Priestesses, The Sacred House. They were paid an obol by every initiate in both the Lesser and Greater Mysteries. The role of Kore was in every probability played by the priestess holding this office for the year. The holders of this office could be married, children are mentioned in inscriptions. There were also other priestesses, *panageis*, The All Holy Ones. These were women ministrants whose office is uncertain. Hesychios called them simply priestess of Athens. They had the right of touching the *hiera* (a sacred object) and they lived in special dwellings in Athens – an auxiliary part of the sanctuary. They probably carried the *cista mystica* (ritual baskets) during the processions. They were called bees and like modern nuns had no dealings with men.

The Mysteries at Eleusis were famed throughout the ancient world. A vast complex of temple and precinct gradually evolved to house the ceremonies which attracted candidates for initiation in large numbers. It was one of the most important religious centres of the pagan world. By tradition Demeter herself had founded these mysteries. Eleusis was born and thrived. The mysteries were open to Greek speaking people of both sexes. The site became a matter of civic pride. The Mysteries were organised by the polis of Athens and supervised by the Archon Basileus. Prominent Athenian leaders shared in the expense for the additions which were required to keep pace with its increasing popularity. Later, the emperors Hadrian, Antonius Pius and Marcus Aurelius also contributed.

These Mysteries, established in the sixth century BC, were finally destroyed. The historian Eunapios, himself initiated at Eleusis, recorded a prophecy given by the last legitimate hierophant foretelling destruction: the role of hierophant would be usurped by a foreigner, the sanctuary would be destroyed, the worship of the two goddesses would come to an end before his own death, the place would be overrun by barbarians and men in dark garments. All this came to pass when Alaric King of the Goths invaded Greece in AD 396, followed by monks.

The Lesser Mysteries were held once a year in Anthesterion, the month of flowers (February). They were held at the sanctuary of Agrai on the banks of the River Ilissos. These Mysteries served to prepare the candidate for the Higher Mysteries in the autumn. The Greater Mysteries were held once a year in the month of Boedromion, September to October. Every fourth year they were especially celebrated. Special messengers went out to invite candidates and proclaim a holy truce.

The Mysteries opened with a procession. The hiera of Demeter were taken from the anaktaron at Eleusis to Athens. Priestesses carried the cista mystica, the sacred baskets securely closed with red ribbons. The hiera were deposited in the sanctuary and the *phaethyntes*, minor officials, would go to the priestess of Athens to announce the arrival of Demeter.

The ritual gathering culminated in a revelation in the sanctuary. We know only that things were enacted, *dromena*, things were shown, *deiknymena*, and things were spoken, *legomena*.

The secret of the mysteries was kept, although numerous clues have been passed down through time. Initiation was taken extremely seriously. Alkibiades when drunk dared to imitate the acts of celebration. He was condemned to death in absentia, his property confiscated and all the priests and priestesses of the state were called upon to pronounce curses on him, despite the fact that he had been on the important Sicilian military expedition and was popular. Diagoras the Melian was condemned for divulging the secrets of the Lesser Mysteries. The Athenians issued a decree against him promising a talent as a reward for his death and two talents for his capture. Pausanias was very careful not to step outside the permitted boundaries. 'My dream forbade me to describe what is within the wall of the sanctuary; and surely it is clear that the uninitiated may not lawfully hear of that from the sight of which they are debarred.' Livy tells of two youths who accidentally wandered into the sanctuary: they were apprehended and condemned to death. Aeschylus was attacked in the theatre when the people of Athens thought he was revealing secrets in his tragedies. Secrecy was preserved. Future generations were left to wonder and imagine. 'We are at best, we are in the situation of eaves droppers, of strangers at the gate.'[21]

All the sources agree that the culmination of the Mysteries was a revelation in which something was displayed. Tertullian suggests a phallus, Hippolytus suggests a grain of wheat. Bruce Lincoln concludes however, 'it is only the recovery of the lost Persephone that could produce such a result.'[22] A scholium of Apolodoros of Athens states that the final revelation was indeed Persephone herself called forth by a huge gong. Otto suggests that the gong signified the bursting forth from the underworlds, but who played the part? He answers his own question, 'a young woman of appropriate age, perhaps a priestess'.[23]

Here I think we have an answer which provides a satisfactory resolution in perfect accord with the traditional function of the priestess, namely to mediate the presence of the goddess.

Imagine if you will, that you have answered the invitation to be initiated into the Mysteries of the sorrowing mother and her daughter. You have already prepared by being initiated into the Lesser Mysteries. The memory of this is still clear in your mind. Now it is the month of Boedromion, the Mysteries have been proclaimed.

You set out on the first part of your journey as part of a great throng walking towards Eleusis. There is much anticipation and excitement in the crowd. The sun beats down mercilessly as you all walk together. You are hot and dusty. At the end of the first day you reach the sea. With a single thought you all rush into the cool waters. The cry goes up, 'Initiates, into the sea.' You need no further bidding, immersing yourself in the salt waters, diving and ducking with sheer delight at the cooling waters. You feel purified.

On the following day, the mood changes. You must sacrifice a pig to Demeter. It is her animal, her epiphany. You take a life. You think of death.

You remain indoors on the next day imitating the mourning of Demeter herself. You think of her sorrow and her search. On the fourth day, you all reassemble and move in procession to Eleusis. The excitement mounts. Priestesses carry baskets on their heads returning the sacred objects to the safety of the sanctuary. You each wear myrtle in your hair and carry myrtle boughs. You remember that the mother of Dionysus, Semele, was exchanged for myrtle by Hades.

Women carry kykeon vessels upon their heads, men carry small pitchers as reminders of the Lesser Mysteries and their lessons. The procession continues. Awaiting you at the narrow bridge is Baubo. It was Baubo who brought the first smile to the grieving Demeter as she searched the land for Kore. Now Baubo will do the same for you. You hear laughter as her coarse jokes resound. You laugh too at her pantomime performance.

Now it is time to consume the mint drink, kykeon, as Demeter herself did. You have become like Demeter in every respect. In your heart you feel what she felt as she searched and grieved.

At a second bridge you are challenged, a time-honoured tradition for those seeking initiation. You answer clearly, 'I have fasted, drunk the kykeon, taken things out of the big basket and after performing a rite, put them back in the little basket, whence I put them back in the big basket.' You remember that you have secretly pounded the grain and watched a transformation take place. What you have performed outwardly will soon take place inwardly.

You pass on, the answer has been given. Now you approach the sacred precincts. You are full of expectation and anticipation. It is now dark. This is the underworld, the kingdom of death. You enter the Telesterion, the Hall of Initiation. A hush descends on the crowd. You stand in a great hall. Towards the centre there is a small rectangular room, a chapel on its own. In front of it you see the hierophant, 'he who makes them (the holy things) appear'. Torchbearers carry flaming brands which flicker. The crowd waits in silence. At a sign from the hierophant, the anaktaron (inner chamber) opens, a brilliant light blazes forth. He proclaims in a loud voice, 'the mistress has given birth to a holy boy, Brimo has given birth to Brimos that is, The Strong One to the Strong One.'

Brimo is a designation for the queen of the dead, both Demeter and Kore in their underworld aspects. You understand; birth comes from death. Dionysus was born amidst the lightning. According to one version his mother was not Semele but Persephone herself.

Now in the half light the hierophant beats the echeion, an enormous contrivance used by the Greek theatre to imitate the sound of thunder. With a voice like thunder he calls forth the queen of the underworld, Persephone herself. Your heart beats faster, was she not lost! In the silence a figure appears. It is Persephone. You see her living form. She who was lost is found, she who descended now arises, she who tasted death lives.

Now as rapidly as she appeared before you, she is gone. The hierophant alone remains. He holds up an ear of wheat, Demeter's sign. The grain is both Demeter and Persephone, the harvest to come already present in the seed. The wheat is mown, the grain will rise again. From death birth will come. The Mysteries of Eleusis are complete.

In the Mysteries we find the central theme of death and rebirth.

Here, after all, is humanity's oldest fear, greatest threat and ultimate mystery. The sacred drama was didactic. The initiate was taken into the underworld, the realm of death and saw the glorious moment of rebirth portrayed as a reality. In effect the initiate was prepared for personal death with the expectation of renewed life. Through a ceremonial form the initiate took on the part of the questing soul, ostensibly searching for the beloved. The beloved is of the same blood, brother to Isis, daughter to Demeter. The beloved symbolises our own fate, snatched from life, abducted like Kore, even murdered like Osiris. The initiates returned to the world, changed through the experience. Salvation had been granted, bestowed by a goddess as saviour.

Plutarch, himself a priest, was quite aware of the correspondence between death and initiation. He described the process of dying in terms of mystery initiation.

> The soul suffers an experience similar to those who celebrate great initiations . . .wanderings astray in the beginning, tiresome walking in circles, some frightening paths in the darkness that lead nowhere; then immediately before the end all the terrible things, panic and shivering, sweat and amazement. And then some wonderful light comes to meet you, pure regions and meadows are there to greet you, with sounds and dances and solemn, sacred words and holy views; and there the initiate, perfect by now, set free and loose from all bondage, walks about crowned with a wreath, celebrating the festival together with the other sacred and pure people, and he looks down on the uninitiated, unpurified crowd in this world in mud and fog beneath his feet.[24]

PRIESTS OF ISIS

Isis is the All-woman, and all women are Isis. Osiris is the All-man, and all males are Osiris. Isis is all that is negative receptive and latent, Osiris is all that is dynamic and potent. That which is latent in the outer is potent in the inner; and that which is potent in the outer is latent in the inner.

DION FORTUNE, *Aspects of Occultism*

Plutarch was a priest at Delphi. Isis was always served by priests as well as priestesses. Her Mysteries were those of the human spirit, of transcendence and mystical union. Men took initiation into the Mysteries of Eleusis alongside women. Women would have easily identified themselves with the grieving mother. Men on the other hand might have found this identification outside the usual male experience. Here lies the essence of the initiation into the emotional life as experienced only between the male and the Divine Feminine. Women do not have to discover this relationship, it is already instinctive. The male initiation to the Goddess begins with the awakening of the emotions.

> In order to attain redemption, he has to be able to stand the impact of the Eros in all its intensity. He must be able to be a witness to the emotion of Isis in her grief over the dead Osiris and, as the ancient story relates, to 'stand in awe of her.' This awe is of the goddess, not of human woman, even though in the experience of many men the power of the Eros may be mediated through a human woman and her emotional experience. [25]

If a man is to come of age he must make contact with Eros, his own feeling nature. He must 'explore the depths of emotional intensity within himself and be able to stand that revelation'. [26] In other words he must undertake initiation to the goddess. The awakened emotional life has the power to transmute raw sexuality without the need for physical sacrifice. The frenzied priests of Cybele who castrated themselves on the Day of Blood, paid a high price for their devotion to the Great Mother, as they demonstrated the abandonment of their masculinity in the most physical way. Those men who would walk willingly in the service of the Goddess find that the first lesson still lies in the transmutation of lust and the subsequent raising of these powerful life energies to a higher level of expression.

The mainstream woman's movement finds little place for men. Its purpose is to empower women. Women who have discovered the Goddess blame men for her disappearance and cherish a newly-found power. They see no value in sharing her mysteries with the enemy. When individuals are securely grounded within the power of their own gender, opposite sexes may come together with respect and mutual trust to stand in the Higher Mysteries which transcend gender, a rare but not impossible ideal.

Men too can be imprisoned by patriarchy, hopelessly bound to expectations and attitudes which they inwardly disavow. When a man has seen the face of the goddess through her priestess, he touches the means of his own release, he is lost to the ways which reduce the Feminine and in finding the Goddess finds himself.

Chapter 12

THE SACRED MARRIAGE

The sacred marriage was celebrated in order that, by a species of sympathetic magic, the resulting fruitfulness might be extended to the people and the whole land.

DOUGLAS VAN BUREN, *The Sacred Marriage*

DIVINE WEDDINGS

Marriage may no longer be every young girl's dream. It is an institution undergoing change. Nevertheless, marriage is still an everyday event celebrated by the families of those coming together in partnership. A contemporary royal marriage still excites intense interest. Once goddesses and gods were married, the people rejoiced, confident in the belief that the land and the people would prosper.

The divine marriage constantly reappears in a number of civilisations which have little else in common with each other. Mesopotamian priestesses were married to the moon god. Egyptian priestesses were married to Amun. Vestal virgins exemplified the Roman wife. Today nuns are married to Christ.

The balance of power in the divine marriage shifted over the generations, reflecting changing social and economic factors which were also at work in the institution of personal marriage. It is not difficult to envisage a time without marriage, either human or divine. When parthenogenesis ruled, permanent union of any sort was meaningless. When the male contribution to reproduction was recognised, the god appeared for the first time.

Ipthyphallic male figures and representations of the phallus appeared in a variety of forms in the late Neolithic period. Human sexuality was raised to a sacramental level in the rite of the sacred marriage. When and how did the sacred marriage originate? Marija Gimbutas poses and answers this question. 'When was the drama of hierogamy introduced into Europe? Was it at the very beginning of the Neolithic period, or on the advent of advanced agriculture? It seems unlikely to have been later than 6500 BC.'[1] A single statuette, the only one of its kind found at the Cascioarele site from the East Balkan civilisation is suggestive of lovers, 'possibly a portrayal connected with the sacred marriage'.[2] It is dated at late in the fifth millennium. The Great Goddess remained the power holder, representing the undying forces of nature. The agricultural year imposed a certain pattern. The crop was destined to rise only to be cut down. Mother Nature was ever bountiful, continuous and fruitful, the life of the year god was brief, but a season. As impregnator of Goddess, woman and land, his reign was over once the seed had been sown. The yearling god exercised no independent power. His reign was short lived, often ending with a sacrificial death. Coincidentally, male images at this time depict 'the sorrowful god', seated, often with head in hands. Is this the yearling god contemplating his own demise?

The primacy of the Great Goddess was now compromised. Male power in myth and reality became assertive, unwilling to be symbolised by the dying consort. The consort became the king, an independent ruler who could now outstay his time. The simple fertility rite did not disappear but became a rite of fertile rulership. The Divine King as god, man and ruler was now the power holder, able to diminish goddesses and quell queens. The sacred marriage continued in a changed form to reflect the new male power base. We clearly see these changes in Mesopotamia.

DIVINE BRIDES AND SACRED GROOMS

The sacred marriage signified the end of the period during which life in nature had been suspended. Now god and goddess united; the male forces fertilised the Great Mother from which all life came forth.

FRANKFORT, *Kingship and the Gods*

The sacred marriage probably evolved from spring fertility rites which involved the whole community. Agricultural societies have invariably evolved sympathetic magical acts designed to unite the fertility of the land with the fertility of people. Intercourse was commonly taken to be analogous to ploughing. Ritual intercourse in a ploughed field was undertaken to fertilise the land. The forces of spring renewal were conceived as the marriage of the Mother Goddess with the god. This drama was enacted by the community according to its own customs. Eventually the communal fertility celebration gave rise to the sacred marriage between honoured representatives.

Human sexuality is a powerful drive, sacramental because it produces life and enables human beings to see themselves as creators. 'The Hieros Gamos and the ritual orgy express on different planes the religious character of sexuality.'[3] The Hieros Gamos represented a sophisticated amalgam of concepts. It was an act performed by representatives on behalf of the group. It recognised both male and female powers and elevated human sexuality into a sacred symbol, raising the union of male and female into a sacred mystery. The sacred marriage was a sympathetic magical act of national significance. It expressed the need of a people to be fertile, to be assured of a future generation of crops, animals and children.

Mesopotamian history enables us to follow the development of this rite in a particular cultural context. The sacred marriage was celebrated throughout the Middle East for several thousand years. The main outlines of the drama can be traced from scattered evidence, hymns, votive inscriptions, cursory allusions and figurative material. Originally it was probably used on an ad hoc basis, most especially when the land or the people were in special need. However, the Sumerians incorporated it early into the cultic calendar at the New Year celebrations, the *akitu*, when it was enacted across the land throughout numerous city states. The participants were the deities of the city states and their consorts, or rather those who impersonated them as bride and groom. The now well-known marriage between Inanna and Dumuzi was but one union among many. In Nippur, Enlil and Ninlil were married; at Lagash, the marriage was between Baba and Ninghirsu; at Ur, between Nannar and Ningal; at Uruk, Innin and her consort were married; at Isin, the sacred marriage was between Ishtar and her consort; at Dilmun, Enki and Nintur were married; at Eridu, the divine participants were Enki and Ninki; at Kes and Adab, Ninhursaga and Assergi were married; at Sippar, the marriage was between Samas and Aia (Aja); at Dilbat, Ninegal and Ninurta were married. Later in Babylon a sacred marriage took place between Marduk and Sarpanitum; at Orsippa, Nabu and Tasmetum were married; Anu and Antum were married at Uruk; Assur and his consort were married in the city of Assur.[4]

The many and varied participants reflected the independence of different areas, changes in religious beliefs, political motives and the infiltration of foreign gods. The rite subtly altered through the centuries. When the Hieros Gamos was enacted infrequently the choice of participants was straightforward, falling upon the most important man and the most important woman of the locality, the local ruler and the queen, or more likely a priestess. When the sacred marriage was everywhere enacted the choice of participants became problematical. Local rulers had by then been eclipsed by a single king who could not take the role of the bridegroom at every sacred marriage. The rite was adapted to incorporate substitution which was followed later by a trend towards abstraction and pure symbolic representation.

Each city state was quite independent and organised its own sacred festivals. Regional differences remained marked. Various cities even had their own calendars which employed the same month name as each other but not in the same order. At Ur an akitu was celebrated twice a year, in the sixth month of sowing and first month after the barley harvest. The sowing akitu was possibly the more ancient of the two. In other cities the akitu was celebrated in the 4th, 5th, 7th, 8th and 10th months. The lunar calendar necessitated the regular use of whole intercalary months. As a result harvest and sowing months often did not coincide with the correct events.

These inconsistencies did not diminish the popularity of the sacred marriage. The festival remained central to the welfare of the people. The Hieros Gamos actualised the communion between gods and humankind. Divine energy flowed directly upon the city and insured prosperity for the year. The earliest evidence for the proceeding of the rite comes from Uruk III. Here we find that the consort had to travel by chariot and by water. The boat was open, with high curved stern and prow, both symbolically ending in sprays bursting into bud. It had a square sail and was steered by two oarsmen. When not in use these ships were kept in the temples on stone bases. In later ages the ship for the akitu was enriched with gold, silver and precious stones. The more ornate ships were probably used only for ceremonial purposes.

The festival produced frenzied activity. Temples were cleaned, repaired and swept. Green boughs were hung, the bride prepared herself. Stores of butter, meat and game were made ready. Vegetables, wines and baskets heaped with fruits were laid out. The bridegroom came bearing costly gifts and ornaments, sacred utensils, even live animals. The bride prepared herself by washing in the river or a ritual bath of water and soda which ritually restored her virginity. She was anointed with sweet-smelling oils and arrayed in festive attire. She wore a pale robe, 'the garment of ladyship' which was described as bright and shining, a crown and a girdle, variously called the 'the girdle of royalty', the 'birth stone girdle', or the 'girdle of casting lots'. The seven little stones used for divining the fates were attached to it when not in use. The bride also wore shoes decorated with symbols, bracelets, necklaces, amulets and a horned cap as a sign of divinity.

The goddess Nina, as bride of the sea, sat on a throne made of fish, carried a sceptre made of fish, wore a crown of fish and was decked in a mantle and shoes made of fish skins.

The goddess Ishtar wore sprays of aromatic cedar twined round her upper body and arms. Her consort offered 'gifts and sprays'. The bridegroom also wore ritual garments including a 'green tiara'. Later the bridegroom Marduk wore a garment of ears of corn. The bride stationed herself between the pair of gate posts decorated with streamers which marked the entrance to her domain. If the bridegroom was Tammuz, the goddess uttered laments for her imprisoned consort. The tale of the descent of Ishtar to the lower world was unfolded. At his restoration to the upper world, rejoicing commenced. After his entry into the temple the oracle was consulted, sometimes in the presence of a large assembly in the Great Hall of Judgment. After the oracle had been given the bridal pair were conducted 'in glad procession' to the nuptial chamber, the *gigunu*, later called *e-nir*. Here they were attended only by a priest to testify to the accomplishment of the act and the goddess Ishara who presided over the ceremony of marriage. She was called 'mistress of the du-ku', that is, the month of the New Year festival, and was responsible for the preparation of the room. Her presence was sometimes symbolised by a scorpion.

The gigunu was located in a sanctuary on the summit of the ziggurat. It was 'the great reed house', built of sweet smelling wood, adorned with precious stones and other metals. It was described as 'glowing like the sun'. Another cult room was the *gu'enna* probably an ante-room where musicians played music just outside the nuptial chamber. This room also housed two thrones where the bridal pair were enthroned and pledged to one another with ceremonial toasts. They were attended by women who brought specially prepared foods symbolising the abundance which their union would bring to the land.

Glad news of the successful accomplishment of the rite was announced to the people. There was an outburst of exaltation, feasting and thanksgiving. Fertility was assured. The divine participants returned to their own temples. 'The going up of the procession is finished.'

BRIDEGROOMS, KINGS AND GODS

Having been thus exalted to the status of a god he was qualified to officiate in the succeeding phases of the sacred drama as if he were in very truth the divine consort of the goddess.

DOUGLAS VAN BUREN, *The Sacred Marriage*

This increased regularity across at least a dozen city states simultaneously produced a problem. As the city states were amalgamated under a single ruler, the king of the country could no longer be present personally in every city where the rite was performed. A substitute had to stand in for the king. In effect, someone had to impersonate the king impersonating the god. The

Sumerians were aware that this created a potential problem for the internal congruity of the rite. The distinctive ritual garments were sent in his stead, for his substitute to wear. A prayer of penance was recited in the hope that the substitution would be acceptable. It is not known how the goddess made her choice but it is likely that he was chosen through some sort of oracular consultation. This development did not diminish the position of the goddess whose role could still be taken by a priestess from the temple in each city state.

From the time of Gudea onwards the priest-king as bridegroom suffered recognisable loss of status. How could the representative enter the rite as a god, if it were clear to all that he did not even bear the distinction of being a local ruler. In keeping with this new lowered status, the priest-king-bridegroom became responsible for all the arrangements including the food required, the cleanliness and repair of the temple. He could no longer present gifts in person but had to present them 'like a servant full of respect for his mistress'. Before approaching the goddess, the bridegroom offered libation and sacrifice. This loss of status was duly compensated: the bridegroom, whether royal or royal substitute, was ritually raised to the level of a god. Having prepared himself, he joined the goddess and in the *guenna*, the room of gold and lapiz lazuli, and with the participation of other gods he was raised in rank to divine status, enthroned, crowned and given the sceptre of righteousness. To further stress the new and less exalted status the union between the goddess and the newly-divinised bridegroom took place not in the gigunu at the top of the ziggurat but upon the earth in the *e-gipar*.

Kings of course did take on the role of the bridegroom and were duly divinised in the same manner. The priest-king was now a god-king, a formidable change of status with long-term political consequences. The account given by Gudea precisely describes the part played by king as bridegroom: 'I am the shepherd, the lordship is given me as a gift.'[5] He performed ablutions, presented gifts and approached the sleeping chamber to pour out libation and make sacrifice. He played upon a flute to please his divine mistress who foretold his fate. Crown and sceptre were conferred upon him along with divine status.

A text known as 'The Deification of Lipit-Ishtar' shows that this king was deified prior to the sacred marriage by being fused with Urash, a fertility god. The text consists of a song cycle and its construction suggests that it was recited as a ritual deification to prepare the king for his exalted function. The first song relates how Anu appointed Lipit-Ishtar as king of the land. The ruler is called 'child of Enlil', a term which serves to establish the divinity into which the king's person will be absorbed. In the second song Anu addresses Lipit-Ishtar directly. The next two songs resemble the first but are addressed not to the king but to the god Urash. Now it is said 'Ishtar, is thy lover may she prolong thy life.' These words are spoken to the king as Urash. The rest of the songs treat Lipit-Ishtar as Urash. The construction of the song cycle suggests it was recited just before the king entered into the presence of the goddess; merging with the god Urash he was raised as it were to her level. At Ur and Isin where kings acted as divine bridegrooms and the divine determinative was used, the rulers were credited with an influence on the prosperity of the land which far exceeded that normally attributed to them.

The appearance of the king as a god is most clearly described in a hymn which glories Ishtar as the evening star. Her bridegroom bears an epithet of Tammuz yet he is king Idin-Dagan of Isin. The purpose of the rite is 'to guard the life-breath of all lands'. He is called Ama-ushumgalana, 'great ruler of heaven', an epithet of Tammuz.

Gudea took the role of the god Ningizzida when the marriage festival was performed and rebuilt the joint temple of Ningizzida and Gestinanna. Those who had undertaken the role of the bridegroom were privileged to set up statues in the temple precincts. Gudea erected statues of the goddess and on his own statue he had inscribed the words 'Gestinanna look upon me with a favourable eye'.[6]

Other kings also played the role of divine bridegroom and celebrated this fact in word and deed. Ur-nammu built a splendid *gipar* for Ningal. His son Sulgi gave a detailed account of what he did for the goddess Ninlil, making her a splendid new bed and providing an orchestra for her. Bur-Sin restored the e-gipar of Ningal at Ur. At Uruk he built an e-gipar for Innin his beloved consort and rebuilt the e-gipar which had fallen into disrepair for Nanna at Karzida.

In the sacred marriage the dependence of the god upon the goddess is strongly emphasised. A hymn to a king of Ur states, 'O Shulgi, thou art created for the pleasure of Inanna.' King Ishme-Dagan said of himself, 'I am he whom Inanna queen of heaven and earth, has chosen for her beloved husband.' The normally domineering Ningirsu was instead dominated by the goddess Baba. In the epic of Gilgamesh it is Ishtar who invites the king of Erech to become her husband.

The deification had a significant political repercussion.

It may well be that only kings were deified who had been commanded by the goddess to share her couch. In a general way the kings who used the determinative before their names belong to the same period as the text mentioning the marriage of kings and goddess; and we have seen that some kings adopted the determinative not at the beginning but at the end of their reigns. If we assume that they did so on the strength of divine command, we remain within the normal scope of Mesopotamian thought, while the view that the king should have presumed of his own accord to pass the barrier between the human and the divine conflicts with everything we know of Mesopotamian belief.[7]

The most famous Sumerian marriage is doubtless that between Inanna and Dumuzi. The courtship and wedding of Inanna and Dumuzi is told in both lightweight literature, popular ditties sung to the rhythm of women's work and in the classic literature of the period. The Uruk Text serves as a narrative piece for the sacred drama describing the tale to the assembly of worshippers.

THE JOY OF SUMER

The people of Sumer assemble in the palace,
The house which guides the land.
The king builds a throne for the queen of the palace.
He sits behind her on the throne.

In order to care for the life of all the lands,
The exact first day of the months is closely examined,
And on the day of the disappearance of the moon,
On the day of the sleeping of the moon,
The me are perfectly carried out
So that the New Year's Day, the day of rites,
May be properly determined,
And a sleeping place set up for Inanna.

The people cleanse the rushes with sweet smelling cedar oil,
They arrange the rushes for the bed.
They spread a bridal sheet over the bed.
A bridal sheet to rejoice the heart,
A bridal sheet to sweeten the loins,
A bridal sheet for Inanna and Dumuzi.

The queen bathes her holy loins,
Inanna bathes the holy loins of Dumuzi,
She washes herself with soap.
She sprinkles sweet-smelling cedar oil on the ground.

The king goes with lifted head to the holy loins,
Dumuzi goes with lifted head to the holy loins of Inanna,
He lies down beside her on the bed.
Tenderly he caresses her, murmuring the words of love;
'O my holy jewel! O my wondrous Inanna.'

After he enters her holy vulva, causing the queen to rejoice,
After he enters her holy vulva, causing Inanna to rejoice.
Inanna holds him and murmurs;
'O Dumuzi, you are my true love.'

The king bids the people to enter the great hall.
The people bring food offerings and bowls.
They burn juniper resin, perform laving rites,
And pile up sweet-smelling incense.

The king embraces his beloved bride,
Dumuzi embraces Inanna.
Inanna seated on the royal throne, shines like daylight.
The king like the sun, shines radiantly by her side.
He arranges abundance, lushness, and plenty before her.
He assembles the people of Sumer.

The musicians play for the queen;
They play the loud instrument which drowns out the southern
    storm,
They play the sweet algar instrument, the ornament of the palace,
They play the stringed instrument which brings joy to all people,
They play songs for Inanna to rejoice the heart.

The king reaches out for food and drink,
Dumuzi reaches out his hand for food and drink.
The palace is festive, the king is joyous
In a pure clean palace they celebrate Inanna's song.
She is the ornament of the assembly, the joy of Sumer.

The people spend the day in plenty.
The king stands before the assembly in great joy.
He hails Inanna with the praises of the gods and the assembly;
'Holy Priestess! Created with the heavens and the earth,
Inanna, First Daughter of the Moon, Lady of the Evening!
I sing your praises.'

My lady looks in sweet wonder from heaven.
The people of Sumer parade before the holy Inanna.
The Lady who Ascends into the Heavens, Inanna is radiant.
Mighty, majestic, radiant and ever youthful –
To you Inanna I sing![8]

In the Iddin-Dagan Text the king himself plays the part of Dumuzi. Dumuzi as the god of vegetation appears frequently in hymns, laments, rituals and myth. He comes into being in the spring, is celebrated as bridegroom in the cult rite of the sacred marriage, is killed by the powers of the netherworld and is lamented and searched for by his mother and young widow. His cult is more complex and fragmented than might first appear. Several different cults enacted different aspects of his being. The cult of Dumuzi Amaushumgalanna, the power in the date palm to produce new fruit, celebrated his sacred marriage but not his death. Among the shepherds, he was the son of Dutter the personified ewe. Among the cowherds, he was the son of Ninsuna, Lady of the Wild Cows. This cult both celebrated the marriage and also lamented for his loss. Textual evidence also indicates a fourth aspect, Dumuzi of the grain. The god is envisaged as the power of the barley particularly in the beer brewed from it. Finally, the god is worshipped under the name of the god Damu, the child representing the rising sap. In this cult special emphasis was paid not to his marriage but the search in the underworld.

The sacred marriage, enacted and celebrated for several millennia, was the prime rite of a people who wanted the deities to walk the land, to be embodied in rulers and sacred women. The contentment of the divine couple annually renewed was seen as the source of happiness, prosperity and fertility of the land and of all living upon it. The bride sang these words to her beloved the king Shu-Sin.

> *Bridegroom, dear to my heart,*
> *Goodly is your pleasure honey-sweet;*
> *Lion, dear to my heart,*
> *Goodly is your pleasure honey-sweet.*
>
> *You have captivated my heart, I stand trembling before you,*
> *Bridegroom, I would be carried off by you to the bedchamber.*
> *You have captivated me, let me stand trembling before you.*
> *Lion, I would be carried off to the bedchamber.*
>
> *Bridegroom, let me give you of my caresses*
> *My precious sweet, I would be laved (?) by honey,*
> *In the bedchamber, honey-filled,*
> *Let me enjoy your goodly beauty;*
> *Lion, let me give you of my caresses*
> *My precious sweet, I would be laved (?) by honey.*

Bridegroom, you have taken your pleasure of me,
Tell my mother, she will give you delicacies,
Tell my father, he will give you gifts.

Your spirit – I know where to cheer your spirit,
Bridegroom, sleep in our house until dawn,
Your heart, I know where to gladden your heart
Lion, sleep in our house until dawn.[9]

The poet describes the preparations for the nuptial rites.

In the palace, the house which guides the land, the house of the king
   of the lands,
In its judgement hall, where the black-headed people gather,
He erected a dais for the 'Queen of the Palace'
The king, the god, lived with her in its midst.
In order to care for the life of all the lands.
To examine closely . . .
To carry out to perfection the divine rules on the day of 'sleeping'.
On the New Years, the day of rites
A sleeping place was set up for 'my Queen'.
They purify it with pots full of rushes and cedar.
They set them up for 'my queen' as their bed,
Over it they spread a coverlet,
A coverlet which rejoices the heart, makes sweet the bed.[10]

The goddess sings again

When for the wild bull, for the lord, I shall have bathed,
When for the shepherd Dumuzi, I shall have bathed,
When with . . .my sides I shall have adorned,
When with amber my mouth I shall have coated,
When with kohl my eyes I shall have painted,
When in his fair hands my loins shall have been shaped,
When the lord, lying by holy Inanna, the shepherd Dumuzi,
With milk and cream the lap have smoothed . . .
When on my vulva his hands he shall have laid,
When like his black boat, he shall have . . .it,

When like his narrow boat, he shall have brought life to it,
When on the bed, he shall have caressed me,
Then I shall caress my lord, a sweet fate I shall decree for him.
I shall caress Shulgi, the faithful, shepherd, a sweet fate I shall
*   decree for him.*
I shall caress his loins, the shepherdship of all the lands,
I shall decree as his fate. [11]

THE AKITU IN BABYLON

The very ancient rite of the sacred marriage was of the utmost
importance if not the essential and pivotal element of Babylonian
religion.

DOUGLAS VAN BUREN, *The Sacred Marriage*

The sacred marriage continued as Babylonians superseded
Sumerians. The rite had changed. It was now held in a special
building, the *bit akitu* situated outside the city in fields near a quay
on the canal. At least seven different towns had akitu buildings
during the first millennium, ranging from north Syria to Babylon.
The last known occasion on which akitu was celebrated was 583
BC. The dominance of the goddess was gone. Marduk had risen
to prominence as the patron god of Hammurabi's home city. The
New Year's ceremony now lasted twelve days. The sacred marriage
was but one rite in a series of rituals and dramatic enactments
which supported, sustained and justified kingship. The
mythology of Marduk, with its themes of imprisonment and
release signified the triumph of order over chaos. The sacred
marriage had now become more symbolic than real although it
remained the vehicle which served to decree the destiny of the
people for the forthcoming year.

At this point the sacred marriage is already several thousand
years old. To expect stasis would be foolish. 'The New Year
ceremonies must be seen as a complex accretion, over a long
period, of a number, probably at least half a dozen, of different
elements from different rites and cults.'[12]

In Babylon the New Year was celebrated during the first twelve
days of Nisan at about the time of spring equinox after the barley

harvest. The actual date of 1st Nisan varied from year to year. It was generally fixed to be as near 21st March as possible. It could be as early as 16th March or even as late as 31st April. We know nothing of the first day's ceremonies. The fifth, eighth and eleventh days were especially important. On the second day the high priest, the *sesgallu*, entered the sanctuary of Bel and drew back the linen curtain and prayed.

> *Have pity on your city of Babylon,*
> *Turn your face upon your temple Esagil,*
> *Maintain the freedoms of the privileged citizens of Babylon.* [13]

Then he opened the temple and admitted the rank and file priests, the singers and musicians. On the third day the High Priest sent for the smith and carpenter to make two small wooden images which stood for the next three days in the temple of Madanu the Divine Judge. On the fourth day he prayed first to Bel and then to his consort Beltiya and addressed her as Sarpanitum. The temple was blessed.

> *She is mighty, she is divine, she is exalted among the goddesses;*
> *Zarpanit, the brightest of stars dwelling in E-ud-ul;*
> *The . . .of the goddesses, clothed with light;*
> *Who dost pass through the heavens, dost heap up the earth;*
> *Zarpanit whose dwelling is exalted;*
> *Shining Beltia, exalted and most high;*
> *Among the goddesses there is none like her;*
> *She accuses and intercedes*
> *She abases the rich and vindicates the cause of the lowly;*
> *She overthrows the enemy, he who does not revere her godhead;*
> *She delivers the captive, and takes the hand of the fallen;*
> *Bless the servant who honours thy name;*
> *Fix the destiny of the king who fears thee;*
> *Give life to the children of Babel, thy dependents;*
> *Plead for them before Marduk, the king of the gods;*
> *Let them tell of thy glory, let them exalt thy kingdom;*
> *Let them speak of thy prowess, let them glorify thy name*
> *Have mercy on thy servant who blesses thee;*

Take his hand in need and suffering;
In disease and distress give him life;
May he go ever in joy and delight;
May he tell thy prowess to the peoples of the whole world.[14]

At the same time the King set out for Borsippa to fetch the statue of the paternal deity Nabu, first born son of Marduk. In the evening after the offering meal the Epic of Creation was recited. On the fifth day, six ceremonies took place including prayers to Bel and Beltiya, temple cleansing and the important negative confession made by the king. Nabu also arrived by canal with the king.

The king prepared to make the negative confession. He was divested of all symbols of office – ring, mace, crown and staff – by the sesgallu. He was then led by the king into the sanctuary, pulled by the ears and forced to kneel before the god. The king made the ritual negative confession.

I have not sinned, lord of the lands.
I have not been negligent of your godhead.
I have not destroyed Babylon.
I have not ordered her to be dispersed.
I have not made Esagil quake,
I have not forgotten its rites.
I have not struck the privileged citizens in the face,
I have not humiliated them.
I have paid attention to Babylon,
I have not destroyed her walls.[15]

Finally the king was reinvested with the symbols of authority. The sesgallu struck him across the face. If the king's tears flowed, Bel was pleased. On the 6th day other gods' statues arrived in Babylon from their home sanctuaries. A slaughterer struck off the heads of the human statues. They were burnt before the god. On the eighth day the statue of Marduk was brought from the temple and enthroned beneath a canopy in the temple courtyard. Then Marduk was taken to the Shrine of the Destinies where the destiny of the king was determined.

Go forth Bel, O king, go forth.
Go forth, our lady, the king awaits you. [16]

The king made ready to participate in the sacred marriage. In a grand procession Marduk, the king, singers and musicians walked the processional way to a quay where the royal party embarked for the akitu building. Finally the procession returned to Babylon for a last assembly in the Shrine of Destinies where the destinies of the land were cast.

The Babylonian akitu festival was quite different from its Sumerian predecessor. The Hieros Gamos was now but one minor episode in a lengthy festival which primarily enacted Marduk's mythology. The captivity, freeing and triumphal procession of Marduk served to empower the institution of kingship. The sacred marriage was now vestigial and probably only symbolic. There was little need to either court the goddess with gifts or delight her with pleasure. Her power was now insignificant. Sumerian predecessors had already raised the king to a god. The balance of power had been transferred. The dying consort had become the divine king.

DIONYSUS AND THE BASILINNA ARCHON

Only this much is certain, a sacred marriage was enacted by a woman high born and blameless, and that the marriage was a mystery.

JANE HARRISON, *Prolegomena to the Study of Greek Religion*

Dionysus was originally a yearling god. His signs were the bull and the phallus, emblems of rampant sexuality designed to fertilise mother nature. The cult of Dionysus gradually evolved independently and became associated with one particular aspect of nature's renewal, the wine harvest. The worship of Dionysus became widespread and was especially popular with women. On the island of Keos, Dionysus was worshipped from the fifteenth century BC by ecstatic women devotees. A Dionysian festival was even incorporated into the cultic calendar of Athens overlaying an older festival designed to placate the spirits of the dead. In the month of Anthesterion, a spring fertility rite included a procession and a sacred marriage to the wife of the chief magistrate. The sacred marriage of the Basilinna, wife of the Archon Basileus to Dionysus, probably originated when the cult was transferred from Attica to Athens in 534 BC. Dionysus himself appeared riding on a ship mounted on wheels. In the ancient tradition of sacred drama, he was personified by an actor wearing a mask.

The Basilinna was expected to be 'high born' and 'blameless'. A scandal erupted one year when a particular wife of the Archon Basileus, the daughter of one Nearira, allegedly broke both conventions and offended Greek sensibilities. She was charged with being neither high born nor blameless. In a trial, the prosecutor alleged that her mother Neaira as both a foreigner and a courtesan was precluded from marriage to a citizen. Her daughter was married to the Archon Basileus who retained the responsibility for many of the older religious ceremonies of the year. The situation clearly outraged all sense of ancestral tradition. The prosecutor reminded the jury that the qualifications regarding the Basilinna were clearly set up on stone stele by an altar in the sanctuary of Dionysus in the Marshes. The Basilinna had a particularly important part to play during this festival. She was to be married to the god, Dionysus.

By tradition, on the 12th day of the month the Basilinna 'offered secret offerings on behalf of the city, and saw what no foreigner could fittingly see, and entered whither no other Athenian of all the many there are, enters except the wife of the Basileus.'[17] She was attended by fourteen Gererai, 'revered', who also served the sacred rites offering at each of the fourteen altars in the sanctuary. They were appointed annually by the magistrate. They each swore a sacred oath in the presence of the sacred herald who acted as servant to the wife of the Basileus. 'I fast and am clean and abstinent from all things that make unclean and from intercourse with man and I celebrate the Theoinia and Iobacccheia to Dionysus in accordance with ancestral usage and at the appointed times.'[18] We have no knowledge of either the Theoinia or Iobaccheia.

The Basilinna was annually married to Dionysus. No details are recorded. It took place in the Boukoleion beside the Prytaneion in the civic centre in Athens. Aristotle tells that in the past days the king Archon used to live in a place called the Boukolion near to the Prytaneion. 'And the proof of this is that to this day the union and marriage of the wife of the King Archon with Dionysus takes place there. In a place called the 'cattle shed' the Queen Archon was married to Dionysus at the festival of the Anthesteria.'[19]

In time-honoured tradition 'our evidence points to someone impersonating the god'.[20] If so, 'it could appropriately be the Basileus and again robed and masked to impersonate the god, he will have emerged from the wedding procession and for the final intimacies of the Boukoleion.'[21]

This particular sacred marriage is an ironic development. Dionysus was once the yearling god occupying a secondary role to the Great Goddess. Now Dionysus was the god annually married to the Basilina as consort. The circle was complete.

HATHOR AND HORUS

That there were annual dramatic performances at Edfu, in which the victory of Horus of Behedet over his foes, his coronation as king of Upper and Lower Egypt and his marriage with the goddess Hathor of Denderah were enacted is beyond dispute.

BLACKMAN AND FAIRMAN, The Myth of Horus at Edfu

Each year Hathor in the form of her statue made several voyages along the Nile from Denderah. One of the most dramatic and spectacular voyages was her journey to Edfu to meet Horus. When the two deities were together a complex series of rituals took place over a fourteen-day period at the Edfu temple site. These ceremonies divided naturally into two phases, the arrival and reception of Hathor and the ceremonies of victorious kingship. Yet again we are faced by incomplete evidence and its interpretation. Certain authorities believe that the meeting of Hathor and Horus can be defined as a sacred marriage. Others remain unconvinced that their meeting carried this connotation.

The goddess Hathor set out in the form of her image

accompanied by her priesthood. The procession departed from the Denderah on the 18th day of the tenth month (Payni). She journeyed in her ship, *nb mrw.t*, the mistress of love.

On the first day Hathor visited Mut of Asheru at Thebes. On the second day she visited the sanctuary of Anubis. On the third day her flotilla arrived at Hieraconopolis where she met the local Horus who accompanied her to Edfu. In the meantime Horus of Edfu together with Khonsu set out to meet the flotilla. Their meeting took place at Wts.t-Hr to the north of Edfu. Together the divinities proceeded to Edfu. Before their departure offerings were made to ascertain whether the time of their departure was propitious. When reassured by a good omen, the barques set out again. The flotilla proceeded on its way landing at the temple of Horus on the first day of the 11th month at the eighth hour, the day of the new moon. Crowds cheered the arrival of the barges. 'The inhabitants in Edfu are in jubilation shouting for joy to the height of heaven.' The divine effigies were placed in the temple. The festival of *Bhd.t* commenced. It was also called the festival of the beautiful embrace, *hb n shn nfr*. An inscription states that the goddess sailed from Denderah 'to consummate the beauteous embrace with her Horus'. It is also stated that on the fourth day of the festival the young Horus was conceived by the goddess. Fairman believes that the Hieros Gamos took place here on the afternoon and evening. There is no suggestion that human representatives took on the mediating roles in this instance. The Egyptians believed after all that cult statues embodied the essence of the deity which might be vivified when the ceremony of the Opening of the Mouth was performed. The ceremonial placing of divine effigies together would have been sufficient to effect a union if it was so intended.

Nevertheless we are not dealing with a sacred marriage in either the Mesopotamian or Greek style. The union of Hathor and Horus was never intended as a pattern for human marriage, nor was it an agricultural fertility rite.

Hathor is a goddess of love and fertility, she bears the title *nb.t htp.t*, mistress of the vulva. She is also called 'mistress of love'. She also has a special relationship with the pharaoh as the rejuvenator of royal power. Unlike Hera and Zeus or Inanna and Dumuzi,

Hathor's partner fluctuates according to the particular mythological scenario. She is most often referred to as the wife of Amun Re. By extension she might be partnered to Horus, another solar figure. She is also the mother of Horus the sky god. Hathor has two sons Ihy, a divine musician and Harsomtus, 'Horus who unites the two lands'. Horus of Edfu is not the sky god but son of Isis and Osiris, avenger of his father, defeater of the enemy Seth, the rightful king.

These confusions and convolutions may prevent us from comprehending the contemporary meaning attributed to Hathor's visit. It may have been a subtle ritual thread in the sustaining rites of kingship. The meeting of Hathor with Horus preceded the main rites of the Behedite festival which depicted Horus overthrowing his enemies. On the morning after the two effigies had shared the temple sanctuary, attention shifted to the fourteen-day festival of Behedet which now took precedence. These ceremonies commenced with a procession headed by five sacred lances to the burial ground of Behedet some distance to the south west where a sacred drama was enacted. It commemorated the victory of Horus over his enemies. The procession visited the upper hall of the temple before making its way to the hall of the House of Life.

Here another series of complex rituals took place. These rites included common Egyptian themes. The red enemy Seth was overcome, symbolised by the slaughter of a red goat and red ox. Geese were dispatched to the four compass points to inform the gods that Horus had rightfully taken both the white crown and the red crown. First fruits were offered, calves were driven. Further ceremonies were performed, a red wax hippopotamus on which the name of the enemies were written was destroyed.

The lengthy festival included feasting and further complex ceremonies. Bleeker contests Fairman's analysis of events suggesting instead that Hathor went to Edfu only in her role as sun-eye, patroness of fertility and goddess of the dead. The issue remains open.

HERA AND ZEUS

The sacred marriage continued to be one of the most
characteristic features of the worship of Hera.

WILLETTS, *Cretan Cults and Festivals*

The marriage rites of Hera which were a central part of her Greek
cult activity, were probably derived from Crete where a sacred
union between the solar bull and lunar cow was enacted. As Hera
became increasingly humanised, the marriage rites took on a
social aspect. The marriage of Zeus and Hera came to represent
the archetypal marriage for Greek society. It is difficult to date
the appearance of ritualised marriage rites in Greece. The
evidence is fragmented. We do not have a full picture of the
proceedings.

M. Eternities Varro, a Roman admiral, visited Samothrace and
described an annual feast of the goddess. 'Her most famous and
ancient temple is in Samos, and a statue in the costume of a bride
was worshipped in her yearly festival celebrated with the rites of
marriage.'[22] It is clear from all accounts that Hera was represented
by a statue, first in the form of a wooden board shaped at the waist,
later by a more lifelike representation. Pausanias mentions the cult
statue at Samos 'there are some who say the sanctuary of Hera
at Samos was founded by the crew of the Argo who brought the
statue from Argos.' He continued, 'you could tell this was one of
the most ancient of all sanctuaries if only from the statue. It was
made by Smilis of Aigina.'[23] Hera's statue stood in the temple.
'People came to it through the temple, through a long corridor,
clothed it, and fetched it to be set up outside, for the ritual
performance in which it was a 'property'. It had first to be clothed
with a beautiful robe, like those of which we possess an inventory
on a marble stele.'[24] The Samian sanctuary also contained a
wooden bed. A terracotta relief showing Hera naked standing
beside Zeus was attached to one of the four posts. The meaning
is perfectly clear.

Pausanias and Plutarch were witness to Hera's wedding rites in
Boetia. The main festival was called the Great Daidala. It took
place every sixtieth year. The Great Daidala was celebrated

throughout the whole of Boetia, and was the end product of a story uniting several layers of the cult. The Little Daidala took place every seventh year, but was celebrated only by the people of Plataia. At the Little Daidala fourteen wooden statues, *xoana*, 'works of art', accompanied the cult statue of Hera. The xoana are also found on Crete. These represented the nymphs, her bridal escort. The first act involved selecting the tree from which to fashion the images. Pieces of meat were laid in an oak wood to draw down ravens. The tree in which the birds alighted was selected. The culminating rites entailed a grand procession up to the peak of Mount Kitharon. The statue decked and veiled as a bride was set on a cart hung with drapery, drawn by white heifers. Other carts followed with the bridal escort accompanied by flute players. At the mountain peak they reached a nuptial chamber in the form of a small house constructed of wood lined with brushwood. Here the beasts contributed by the cities were sacrificed. Each participating city sent a cow and a bull, probably a resonance of the primal Cretan union. After the sacrifice the bridal chamber and all the wooden images were put to the torch.

Another nuptial chamber was constructed for Hera and Zeus at Paestum. This little house contained a bed too small for a human and offerings of honey in great bronze jars. This nuptial chamber was sealed with blocks of stone.

The Olympic games held to honour Hera were founded by a woman named Hippodrome to give thanks for her own marriage to Pelops. These games were held every four years and organised by a committee of sixteen women helped by women assistants. Young girls raced in honour of Hera in three age groups with right breast and shoulder bared. The sixteen women also wove a robe for Hera and arranged two dances. The performance of a marriage drama may have been part of the celebrations.

The other features of Hera's cult were the ritual bathing which preceded the marriage itself and the disappearance and search for the cult statue. The annual ritual bath which restored Hera's virginity preceded the wedding rites.

There can be no doubt that in the great classical temples to Hera, marriage was ritualised. It was a rite of passage for women enacted by women.

The history of the Sacred Marriage clearly reflects the changing status of women. It was once the divine union which brought blessings to the land and its people. But it became the social model for a marriage between a faithless husband and a jealous wife. The marriage of Zeus and Hera, tempestuous and ultimately broken, was a model upon which Greek marriage was fashioned. An archetypal pattern descended into the most mundane application. The balance of power had swung dramatically in the opposite direction. Marriage itself was rejected by many women who sought neither the union of opposites nor the Hieros Gamos.

GLOSSARY

E-gipar, a suite of rooms, possibly even a collection of buildings containing the gipar

Gigunu, 'the seat of joy', a chamber situated at the top of the ziggurat

Gipar, a chamber within the temple precinct, but not on the ziggurat where the sacred marriage was enacted, when the divine bridegroom was subjected to a loss of status

Guenna, a cult room, probably an ante-room of the gigunu. Possibly the throne room

Chapter 13

VOICE OF THE ORACLE

Each generation now should produce its seers.

The Tibetan, TIBETAN, 'A TREATISE ON WHITE MAGIC'

It is commonly asserted that women are more intuitive and psychic than men. When a man shows qualities of intuition he is usually said to be drawing on his own feminine nature. Women certainly have a natural affinity for sensing, intuiting and attuning to non-verbal expression, responding to mood, atmosphere and body language. Such sensitivity may have evolved through an instinctive body awareness, even from child-rearing itself. Rhythms of menstruation, social intimacy and family bonding have created an evolutionary push for the development of subtle sensitivities. Women have learned to communicate through the body and the unspoken emotions, to sense a child's needs, to recognise unvoiced feelings and attune to personal tides. This refinement of feeling, instinct and intuition is possibly the inheritance of the generations. The ability for natural rapport is often latent, unrecognised and undeveloped. When such qualities are valued, utilised and cherished, empathy may flower into compassion, intuition into wisdom, images will turn into visions, feelings will coalesce into certainties.

It is possible that such evolutionary factors have produced some physiological effects. The human brain reflects our evolutionary history. It contains reptilian, mammalian and neomammalian areas. The cortex, the roof brain, reflects the unique characteristics of human development, symbolic representation and abstract communication. The corpus callosum, which serves as a bridge between the left and right hemispheres, appears to be weightier and more complex in women. This may be related to a woman's natural integrative experience of life. Men certainly seem more at ease when separating, analysing and rationalising. The activity of the left brain hemisphere is incomplete, unbalanced and usually antithetical to indirect thinking. Higher states of consciousness which include psychic activity and supra-mundane experience seem related to brain function through the activity of the pituitary and pineal glands.

These higher states of consciousness, once belittled and disbelieved, have now been witnessed by the electronic brain monitoring of the late twentieth century. There is a clear relationship between meditation and brain rhythms. The brain-consciousness interface still holds many secrets. We may find in the future that different psychic functions engage quite specific areas of the brain. The left hemisphere of the brain is not capable of registering higher states of consciousness alone. Its function is to dissect not to synthesise. The cortex is the youngest, most sophisticated and characteristically human part of the brain. It may prove to be the case that psychic and higher consciousness functions are predominantly related to this area. The more primitive brains which control instinct, drive and basic emotion function automatically. The cortex responds to the type of external stimulation characteristically found in spiritual traditions, intense internal imagery, concentration, abstract thought patterns and transpersonal identification. It may prove that higher states of consciousness, far from being aberrant, represent the true flowering of humanity's unique abilities.

DIVINE WILL

The gods know all things and in sacrifices, omens, voices, and dreams they give forewarnings to whomever they wish.

XENOPHON

It is an ancient belief, going back to heroic times but since confirmed by the unanimous opinion of the Roman people and of every other nation, that there exists within mankind an undeniable faculty of divination. The Greeks called it *mantike*, that is, the capacity to foresee, to know future events, a sublime and salutary act that raises human nature most nearly to the level of the divine power. In this respect, as in many others, that we have improved upon the Greeks by giving this faculty a name derived from the word god, *divinatio*, whereas according to Plato's explanation the Greek word comes from *furor* (*mania* from which *mantike* is derived). What cannot be gainsaid is that there is no nation, whether the most learned and enlightened or the most grossly barbarous, that does not believe that the future can be revealed and does not recognise in certain people the power of foretelling it. [1]

Many centuries have passed since Cicero wrote these words in *De Divinatio*, yet many people undoubtedly still hold the same opinion. Society has changed beyond recognition since Cicero's time, but human nature seems to change little.

Ascertaining the divine will has always been important. It was naturally felt that significant decisions which affected the lives of the whole group were more likely to succeed if backed by divine sanction. Every civilisation has produced its seers, oracles and, it has to be said, charlatans masquerading as mystics. Every civilisation has tried to know the future, to forestall disaster and comply with the divine will. According to Sumerian myth, a legendary king of Sippar received the gift of divination from the gods. It was then handed down to the priesthood, into the keeping of the guild of diviners, the *baratu*. These diviners paid great attention to dreams and visions. A special chamber in the temple was set apart for dream incubation. Dreams were interpreted according to traditional principles passed down through the generations.

Babylonian seers, *mahhu*, 'ecstatics', were frequently female. The oracle of Baia of Arbela uttered the following, presumably prior to the battlefield.

Fear not Easarhaddon, I, the god Bel, speak to you. The beams of your heart I strengthen, like your mother who caused you to exist. Sixty great gods are standing together with me and protect you. The great god Sin is at your right, the god Shamash at your left; sixty great gods stand round about you, ranged for the battle. Do not trust men. Turn your eyes to me, look at me, I am Ishtar of Arbela; I have turned Ashur's favour unto you. When you were small, I sustained you. Fear not, praise me. Where is the enemy that blew over you when I did not notice? The future is like the past I am the god Nabu, lord of the tablet stylus, praise me.[2]

Discovering the will of the gods was once of vital significance to the smooth running of countries. The divine will was treated as the final arbiter of the decision-making process. Matters great and small were presented to the gods. Kings, governments and cities wanted to know what the gods demanded of them in order that they might best comply.

Alexander the Great went to the oracle of Ammon and was proclaimed as 'a son of Ammon'. Hatshepsut 'was making supplication at the stairway of the lord of gods, a command was heard from the great place, an oracle of the god himself.' Elizabeth I was guided by the contemporary astrologer John Dee. The Emperors Trajan and Hadrian visited the oracle at Didyama. In Sumer the priestess fixed the fates for the year at the New Year's ceremonial. Kings and queens, perhaps more than any others, have desired to know the future: the destiny of nations is no light burden. Monotheistic religions have no time for such indulgence while paradoxically deferring to 'the will of God', which is constantly sought and invoked.

People still hanker for the added security of another perspective when taking an important decision. In a tarot spread the last card is often indicative of the 'final outcome', the conclusion to both past and present events. We are fully aware that each decision is like a crossroads. Insecurity born of the moment breeds a compulsion for security. We are wracked by the possible outcome of our decision making. In effect we want to peep ahead, to check that our chosen road is not potholed or fraught with trouble. Contemporary modern life is comparatively secure. When lives were at the mercy of harvest, the weather, a fragile peace treaty or an outbreak of disease, the right decision assumed monumental proportions. The right decision would be blessed by the gods.

Interpreting the words of the deities has always been a part of sacred life, taking place under ritualised conditions in places sanctified for the purpose. Speaking with the gods was thought to be a dangerous business safeguarded only by proper precautions and correct procedures. To cross the boundaries between the mundane and the supra-mundane was seen as a journey, undertaken by either the individual or the deity descending to take possession of the mediator. In either case the individual closed down to the ordinary world, usually by entering a state of mind often loosely labelled as trance. New models of consciousness are continuing to expand our knowledge of the brain/mind interface. The holographic model is promising and exciting, uniting the scientific and mystical into a whole. We need to understand the mind and the nature of the human being if we are to comprehend the function and meaning of consciousness throughout its entire range of possibilities. William James was not the first to recognise the existence of other quite different but equally valid states of consciousness. 'Our waking consciousness is but one special state of consciousness, whilst all about it, parted by the filmiest of screens, there lie potential forms of consciousness entirely different.'[3]

ALTERED STATES OF CONSCIOUSNESS

There exists a wide spectrum of ancient and Oriental spiritual practices that are specifically designed to facilitate access to the perinatal and transpersonal domains.

STANISLAV GROF, *The Adventure of Self Discovery*

Psychic phenomena such as clairvoyance, clairaudience, visions, prophetic dreams and intuitions are thought of as being feminine qualities, whether possessed by men or women. In order to receive subtle impressions, the mind needs to be passive and receptive. This is not weakness, but a subtle and refined attunement. Quite simply if the mind is dominated by uncontrolled and egotistic thoughts, there will be no space for the silence of receptivity.

Living spiritual traditions rooted deeply in the distant past possess a core of esoteric practices and techniques which, it is claimed, have the power to awaken higher and more subtle senses in the individual. Such practices typically involve mental functions, self-awareness and spiritual exercises in combination. It is claimed that steady and committed application can awaken functions of higher consciousness. The path to higher consciousness is of course open to both men and women. However, women generally seem have naturally sensitised abilities. Mental training can turn receptivity into reception, intuition into inner tuition and insight into inner sight.

Normally, the mind is distracted by a wide range of sensory data. Attention flits from one sensation to another. The trained mind, however, is able to hold its focus on a given subject for sustained periods of time. The mind can turn inwards upon itself to a different quality of experience. When the external stimuli have been reduced as far as possible, the body is passive yet the mind is active. The outer senses are closed, the inner senses are opened; the inner ear listens inwardly, the inner eye opens inwardly; the inner senses open to subtle feelings and realisations. This state can be reached through a variety of processes. An altered state of consciousness can be attained through external means such as drumming, dancing and chanting which establish rhythmic patterns. These are typically shamanic techniques. An altered state of consciousness and shift of personal energy may also be achieved through internal discipline using the creative imagination.

In a controlled and altered state of consciousness it is possible to transcend the normal limitations imposed by the senses and function from a different level of mind and being. These functions are quite varied and separate in themselves. Mediumship, pychism, seership, and mediation are quite different one from the other. Mediumship is the ability to communicate with the spirit world and its inhabitants. Psychism is the general ability to pick up information from non-physical sources. Seership is the ability to see across the boundaries of space and time. Mediation is the ability to stand between the deities and the world. Testaments from every culture and time serve to show that such experiences are universal and indeed still possible.

THE LIVING ORACLE – THE STATE ORACLE OF TIBET

The protector is here, in the room.

JOHN AVEDON, *In Exile from the Land of the Snows*

The State Oracle of Tibet is unique today. It still functions in an official capacity as guide for political and spiritual decision-making. The relationship between the gods and the state, decision-making and the oracle was once common, accepted and accorded its due respect. Such a relationship is now very rare, possible only in a culture rooted in spiritual certainty. The Tibetan Oracle, as a vestige from a previous age, may give us a glimpse of the psychic and spiritual processes now all but vanished from the world. Its existence may help us to understand the oracles of the ancient world.

The Tibetan Oracle continues alone in the world. It is sustained by a belief system which recognises and values the possibility of supra-mundane contact. It is upheld by the rigorous testing of the oracular vehicle and validated by the scrupulous recording of all oracular statements. Such safeguards preserve the integrity and continuity of the oracle.

We cannot know if the ancients applied such strictures. We know only too little about the selection and training of those acting as the oracular mouthpiece of the gods.

The State Oracle of Tibet offers a living example of mediation, a model of oracular possession which represents the ideal regardless of the oracular vehicle's gender.

The current oracular vehicle was confirmed in his position after a series of profound and dramatic experiences. These included classic shamanic episodes, sudden illness, outbursts of irrationality, fits, seizures, hallucinations, trance, terrifying dreams and spirit possession. These experiences culminated in a series of rigorous tests by the authorities. Finally Lobsang Jigme was proclaimed as the State Oracle early in 1945. The role is highly honoured and respected. It is, however, known for its unique physical and psychic pressures. Lobsang Jigme's predecessor ran away in sheer terror after he had been singled out through possession by the Protector.

A consultation with the State Oracle took place on 14th February 1981. The account provides an insight into a specialised and rare form of oracular working.

The ritual consultation begins with a period of substantial preparation lasting two days. The oracular vehicle undertakes meditation, mantra, prayers and a special diet. As the time approaches he is dressed in a traditional costume of eight layers. It is so heavy that he cannot walk unaided. Finally, at the appointed time, the State Oracle enters the hall. He is prepared to be the vehicle for Dorje Drakden, 'the Renowned Immutable One'. The ceremony begins with the sounds of horns, cymbals, drums and chanted invocations. Three assistants help the State Oracle to a seat, so encumbered is he by the costume that even walking is difficult. The mediation begins.

> He is already starting to enter the first levels of trance. A slight quivering rolls up and down his body. His breathing is short and loud. . . . The whole countenance becomes pure and clear. The medium assumes a piercing, distant look. He is immersed in the visualisation of himself as a tutelary deity standing at the centre of a celestial mansion. . . . The moment has come, the kuden begins to be possessed. . . . Abruptly his head jerks back to the right and he commences to hyperventilate. Each breath is ejected in a compressed hiss like a radiator . . .
>
> The medium's figure visibly expands, swelling two inches, so that the belts of the costume, purposely left loose before now cut into the robes. The heart beat is such that, in a separate movement all to itself the mirror on his chest bounces . . .
>
> His voice is startling. Each word is crisply enunciated, yet in an ethereal, halting, hollow tone suggesting immense age and distance. . . . The secretaries can see his entire body seething with energy vibrating like an electrified filament . . .
>
> The message itself is delivered in a high lilting metred verse . . . [4]

At the end of the session the *kuden* (medium) needs time to recover. On a low bed attendants loosen the heavy costume and massage his body back to normal consciousness. At this particular session the State Oracle was joined by a second oracle, the Gadong Oracle. Unlike the State Oracle, the medium is not a monk but a layperson. This oracle traditionally passes from father to son in one family. At this point in his training the medium had only served for a year. He was still having difficulty with the mediation which was both painful and violent. The session was cut short. He collapsed, to be carried out by attendants who revived him.

True oracular mediation is not easy or common.

ANCIENT ORACLES – DIDYMA

Ever since she has taken on her priesthood, the gods have been appearing in visitations as never before, to the girls and women, but also too, to men and children. What does such a thing mean? Is it the sign of something good?

INSCRIPTION ERECTED OUTSIDE THE TOWN OF MILETUS

The oracle of Apollo at Didyma outside Miletus was very popular in its day. Historical accounts give a clear picture of the proceedings at this site. In the second century BC questioners travelled down the sacred way from nearby Miletus, or arrived by boat. Before them stood the enormous oracular temple. Consultation was expected to be a lengthy process, so questioners could lodge for a day or two. The temple site here was complex and spacious accommodating visitors, altars, various areas, shrines and temple staff. Prophecy was given by a priestess. In AD 200 the priestess came from a well-educated family. Sadly, we know practically nothing of the lives of the women who served here. By contrast, it was customary for the priests of Apollo to inscribe their names and careers on the newly-constructed buildings which stood in Didyma's sanctuary. The prophetess was attended by a prophet who recorded her words. This prophet was often part of the civil service from Miletus.

Iamblicus tells us that the prophetess lived a chaste life. She bathed and prepared for a forthcoming oracle by fasting for three days and making sacrifice. She lived in the inner shrine. Iamblichus says that she was 'already possessed by the divine light, enjoying it for a long while'. It was noted that she 'breathed' as she received the god. She sat upon a cylindrical block beside a small sacred spring which welled up at the rear of the courtyard.

Her inspired words were turned to verse by the attendant prophet. Copies of her words were made available at the nearby record house.

The prophetess gave her oracle in an unroofed inner shrine. While delivering her message the priestess held a rod 'handed down from the god', like the rod which Apollo was said to have cut from a bay tree and given to the legendary founder of the Didyma priesthood. Like the Tibetan State Oracle who literally assumed the mantle of Dorje Drakden, the priestess at Didyma assumed the authority of the god by taking up the rod as a visible sign of empowerment.

The priestess at Didyma, like the current State Oracle of Tibet, followed the characteristic stages of divine possession, preparation, mediation and finally recovery.

CLAROS

What is the nature of God?

QUESTION TO THE CLAROS OREACLE

At Claros, another major Apollonian oracular site, prophecy was given by a male prophet in a darkened underground chamber. Visitors first entered a sacred valley and approached the temple through a big triple gate which stood before the shrine. Beyond it there was a sacred grove, leading to a Doric temple of Apollo. The approaches were lined with republican statues. The altar was enormous as were the colossal statues of Leto and Apollo. Visitors were prepared to consult the god. Iamblicus tells us, 'many religious rites were performed before the god was consulted'. The prophet himself fasted. A sacrifice was made on the great altar. It seems that some visitors were initiated into a mystery rite, as a preliminary to consultation. Here, the gods were questioned by night. At the beginning of the second century AD there was only a single prophet available. By AD 130 he had been joined by a *thespode*, a singer of oracles who served for life. We know little of the education or training of either of these officials.

When the appointed sacred night drew close, the underground lamps were lit. The staff and questioner met by torchlight, they journeyed to the inner shrine, bent double as they passed through the underground tunnel roofed in dark blue marble. They reached an open underground cavern. Here the sides of the room were fitted with stone benches, in the centre a deep blue marble omphalos (a stone representing the navel of the earth) indicated that they had reached the oracular centre of the earth. A narrow corridor led from the first chamber to a second where the sacred spring bubbled. The prophet drank the water and was inspired to speak. The thespode put the utterance into verse.

The oracle was highly popular, and people would undertake long journeys for a consultation. In the second and early third century official delegations went to Claros, arranging for their names to be inscribed wherever space still permitted on marble blocks. Three hundred texts have been recovered. The earliest civic inscription was the envoy from Perinthus who visited the oracle in AD 110. Civic envoys came on a regular basis, often with their own choir. The site was visited by individuals including a nephew of the Emperor, a philosopher, a merchant from Pontus and the helper to the orator Aelius. The novel composed by Xenophon was centred on the oracle.

DELPHI

There are a lot of different stories about Delphi, even more about Apollo's oracle. They say that in the most ancient times the oracle belonged to Earth, and Daphnis was its prophetess whom Earth appointed; she was one of the nymphs of the mountain.

PAUSANIAS, *Guide to Greece*

Delphi remains the most famous oracular site of the ancient world. It is also the site most shrouded in mystique and misinformation. Legend tells that a herdsman with a flock of goats came upon a place – in some versions it is referred to as a chasm – whereupon the goats began to behave strangely. This original site became the home of the Delphic oracle, the centre of the world marked by the world navel, the omphalos. In memory of the founding legend, goats were traditionally sacrificed to ascertain if it was a propitious day to consult the oracle.

This oracle was always under the authority of a priestess. Paradoxically, women could not consult the oracle here except through a male intermediary. According to Diodorus Siculus the role of priestess here was once taken by a young woman but Echecrates the Thessalian carried her away and raped her. Thereafter, the office was filled by a woman over fifty. She continued to wear the dress of a young woman in memory of the previous prophetess.

We know little of the selection process for the women who served here. Plutarch tells us that 'the woman who at present occupies the position belongs to one of the soundest and most respected families to be found in Delphi and has always led an irreproachable life.' He continued, 'the woman is committed to a strenuous existence and for the remainder of her life must remain pure and chaste.' Euripides states that the priestess was selected 'from all the women of Delphi'. Furthermore, upon taking office she became 'the god's bride'.

Contemporaries were just as fascinated as later enquirers by the mantic work of the Pythia. Their guesswork and speculation has unfortunately become the cast iron certainty of later generations. Classical authors have handed down an image that still persists today. The term Pythia, now synonomous with the Delphic priestess, is a late term popularised in the nineteenth century. It was not used by ancient writers with reference to Delphi. It is still commonly believed that the priestess mounted a tripod, inhaled vapours which poured from the ground, entered a state of frenzy and made wild and mainly unintelligible sounds which were then interpreted by a prophet in attendance. The stereotype of divine madness is hard to break. Farnell, in 1907, described the work of the oracle accordingly.

> The pythoness ascended into the tripod, and filled with divine afflatus which at least later ages believed to ascend in vapour from a fissure in the ground, burst forth into wild utterance which was probably some kind of articulate speech and which the Hosioi, the 'holy ones', who with the prophet sat around the tripod, knew well how to interpret.[5]

Classical observers with a limited knowledge of spiritual psychology looked for explanations only in the external sources. They speculated on the effects of vapours and gases or the supposed intoxication brought about through chewing bay leaves. The truth behind genuine oracular ability lies in the mind. External components are at best mere triggers.

However, very few of the authors who wrote so extensively about Delphi took the trouble to visit the oracle. Instead rumour, elaboration and hearsay created a classical game of Chinese whispers in which the statements of one commentator became the distortions of the next. Neither Strabo nor Lucan knew Delphi. Plutarch alone is a unique authority on Delphi; he was a priest here.

Joseph Fontenrose has closely examined all the classical sources and finds no good case for this traditional view. He reports that the fabled chasm only appears as an element in one myth. Those who were acquainted with Delphi – Aescylus, Euripides, Pindar, Herodotus, do not mention the chasm or the vapours. The site itself has revealed neither chasm nor vapours. It is not a volcanic site which might give rise to fumes and gases, but is built on limestone and schist. The frenzy so often attributed to the priestess by some late writers originates from a misunderstanding of Plutarch's use of the word 'mania' meaning transport, rapture, inspiration, and ecstasy. The Greek word 'mania' was translated into the Latin 'insania'. Herodotus always represented the priestess speaking directly to the consultant under Apollo's inspiration. He attributed her inspiration to the god's impulse, Apollo put visions into her mind, and a light in her soul which enabled her to see the future. She revealed the vision in her own words.

Plutarch described the priestess as frenzied and wild only on one occasion, which may be understood as a deliberate cautionary tale. Plutarch's Lamprias tells his company about foreign envoys who had come to consult the oracle. The priests poured cold water over the sacrificial goat in the usual manner but the animal remained unmoved, a sign that this was not a good day for an oracle. The priests, however, continued to drench the goat, in effect forcing the goat to shudder as the propitious omen. The priestess was reluctant to proceed: 'at her very first remarks it became evident from the roughness of her voice that she was not in control of herself.'[6] Finally she rushed out, fell unconscious and died a few days later. This tale, fictionalised by Plutarch, indicates an usual occurrence. The story pointed out that proper procedures were not observed. This tale has been falsely used to demonstrate the wildness which overcame the priestess as a matter of course.

A second tale of wild possession was recounted by Lucan who had not visited the oracle. His tale recounts a consultation with one Phemonone, the traditional name of the first priestess. Accordingly, in 48 BC, Appius Claudius wanted to know the outcome of the civil war. The priestess was reluctant to speak and only pretended to respond. Finally, when threatened with punishment, she submitted. 'She raged madly about the cave and finally announces Appius' fate. She finally pronounced, "Appius will have no part in the war, but will have peace alone in the valley of Euboea."'[7]

This answer referred of course to the imminent death of Appius. The priestess never recovered from the delivery of this message and fell to the ground. The story states that she died not long afterwards.

This story is in all probability based on Virgil's account of the Sybil of Cumae, and not on any personal experience. The literary tradition which grew up around Delphi served to increase its magnetic attraction. These stories fuelled an image of the oracle as frenzied and uncontrollable. Contemporaries were both fascinated and bewildered by the workings of oracles.

It seems likely that the priestess prepared herself by bathing in the waters of the Castilian spring. She probably drank from this too. She burned bay leaves and barley before the altar and wore a bay leaf crown. She also held a bay leaf sprig in her hand, shaking it on occasion. She sat upon a *holmos* – a tripod-like hollow seat – and delivered her words clearly, inspired, transported, enraptured by the experience. In the Prologue to *The Eumenides* the prophetess offers a prayer to the Earth as she prepares to be inspired.

Figure 10 The Delphic Consultation. The priestess does not appear frenzied. She calmly uses a shallow bowl for scrying, and holds bay leaves in her hand.

First in this prayer I honour before the other gods Earth, the primal prophetess. After her Themis, who was the second to sit here in her mother's oracle, as a tradition says. In the third place, willingly and not perforce, after her sat another child of Earth, the Titaness Phoebe. She gave it as a birthday gift to Phoebus who takes his name from her. [8]

It is now difficult to judge the exact psychic function of the oracular vehicle. Was she possessed in a similar manner to the

State Oracle of Tibet? Were her abilities mediumistic or simply psychic? Possession can be dramatic. It is, after all, the superimposing of one mind and being upon another. However, once the merge is effected the oracular vehicle becomes calm and perfectly lucid. Mediumship is less strenuous, involving contact but not merger between two minds. Psychic abilities such as clairvoyance involve less personal strain.

We find that people's interests do not change much over time. 'Am I to stay in the job of tax collector?' 'Which of the two women should I marry?'[9] At Didyma in the third century the treasurer of the site, Hermias, asked if he might move the altar, hemmed in by new buildings, to join altars of other gods in the circle around Apollo's main altar.[10] Damianos, a prophet from Cyzicus, had noticed there was no altar to Kore among the 'encircling altars of many gods'. Could he place one by the altar of Demeter? 'Perform the honour of joining the encirclement', was the reply.[11] Damianos continued with a second question: would Apollo be the legislator of a pious form of address in hymns for Kore? 'Let us invoke her as Saviour with fair cries at times of sacrifice, gentle to encounter with her mother Demeter.'[12] At Claros the oracle gave Prisca, a priestess of Artemis, a glowing testimony, applauding her virtue and wisdom. She had already served the goddess for sixty years in the city of Stobi.[13] The city consulted the oracle in the mid 160's during the plague years. At Didyma in the late second to early third century, the oracle was consulted regarding the suitability of Saturnilla for the priesthood of virgin Athena. Saturnilla was high born, married but probably widowed, having borne her children. The oracle confirmed her appointment despite the fact that she was not a virgin, her good birth counting in her favour.[14] At the same oracular site the oracle appointed the prophetess Tryphosa, the only female prophet known by name to us in the Imperial period.[15] Apphion, a bull tamer also known as Heronas, from Alexandria asked would he 'acquit himself gloriously at all times in his acts of dancing on tiptoe and training bulls and will he be serving Apollo with a fair name.'[16] Monarchy too asked questions. King Agesiopolis of Sparta asked whether it was sanctioned to accept the Argive truce.

The Emperor Trajan asked about his prospects in the war in the East.[17] The Emperor Carus marched against the Persians backed by the oracle.[18] Seers travelled with the army. Xenophon, a skilled officer, asked the Delphic oracle to which gods he should sacrifice in order to make a safe return voyage.[19] The Spartans asked whether they should found a colony in Trachinia.[20] The Athenians asked about letting lands within the Eleusinian orgas.[21] The Athenians asked how to improve the dress and adornments of the goddesses Artemis, Demeter and Kore.[22] The Emperor Hadrian in curious mood asked about Homer's birthplace. At Dodona, Heraclides asked whether the child carried by his wife is his, another asked if it would be profitable to buy a house in the town, a third asked if he would do well by breeding sheep.

Oracular possession in Greece, at the time of Delphi's fame, was considered to be under the auspices of the god Apollo. This is clearly a fairly late attribution as these sites were considered sacred before the coming of Apollo. The defeat of the serpent at Delphi is a clear reference to the eclipse of the older earth religion by the solar powers. It is likely that Apollo was introduced as a god of prophecy during the dark ages from Asia Minor. Paradoxically far from being solar and Apolline in character, the oracular activities assumed a chthonian expression, underground, often nocturnal and delivered by darkness. The now-famous oracle at Delphi and the lesser-known shrines of Claros, Dodona and Didyma were also Apollonian sites. These oracular sites still maintained links with the distant past. At Claros clients travelled down into an underground cavern complete with omphalos. At Didyma the priestess lived in an inner shrine. Both shrine and cavern imitated the natural caves of the ancestral past. Delphi, too, had its omphalos linking these sites to the earth mother despite the Apollonian veneer.

At the oracle of Zeus Trophonios, the questioner undertook a powerful journey into the earth which retained all the hallmarks of a rite of rebirth with bee priestesses drawing the candidate from the earth like attendant midwives.

Pausanias, who himself consulted this oracle, presents a clear picture for us. The client prepared for several days by staying in the shrine of Good Spirit and Good Fortune where he made sacrifice. He bathed in the river Herkyna, taking no hot baths. At a favourable time proclaimed by the diviners, the incubant was taken to the river to be washed and anointed with oil by the Hermai, two boys acting as servants. When ready the candidate was taken by priests to drink of two springs, the Waters of Memory and Forgetfulness. These symbolised the candidate's need to remember all that was to take place and to forget everything up to that moment. Next the candidate gazed upon a secret image, a statue made by Daidalas, and put on a linen tunic tied with ribbons, and a pair of solid boots. Now it was time to face the oracle. The candidate was taken to the oracle's entrance. Holding cakes of honey the incubant approached the cave by first descending a narrow ladder to an opening in the ground. Now the oracular journey became quite terrifying.

> The man going down lies on the ground with honey cakes in his hands and pushes his feet into the opening and then tries to get his knees in. The rest of his body immediately gets dragged in after his knees, as if some extraordinarily deep, fast river was catching a man in a current and sucking him down. From here on, inside the second place, people are not always taught the future in one and the same way: one man hears, another sees as well. Those who go down return feet first through the same mouth.[23]

The temple attendants were priestesses called *melissae*, bee maidens who finally drew out the incubant and set him on the throne of memory, Mnemosyne, the mother of the muses, asking him all that he had seen and learned. 'Everyone who goes down to Trophonios is obliged to dedicate the story of whatever he has seen or heard, written out on a wooden tablet.'[24] The words of one incubant were put to song. According to tradition this oracle was founded when ambassadors were sent to the oracle at Delphi to enquire when the drought would end. The priestess commanded them to go to Zeus Trophonios and find a cure from him. When they arrived at Lebadeia they were unable to find the oracle but instead saw a swarm of bees who led them into the earth. As Zeus himself was said to have been born in a Cretan cave which he shared with a swarm of bees the new oracular site was dedicated to him.

This oracular site, despite its attribution to Zeus, nevertheless embodies images and themes that belong to the goddess. The original founding by bees, and the melissae, the bee maidens, point directly to the bee goddess of Crete. The honey cakes carried by the incubant were a suitable offering for the goddess in her bee epiphany and made subtle reference to the process of transformation willingly sought by the candidate. This oracle offered far more than a few verses of prophecy. It offered the experience of rebirth literally undertaken, a vision quest into the earth. Consulting the oracle here cannot have been lightly undertaken, the experience was too daunting for the idly curious.

THE SIBYL

Nor countenance, nor hue, nor braided locks
stayed in one fashion: but her bosom heaves,
her heart swells with wild frenzy: and more vast
she seems; nor mortal rings her voice.

VIRGIL, *The Aeneid* BOOK VI

Legend and myth, fact and romance intermingle to tell the story of the Sybil. There may once have been but a single prophetess bearing this name whose success or reputation was such that others also took the same title. The Sibyl is first mentioned by Heraclitus in 500 BC. Ovid tells us that the Sibyl was unwilling to give up her virginity in exchange for immortality. In the latter half of the fourth century Heraclides Ponticus mentions more than one woman, each acting as the Sibyl. He wrote specifically of a Sibyl called Herophile in Erythrae in Asia Minor. In the year 162 Erythrae staked its claim as the home of the original Sibyl. Her cave was duly visited by the Emperor Versius and adorned with statues.

According to tradition, the Sibyl was granted a wish by Apollo. She asked to live for as many years as the grains in a handful of sand. Her prayer was granted but she had forgotten to ask for youth and was fated to live for a thousand years shrinking away with age.

Oracles, reputedly Sibylline, came to form the basis of many written prophetic collections. The most famous of these were the Roman Sibylline Books which were kept as a confidential state archive, consulted only in times of emergency. According to Roman legend, the Sibyl as an aged woman went to Tarquinius Superbus and offered him nine volumes of written prophecy at a high price. When he refused she burned three volumes and later returned offering him six volumes at the original price. He sent her away yet again. She returned with only three books. Finally he purchased the last three volumes. The Sibyl became so identified with Rome that her image even appeared on coins.

Cybele was brought to Rome as a direct result of the Sibylline oracle. In 204 BC the Romans were faring badly in the Punic wars. The Sibylline books stated that, 'if ever a foreign foe should invade the land of Italy, he could be driven out if the Idean Mother should be brought from Pessinus to Rome.' Envoys were duly despatched to king Attalus who remained unimpressed by their request. It was only after a minor earthquake that he agreed to allow a small statue of Cybele to travel to Rome. In the same year Scipio transferred the battle to Carthage and later defeated Hannibal there. Cybele was treated as the saviour of the nation. The Sibylline prophecy was fulfilled.

Virgil includes an oracular consultation with the Sibyl in Book VI of the Aenead.

> *They had gained*
> *The threshold, when the maid exclaims: "Tis time*
> *to ask the oracles; lo! the god, the god!'*

Aeneas speaks

> *And thou most holy seer, who dost foreknow*
> *The future, grant – I do but ask the realm*
> *owed to my destiny*

The Sibyl begins her reply

> *O thou that hast*
> *Outborne at length the sea vast perils, know*
> *Yet worse on shore awaits thee.*

She delivers a message of gloom.

> *In such*
> *Words from the shrine doth Cumae's Sibyl chant*
> *Her awful riddles, and echo through the cave,*
> *In darkness shrouding truth; so shakes the reins*
> *Apollo in her raving mouth, and plies*
> *Deep in her breast the goad. Soon as he had ebbed*
> *Her frenzy, and the frantic lips were still.* [25]

Virgil was undoubtedly drawing upon myth, folklore and his own poetic imagination. His poetic licence has, however, passed into the realm of cast-iron certainty. He created the stereotypical model for divine possession, frenzy bordering on madness.

SAGAS AND SEERESSES

> *They established laws,*
> *they meted out life*
> *to the sons of men,*
> *and declared their destinies.*

FUNCTION OF THE NORNS

The seeress is an important figure in the Icelandic literary tradition. She is called *spakona* from *spa*, to prophesy, or more often, *volva*. In the sagas the volva is depicted visiting homes, making predictions and conducting divination ceremonies. She is a respected and important member of the community.

A special rite known as the *seior* was sometimes used to obtain knowledge of the future. The word seior was connected with song or singing. It seems that a small choir may have sung to assist her. She sat upon a high seat, a raised platform called a *hjallr* which symbolised her ability to see above the ordinary world. She entered the trance state, sighing or breathing deeply before speaking. The most detailed account of this ceremony is in *Eriks Saga rauda*. The seeress first assured the people that the famine would end. She then prophesied the future of individuals present. In another account she was consulted by individual members.

Stories abound concerning the power and uses of second sight. In Saxo's *History*, a woman with second sight was paid by the wicked king Frothi to discover the whereabouts of his nephews whom he intended to kill. The boys had been hidden by a man skilled in magic. The seeress revealed that they had been brought up in secret and called by the names of dogs to hide their identity. The story reached a dramatic climax at this moment. The boys were present in the hall in disguise. Realising that they would be discovered any minute, the boys intervened in her spell-making by showering her lap with gold. She pretended to fall ill and collapsed without giving them away. Here, second sight was on sale to the highest bidder.

In *Eriks Saga* we have another story involving a seeress. The 'little seeress' was invited by an Icelander in Greenland to hold a divination ceremony. People were anxious about the shortage of food. Before the ceremony began the seeress was given a meal composed of the hearts of all living creatures procurable. She sat on a special platform. She wore a special costume including a cloak decorated with ornamental stones. The hood was of lambskin lined with catskin, her gloves were also of catskin, her boots were of calfskin. She held a pouch containing charms, a staff with stones on one end bound with brass and a knife with an ivory handle.

The seeress asked that a special spell song be sung to assist her. Its name was connected with the idea of shutting or closing. Its purpose was probably to enable her to shut out the external world and enter the trance state. The only person who knew the spell was a girl on a visit from Iceland. She consented to sing, at first unwilling as she was a Christian. The spakona thanked her for her song and in return for her help named the illustrious descendants yet to be born into the girl's family. The seeress said that many spirits had come and thought the song fair to hear. As a result of their help she was able to see. 'Those which before would have returned away from us and given us no hearing; but now there are many matters open to my sight which before were hidden from me and also from others.'

It is not surprising to find a strong prophetic tradition here. Shamanic practice originated in these cold lands. Destiny and divination are at the heart of Northern mythology. Destiny is held in the World Tree. Odin himself consulted a seeress when he desired to know his fate.

The three Norns Uror, Veroandi and Skuld held a person's destiny. Uror is the word used elsewhere for fate. She is connected with the well of destiny to which Odin came to discover the future. Veroandi is the present participle of the verb to be. Skuld has the meaning of something owed as a debt. The Norns are depicted weaving, or cutting into wood, spinning the web of fate or notching the allotted life span. Each image is connected with fate or destiny. Gods, kings and men alike might seek to know what fate held. Accordingly, the seeress declared the destiny of the young and forecast for the coming season often at major religious gatherings. Tacitus spoke of a famous seeress, Veleda of the Bructeri in the Rhineland. Her name is derived from *veles*, meaning seer. Presumably this was her official title, not her personal name. In the *Histories* Tacitus says, 'Veleda enjoyed extensive authority according to the ancient Germanic custom which regards many women as endowed with prophetic powers, and, as the superstition grows, attributes divinity to them.'[26]

He refers to them again in Germania. 'They believe that there resides in women an element of holiness and a gift of prophecy; and so they do not scorn to ask their advice, or lightly disregard their replies. In the reign of the Emperor Vespasian we saw Veleda long honoured by many Germans as a divinity; and even earlier they showed a similar reverence for Aurinia and a number of others.'[27]

Veleda obviously wielded considerable authority. She was included among the arbiters when an agreement was made between the Romans and the people of Cologne. She did not meet the Romans directly but remained in a high tower while one of her relatives carried questions and brought back answers, 'as if he were a messenger of the gods', says Tacitus. When a flagship of the Roman army was captured, it was taken up river and presented to her.

She was renowned for her prophecies and was said to have correctly foretold the destruction of the Roman legions in AD 69. The Roman general Cerialis was thought to have carried on a secret communication with her, urging Veleda to use her influence to dissuade the Germans from further revolt. In 78 BC she was brought to Rome in circumstances that remain unknown. Statius refers to her as a captive.

Veleda was well known outside her own tribe. Tacitus also mentions other women like Veleda who were honoured for their second sight. He mentioned Ganna a priestess of the Semnones who was honoured by Domitian and a wise woman of the Chatti whose name he does not give.

DREAMS AND DREAMERS

During the dream, we believe we are awake.

ROBERT BOSNAK, *A Little Course in Dreams*

The sleep state has always fascinated people. It appears to be suspended between life and death. It is an in-between place, a state of paradox, outwardly passive but inwardly active. In sleep laboratories, white coated scientists attempt to probe the mechanics of sleep, to evaluate the psychological and physiological functions, to explore the possibilities of an active higher consciousness at work. Yet the dream state remains as enigmatic as ever. We know something of the mechanics of the process. Perhaps this is the best empirical science can hope for. The gulf between describing the dream state and understanding its role in spiritual life remains as wide as ever.

The sleep state was once in the hands of the priesthood. Metaphysical practitioners, whether shamanic, cultic or alone, have always paid attention to dream messages. In sleep the gods might speak.

Jung's outer work was driven and propelled by his inner life. His work validated what the ancients knew and simply accepted, namely that a dream may convey meaning and resolution. 'The collective unconscious which sends you these dreams already possesses the solution; nothing has been lost from the whole immemorial experience of humanity, every imaginable situation and every solution seems to have been foreseen.' Esoteric tradition still maintains that the natural dreaming function can be refined to problem solve, seek resolution and locate a higher source of knowledge. The mind can be trained to transform the sleep state. Continuity of consciousness during both waking and sleeping is a goal of all esoteric traditions. Incubatory sleep was widely practised in the ancient world. Temples commonly contained incubation chambers. At Pergamum there were even lesser and greater chambers. Serapis, Isis and Aesculapius were thought especially to send dreams to devotees. Hopeful dreamers prepared by abstaining from wine and heavy foods or by fasting. Plutarch tells us that sixteen spices were burned by Egyptian priests to encourage dreaming. Dream spells and inscribed amulets might be purchased. Libations were poured and prayers were offered in the hope of a propitious dream. A member of the priesthood might dream for a client.

Dreams then as now require interpretation. The symbolic language of the unconscious can be obscure to those not used to its broad vocabulary. The Chester Beatty Papyrus is a record of Egyptian dream interpretation. The House of Life was known for its dream interpreters. A Babylonian dream guide was found in Nineveh in the royal library. Artemidorus of Daldis wrote the *Oneirocritica* in which he explained the current theory of dream symbols. He, like a modern investigator, questioned dreamers far and wide, travelling extensively with the sole purpose of collecting numerous case histories. For instance, to dream of Aphrodite naked was inauspicious, to see her topless was, however, favourable. Divinities usually spoke in riddles. Woods and mountain chasms signified distress, especially for the rich, for in such places things were cut up and thrown away. Dreams of a garden signified being slandered for promiscuity, the seeds of malcontent and the seeds of the garden being akin.

Priestesses specialising in dream interpretation were part of the Isian tradition. Indeed Isis was expected to make her wishes clearly known to devotees. The fictionalised character Lucius followed the instructions of Isis who spoke to him in a dream. 'The kind goddess, who was still watching over me visited me in a dream and warned me that I must be prepared for a new initiation and a new vow.'[28] Having been summoned to initiation Lucius then had to wait for the goddess to instruct a priest. 'The day on which a postulant might be initiated was always indicated by signs from the goddess herself and it was she who chose the officiating priest.'[29]

Does the goddess still summon the individual to initiation? Does the goddess speak in dreams today? Of course. Nora Hall recounts her own dream which she called, 'The Moon Speaks to Me'.

> *Rise up, blue princess, from your plastic church steeple bed,*
> *Find a better place to lay your head:*
> *Instead of looking to the Father, Son and Holy Ghost*
> *Look to Artemis, Aphrodite, and Gaia as guides.*[30]

Anyone who serves Deity in Feminine form may have their own dream to tell.

Chapter 14

THE MANTLE OF THE GODDESS

You must consciously withdraw from the world around you without losing consciousness. Gradually you still your roving thoughts, your active mental brain; you refuse to admit the sounds you hear, not by sending them away from you but by withdrawing from you, and gradually you will be able to see yourself standing within the envelope of your body, but be able to leave it with your mind.

DIRECTIONS FOR CONSCIOUS MEDIUMSHIP, The Dancers to the Gods

MAGICIANS AND PRIESTESSES

The twentieth century is coming to its close. The Age of Pisces is closing too. There is a palpable sense of history. Our civilisation remains young. Two thousand years is but a brief episode in the human story. Culture constantly redefines itself. Every generation expresses itself anew. Change is the order of the day. This century has been dramatic and extraordinary, a witness to paradox and revolution. Technological advance has been matched by spiritual retreat. Material progress walks hand in hand with famine. Ecological nightmares now threaten. Political upheaval has rewritten the map books.

As we approach the close of the century, we can with hindsight look over our shoulder and see how the threads of the past have woven together to bring us to this point in time. One of the many significant and continuing themes of this century has been the liberation of women. Women have redefined their own lives in political, economic and spiritual terms.

The history of the Suffragettes is well documented. While they were making the first breakthrough into the armour of the establishment, a smaller and lesser-known circle of women was also breaking barriers of another kind. Florence Farr, Annie Horniman, Maud Gonne and Moina Mathers served in the Mysteries when most women could only serve their husbands. They were the women of the Golden Dawn.

Moina Mathers worked openly as a priestess of Isis and received many of the initiation rituals for the Golden Dawn. In modern parlance she functioned as a chaneller. Annie Horniman was a gifted astrologer and tarot diviner. Florence Farr taught tarot and Enochian magic, wrote several books on renaissance alchemy and painted Egyptian gods and goddesses. She commissioned her lover, Bernard Shaw, to write *Arms and the Man*. Annie Horniman built the Abbey Theatre and founded the Daughters of Erin to spread Irish history, mythology and language. She led The Women Prisoners Defence League and was jailed several times. But these women were unlike other contemporary reformers and intellectuals. They worked directly with goddess energies at a time when the Divine Feminine was unrecognised.

The Golden Dawn left its mark. It re-established the tradition of the Mystery school. Its direct inheritors were Dion Fortune, Christine Hartley and Charles Seymour among others. The work of this group remained closed until the mid century when the Mystery Schools opened up to take students through correspondence courses, a revolutionary step which is nevertheless in keeping with the spirit of Aquarius. Within the Mystery Schools the relationship between a goddess and the priestess is of a specialised nature.

In society at large the image of the goddess has resonated as a clarion call for a renewed wave of female liberation. Women have gained intellectually from rediscovering historical truths about the Goddess. Women have gained emotionally from taking the Goddess as a role model in a world long starved of powerful and confident images. Women have gained psychologically from understanding the Goddess as an archetypal pattern. The main thrust of the feminist movement views the Goddess in these terms. We value psychology, emotional liberation and historical perspective. Psychology has provided us with an understanding of the power of the mind. We now have a general tendency to interpret all non-physical experiences in psychological terms. We feel safe interpreting the gods and goddesses in psychological terms as archetypal manifestations. We are very loathe to perceive Female Divinity as something separate yet connected, distant but ever present, cosmic yet personal. Indeed it has been suggested that the desire to envisage divinity externally is simply the result of patriarchal conditioning. It is far safer to see the Goddess as an exiled role model or psychological pattern.

There can be no doubt of the liberating and creative impact of feminist spirituality upon real lives. Art and creativity in every shape and form speaks for the impact of feminist spirituality. These testaments speak for themselves. Less well known and understood are the testaments of women who have experienced the goddess not as artistic inspiration but as living presence.

THE GARMENTS OF ISIS

O daughters of Isis, adore the goddess, and in her name give the call that awakens and rejoices. So shall ye be blessed of the goddess and live with fulness of life.

DION FORTUNE, *Aspects of Occultism*

The priestesses of Isis were once called The Garments of Isis. They were the vehicle for the presence of the goddess in the physical world. These priestesses were known for states of bliss and divine rapture which communion with Isis brought.

We are fortunate to be able to share the magical diaries of Christine Hartley and Charles Seymour. Strict record keeping is part of magical discipline. Magical diaries are rarely opened to public view, and publishing such extracts would once have been unthinkable. Here we have experiences which cannot be contained and described in psychological terms. Here are dynamics which stretch the mind and the imagination. Extracts from the diary record the presence of Isis experienced through a Qabalistic structure.

Friday, October 15th 1937 (account by Seymour)
Banished as usual and then invoked in the name of Isis. Up came the power at once. Built Malkuth in the aura, then Yesod in the form of the horned moon. Up came a great silver star which filled the whole room. CCT took charge – journey in the silver litter, past the lotus pool into the hall of the sphinxes and then into the sanctuary. CCT sat on the knees of the goddess with her head between the breasts of the image.

Then came a tremendous head of power. I could see CCT bathed in a sort of silvery mist with the physical eyes, she got up and held out her hands as if in blessing and a stream of pale silver light came off them and on to me. It was so clear that I could feel it physically.

Hartley's report of the same experience adds another dimension to our understanding.

Then at one time the Goddess came right down and I was her mouthpiece and spoke as she dictated, and then I was the priestess giving the responses. It was most strange and very wonderful. I seemed to be carried on without deliberate volition on my part and all I had to do was to keep myself well held in so that the power should flow freely.

Thursday, October 21 1937 (account by Seymour)
Then with a burst of power that shook me, the Goddess took possession of her priestess, there was not much said – a sort of chant of the names of the Goddess which brought a rush of power and then she gave her blessing. It was like sitting in a blast of hot air.

In Hartley's report of the same event we find the following:

Then the power began to come through and I got carried up because the Goddess came down and used me as a vehicle. I cannot remember what I said but she spoke through me and I kept trying to get the right words as if I were translating.[1]

In these reports, we have an important and quite rare glimpse of the experience of mediation which may also be called conscious mediumship. The priestess is divinely possessed, even physically transfigured by the presence of the goddess. The priestess becomes the living vehicle for the presence. She is the channel through which the silvery white light passes from the supra-mundane planes into physical manifestation to be received by an individual or a group. The priestess may speak or bestow a blessing. She may simply bring the presence into the physical world. Imagine this experience set against a wider canvas, groups of initiates receiving the blessing of Isis in the temples of Egypt.

Hartley and Seymour worked in the 1930s. However, the Isian current is still alive. The following account is the report by a priestess of Isis dated 1990. Unlike the workings between Hartley and Seymour which were small and private, the following account is the record of a large working in a group which had come together over a single weekend. Such an event would have been unimaginable to the esoteric practitioners of the 1930s for whom secrecy and training were paramount. Times have changed greatly. Meditation, visualisation, even ritual skills are now accessible generally through groups, workshops and written material. Where training was once confined to small groups, individuals now train themselves through direct inner experiences. It is possible for individuals to acquire as much expertise as that previously gained only in secret groups. Recording all experiences remains unchanged, it is part of standard esoteric practice.

Report

As the rehearsal proceeded, it became impossible for me to stay in the room. The energies in the hall were accelerating too fast for me. I stepped outside into the ante-chamber. I was quite unable to sit still while the energies in the hall were still mounting. Like an expectant parent pacing a hospital corridor, I needed to move. I began to dance, with slow yoga-like movements. As I danced I felt a great descent of power. A winged mantle was placed about me. Contact had been made.

There was now a short break for tea and robing. Others left the hall chatting in small groups. I found it difficult to even speak. I went straight to my room. Time seemed to hang. Mentally I walked the tightrope, holding on to physical reality and my sense of self while not losing contact with the presence in which I was immersed. Finally I was ready, robed in swathes of shimmering green, deep rich brown and gold, a sistrum in my hand. I looked into the mirror and saw the face of another.

I left the room and made my way slowly to the hall. Walking was not easy I felt unsteady on my feet. The participants were already seated. My entrance was not scheduled. It was to be a surprise, symbolic of divine intervention. I sat on a great throne-like chair in the ante chamber facing the closed door to the hall.

As the ritual commenced, the mediation deepened. As the group opened and called upon the deities to be present, I-She answered aloud in the silence of the ante chamber. This continued throughout the opening sequence. I-She answered with word and gesture.

Although I was seated beyond the hall outside the closed door, it was as if the door had become transparent. It was no barrier. Within the hall planetary energies were mediated through a group dance. I saw the planets amidst the heavens. When the maze dance of the zodiac was performed, I saw the living starry constellations as great beings. As each one passed before the throne beyond the closed door, salutes were given.

With the planetary energies in attendance, the group enacted the Trial of Earth, more properly the trial of humankind. Gaia was not on trial. The trial was called to assess whether the Earth's planetary body and human consciousness together were ready to take a cosmic initiation. Unusually in this highly structured ritual, participants were at this point free to speak as the spirit moved. Voices weighed responsibilities, understanding and destiny. Individuals spoke of past failings, of present crises and future possibilities. Finally after long and careful debate, the decision was unanimous. The Earth would proceed towards its own initiation. I-She was filled with joy. The time approached for my entrance.

I stood in readiness. A crown was placed on my head with a mantle of stars. I-She was called from within the hall. The doorway became a star gate. I-She entered and saw the assembled company. It was planned that I should walk around the hall and finally come to stand before the person enacting the role of the Earth, a minute's walk at most. My step was unsteady. Every foot was placed slowly and with great deliberation as I waded through the collected energies of the room. Finally I reached my appointed place before the Earth. It seemed as if I stood before the whole of humanity, confused, bewildered, child-like and vulnerable, reaching out for that dimly sensed and not at all understood. I was wracked by a compassion so intense that my whole body shook. My sight was blinded by tears. The immortal words of Isis were spoken.

'Behold I am come.'

The sistrum was raised above the Earth with a suddenness and force that surprised me. It felt as if humanity was being roused from a deep slumber.

Finally I-She left the hall to sit again on the great chair. This time the door was left open. I sat and looked upon the harmony of the spheres enacted in dance by the participants. The joy within the room was palpable. I sat at the gate, the participants dancing in a great circle passed before the throne. I-She acknowledged each one with salute or gesture. The sense of rapture was so intense that my body began to shake violently. I felt the mediation had reached a critical level. It was time to withdraw. In one sharp gesture, I reached up and pulled a veil down over my eyes. Contact was severed. My work was done. I stood and turned leaving the ante-chamber. The participants still danced. I withdrew. I did not look back.[2]

Other women too have experienced the call of a particular deity. Sarah Robinson writes of her experience with Brighid.

My own experience of the vocational call was that I was working at my desk one afternoon three years ago. I was preparing for an Imbolc festival when the atmosphere changed. It felt very still, cut off from the rest of the world. Then a shimmering form like a column materialised across the room about six feet away. I heard in my mind a female voice saying, 'My name is Brighid, I have always been with you.' Then it seemed as if a hand came out of the light holding a Celtic cross, the circle of which rotated like flames. The whole thing became a swirl of red and faded away. I came back to my senses with a feeling of such happiness that it was a painful.

I should say that up to that time I had followed the old religion for eleven years and had gone through the initiations and trained as a psychotherapist and later as a healer. I had never had a vision of this magnitude before or since.

It is through Her direct guidance that I became a Priestess-Hierophant and founded the priory. I have now met and ordained other priestesses of Brighid – all of whom had very similar experiences of Her. It really feels like a sisterhood in physical terms, with Brighid as a very approachable and personal deity.

When I look at the people in my Iseum, all of them craftsmen, poets and healers, it is so obvious that She had brought us together. Since then She has come into my mind at times with pieces of knowledge or instructions which we carry through implicitly.[3]

Some women spontaneously experience the divine presence, others seek out the goddess. In the following account the devotee undertook a series of exercises designed to bring about an experience of the goddess in a particular form. Vivienne O'Regan remembers a series of experiences.

I cannot recall exactly when my relationship with the goddess first began or when the desire to function as her priestess was born. It must have been shortly after I encountered the mysteries in 1973. The novels of Dion Fortune were a major formative influence on me. Reading these novels began to stir my own far memories.

I began to use creative visualisation and meditation to access the Temples of the Neters. I also discovered that I was able to mediate the presence of the goddess. In my dream life I often found myself serving at the altar of the goddess.

These early experiences centred around my relationship with the cat goddess Bast. I had connected to her early on as my tutelary goddess. In order to consecrate myself to her, I undertook a two month series of daily devotional rituals and meditations. The aim of these practices was to direct every thought and action of daily life towards the beloved deity, Bast. It is like being intensely in love.

I prepared for my ordination. I built a shrine to Bast which included a picture of Her statue, a collection of personal objects and a necklace of tiger's eye. I made a robe in colours which I felt were appropriate for Bast. I wore this during my meditations and rituals. I wrote my own ritual which lasted about forty-five minutes. I performed it twice daily.

During the day I used a short phrase praising Bast as a mantra. My record of this time reveals my feelings of inadequacy and unworthiness. I began to have vivid dreams. I dreamed that I had given birth to kittens. In another dream I followed a great lioness.

This series of devotions lasted from the summer solstice to the autumn equinox. As the end approached I arranged to spend the last three days in retreat. On the day before the final conclusion I focused deeply on my love for the goddess in her Bast form. I dreamed of being in a place with a number of other women. I stood before a mirror and pressed my brow to the glass. I saw a lotus pool. A huge lioness entered and leapt the length of the pool. I awoke. I went outside and made adoration to the setting moon and rising sun, I was joined by Tyger the neighbour's cat. We sat and played together beneath the trees. I felt as if I was living on pure love.

I slept again and saw great statues of Horus, Anubis and Sekhmet. These statues felt somehow alive and seemed to speak to one another about humankind and their worship. I saw Bast in the form of a black panther devouring a sacrificial antelope. I ran forward to her and she turned into a large house cat and curled up satiated after her meal. My husband dreamed that I was an antelope about to be sacrificed.

As I began the evening's ritual, it seemed to me that the statue moved just slightly. I heard a voice in my head, 'I will come.' I cried. That night I dreamed of eating meat although I was a vegetarian. During the next night, the Equinox itself, I enacted the ritual for the last time. As Bast's cult was ecstatic I'd incorporated music and dance into the ritual. I danced myself into an ecstatic state and collapsed in powerful altered state while lying before the altar. I was aware of a great deal of energy. A ball of golden and red light entered my body at the base of my spine.

These experiences proved formative. I decided to train as a psychotherapist. The priesthood of Bast had been concerned with mental and emotional healing. Psychotherapy felt like an appropriate way to express my vocation in the world. I have always kept a shrine to Bast wherever I have lived. She will always dwell in my heart.[4]

THE FUTURE

We stand on the threshold of a Goddess religion which, by virtue
of its membership and its aims, is non hierarchical, decentralised,
and locally-manifest, in many and various ways.

CAITLIN MATTHEWS, *Sophia Goddess of Wisdom*

The priestesses of the past have gone. We may look over our
shoulder into the distant past but we must face our own future.
We stand as the twenty-first century fast approaches. The Age of
Aquarius beckons. If a genuine female priesthood is to have any
relevance we must look to the needs of our own times. There is
no value in re-living the past. We are not a neolithic people with
a limited understanding of the world. We are neither hunters nor
growers but workers. We do not live within hierarchical dynasties
nor do we dwell amidst temples. Nevertheless, the qualities which
the Divine Feminine might bring to the world are sorely needed.
We may be able to explore outer space but we have not learned
to live peacefully together on the earth.

We live during a potent and potentially dangerous time. Old
values fade, new ones take root but the interim feels uncertain
and unstable. Those who are deeply enmeshed in Piscean values
cannot embrace the fluid, global consciousness of the Aquarian
spirit. The disintegration of this foundation feels threatening and
fearful. Those who reach out to a new Aquarian horizon are
mistaken if they only perceive freedom without responsibilities.
The Aquarian Age has its principles too. We are in a time of
transition, the classic initiatory sequence, death and rebirth on
a grand scale. How we emerge from this testing time lies within
our own hands. Our collective response will be dependent on our
group understanding and aspiration. We will shape our own future
and define our place within it. The role of the priestess awaits
redefinition in the twenty-first century. A female priesthood has
much to offer. Its keynote has to be service, not power. Its aims
have to be integrative not separatist. To stand as a mediating body,
it must touch both spiritual and material realities in balance.

Feminism has just discovered the Divine Feminine, the
Mysteries have never lost touch with Her presence. Might not the

outer strength of liberated women and the inner strength of enlightened women merge to found the Daughters of Aquarius. Time alone will tell.

NOTES

1 – *The Fall from Grace*

1. Aristotle, *On the Generation of Animals*, Book I, section II, 20
2. Ibid. Book II, section III, 2
3. Ibid. Book II, section III, 1
4. Ibid. Book I, section II, 20
5. Ibid. Book II, section III, 3
6. Aristotle, *Politics* I.5
7. Quoted in Ranke-Heineman, *Eunuchs for Heaven*, 3
8. Ibid. 5
9. Ibid. 43, 'In genesim homiliae', 15, 3, 4
10. St Augustine, 'De bono conjugali', 2
11. St Augustine, 'De civitate Dei', 14, 24
12. St Augustine, 'Confessiones', VI, 15
13. Possidus, 'Vita', 26
14. Clement of Alexandria, 'Paidagogos', III, 79, 4
15. 'Sacr. conc. collectio', 9, 915
16. Ambrose, 'De poenitentia', I.16
17. 'Apostolic Constitutions', III, 6
18. Quoted in Ranke-Heinemann, op. cit. 114
19. Ibid. 121
20. Cardinal Robert Courson, 'Summa theologiae moralis', 128
21. Cardinal Huguccio, 'Summa', 2, 13

2 – *In the Beginning*

1. Eliade, *A History of Religious Ideas*, Vol. 1, 5
2. Ibid. 8

3. Ibid. 21
4. Marshak, *The Roots of Civilisation*, 316
5. Ibid.
6. Johnson, *Lady of the Beasts*, 11
7. Marshak, op. cit. 293
8. Ibid. 297
9. Ibid. 283
10. Ibid. 312
11. Eliade, op. cit. 8
12. Bronowski, *The Ascent of Man*, 54
13. Campbell, *The Masks of God*, 288
14. Todd, *Catal Huyuk in Perspective*, 134
15. Ibid.
16. Mellaart, *Catal Huyuk*, 11
17. Gimbutas, *The Goddesses and Gods of Old Europe*, Preface
18. Eliade, op. cit. 41
19. Ibid. 40
20. Ibid.
21. Gimbutas, op. cit. 55
22. Ibid. 236
23. Ibid. 237

3 – Mesopotamia – the Betrothed

1. Jacobsen, *Treasures of Darkness*, 78
2. Hallo, *Early Mesopotamian Royal Titles*, 30
3. Bernhard and Kramer, *Eenki und die Weltordnung*, L 400–1
4. A. Sjoberg, E. Bergmann, *The Collection of Sumerian Temple Hymns*, 46, L. 500–3
5. Publications of the Babylonian section, University Museum, University of Pennsylvania, X^2 no. 16 obv.i. 25–6
6. Hallo and Van Dijk, *The Exaltation of Inanna*, 'The Appeal to Inanna', l. 112–15
7. Hallo, *Exaltation*, Addenda
8. Gadd, *En-an-e-du*, 31
9. Ibid. 31
10. Ibid. 39
11. Hallo, *Exaltation*, 'The Indictment of Lugalanne', l. 84–90
12. Gadd, op. cit. 28

4 - *Egypt - The Epiphany*
1. Herodotus, *The Histories*, Book Two, 2, 35
2. Westendorf, *Lexicon*, 1101
3. Ibid.
4. Budge, *The Gods of the Egyptians* Vol 1, 437
5. Ibid.
6. Blackman, *Position of Women*, 28
7. Ibid. 11
8. Ibid. 28
9. Ibid. 30
10. Bleeker, *Hathor and Thoth*, 26
11. Springborg, *Royal Persons*, 135
12. Frankfort, *Kingship and the Gods*, 356 note 19
13. Lichtheim, *Egyptian Literature*, 184
14. Galvin, *Hereditary Status*, 42
15. Ibid., 45
16. Lichtheim, op. cit. 18
17. Blackman, op. cit. 21
18. Ibid. 23
19. Galvin, *The Priestesses of Hathor*
20. Ibid.
21. Blackman, op. cit. 22
22. Ibid.
23. Westendorf, ibid. 1101
24. Lichtheim, op. cit. 356
25. Ibid. 107
26. Ibid. 107–8
27. Ibid. 108
28. Zabkar, *Adaptation*, 128
29. Springborg, op. cit. 3
30. Ibid. 4
31. Ibid.
32. Zabkar, *Six hymns to Isis at Philae*, 119
33. Ibid.
34. Ibid.
35. Ibid. 118
36. Frankfort, *State Festivals*, 1
37. Bleeker, *Egyptian Festivals*, 121

38. Ibid. 102
39. Springborg, op. cit. 157
40. *The Egyptian Book of the Dead*, 30A:8
41. Coffin Texts, Spell 36:137
42. Wente, *Hathor at the Jubilee*, 88
43. Bleeker, *Sacral Kingship*, 26
44. Ibid.
45. Murray, *Egyptian Temple*, 158
46. Robins, *The God's Wife*, 71
47. Blackman, op. cit. 12
48. Robins, op. cit. 78
49. James, *The Cult of the Mother Goddess*, 68
50. Brusch, *Egypt Under the Pharaohs*, 420
51. Gardiner, 'Speos Artemidos Inscription'

5 – *The Sacerdos Perpetua*
 1. Pomeroy, *Women in Hellenistic Egypt*, 57
 2. Ibid. 58
 3. Heyob, *The Cult of Isis*, 102
 4. Ibid.
 5. Ibid. 125
 6. Ibid. 106
 7. Ibid.
 8. Ibid.
 9. Ibid. 87
10. Ibid. 91
11. Ibid.
12. Ibid. 92
13. Ibid.
14. Ibid. 85
15. Ibid. 86
16. Ibid. 90
17. Wilde, *Water in the Cultic Worship of Isis and Serapis*
18. Heyob, op. cit. 99
19. Apuleius, *Golden Ass*, 231–6

6 – *Crete – The Power Holders*
 1. Evans, *The Palace of Minos*, vol 1. 14

2. Graves, *The Greek Myths* vol 1. 88, 1
3. Castleden, *The Knossos Labyrinth*, 169
4. Ibid. 178
5. Willetts, *Cretan Cults and Festivals*, 75
6. Ibid. 180
7. Ibid. 251
8. Harrison, *Themis*, 19
9. Willetts, op. cit. 166
10. Ibid. 44
11. Homer, *Odyssey*, Book 19
12. Willetts, op. cit. 219
13. Homer, *Odyssey*, Book 19
14. Graves. op. cit. 881
15. Willetts, op. cit. 91
16. Ibid. 118
17. Ibid. 117
18. Ibid. 80
19. Graves, *The Greek Myths* vol 2, 128, 129
20. Willetts, op. cit. 117
21. Castleden, op. cit. 116
22. Ibid.
23. Ibid. 79
24. Ibid.
25. In 1979 a small sanctuary was discovered at Anemosophilia on the hillside north west of Arkhanes. It consisted of three narrow oblong rooms, and a 10-metre-long hall. There were altars and in the central hall a pair of clay feet which probably once supported the cult image. In the northern room were the remains of a youth, and the bones of his sacrificers.

   Peter Warren, excavating a Minoan house in the western part of Knossos about 100 metres from the Bull Head Sanctuary, found a mass of children's bones, about 299 in total, knife marks on the bones indicate butchery, see Castleden, op. cit. 123

7 – Greece – The Cult Officials

1. Feaver, *Historical Development in the Priesthood of Athens*, 131
2. Woodhouse, *Priest, Priesthood, Greek* 303

3. Plato's Laws, Book VI, 759
4. Feaver, op. cit. 142
5. Ibid. 137
6. Grant, *Hellenistic Religions*, 26
7. Plecket, *Epigraphica II, Texts on the Social History of the Greek World*, 211
8. Ibid. 216
9. Ibid. 217
10. Ibid.
11. Parke, *Festivals of the Athenians*, 183
12. Pausanias, *Guide to Greece* 1, I, 27.3
13. Worsfold, *History of the Vestal Virgins*, 21

8 – *Japan and Okinawa – The Shamans*
1. Hisako, *Daughters of the Gods*, 57
2. Blacker, *The Catalpa Bow*, 110–1
3. Ibid. 138
4. Ibid. 139
5. Hisako, op. cit. 56
6. Fayu, *History of Okinawan Women*
7. Hisako, op. cit. 59

9 – *The Temenos – The Sacred Enclosure*
1. Dames, *The Avebury Cycle*, 122
2. Ibid.
3. Ibid. 81
4. Ibid. 123
5. Dames, *The Silbury Treasure*, 83
6. Ibid.
7. Ibid. 55
8. Zuntz, *Persephone*, 52
9. Ibid. 51
10. Ibid.
11. Murray, *Egyptian Temples*, 1
12. Bleeker, *Hathor and Thoth*, 78
13. Pausanias, *Guide to Greece*, 1, II, 17.1
14. Kerenyi, *Zeus and Hera*, 122
15. Pausanias, op. cit. 17.7

16. Scully, *The Earth, the Temple and the Gods*, 57

10 – *Women's Mysteries – The Language of Empowerment*
 1. Wehr, *Jung and Feminism*, 22
 2. Ibid. 23
 3. Ibid. 24
 4. Esther Harding, *Women's Mysteries*, 241
 5. Ibid. 34
 6. Ibid. 208
 7. Ibid. preface xiv
 8. *The Oberver*, Jan. 26 1992, 'Why Nobody was There for Little Chanel' by Sandra Horley
 9. *The Observer*, Jan 26 1992, 'China's Baby Girls', by Jonathan Mirsky
 10. *Observer* supplement, Jan. 26 1992, 'India's Child Brides', by Peter Hillimore
 11. Judith Brown, *A Cross Cultural Study of Female Initiation Rites*, 849
 12. Harding, op. cit. 209
 13. Perera, *Descent to the Goddess*, 63
 14. Ibid. 94
 15. Kerenyi, *Zeus and Hera*, 157
 16. Souvinou-Inwood, *Studies in Girls' Transitions*
 17. Ibid.
 18. Lincoln, *The Rape of Persephone*, 228
 19. Ibid. 223
 20. Bolen, *Goddesses in Everywoman*, 2
 21. Harding, op. cit. preface xv
 22. Carole Christ, 'Why Women need the Goddess', *Politics of Women's Spirituality*, 76
 23. Shuttle and Redgrove, *The Wise Wound*, 179
 24. Harding, op. cit. 11
 25. Ibid. 127
 26. Ibid. 31
 27. Ibid. 240

11 – *Transcendent Mysteries – Things Sacred and Glorious*
 1. Haich, *Initiation*, 463
 2. Spence, *The Mysteries of Egypt*, 208

3. Seymour, *The Forgotten Mage*, 222
4. Ibid. 85
5. Gardiner, *The House of Life*, 164
6. Festival songs of Isis and Nephthys, Egyptian Hieratic Papyri in the *British Museum Hieroglyphic Transcripts* I
7. Blackman, *Position of Women in the Egyptian Hierarchy*, 26
8. *The Burdens of Isis*, 21–2
9. James, *Initiatory Rituals, Myth and Ritual*, 147
10. Blackman, op. cit. 29
11. Seymour, op. cit. 101
12. Ibid. 61
13. Ibid.
14. Burkert, *Ancient Mystery Cults*, 89
15. Ashcroft-Nowicki, *First Steps in Ritual*, 25–33
16. Grant, *Hellensitic Religions, The Praises of Isis*, 128
17. Apuleius, *The Golden Ass*, 227
18. Ibid. 228
19. Ibid. 241
20. Report kindly shared with the author
21. Burkert, op. cit. 90
22. Otto, 'The Meaning of the Eleusinian Mysteries', *The Mysteries – Eranos Yearbook* 2, 14–31
23. Ibid.
24. Plutarch, quoted in Grant, *Hellenistic Religions*, 148
25. Harding, op. cit. 227
26. Ibid. 227

12 – *The Sacred Marriage*

1. Gimbutas, *The Goddesses and Gods of Old Europe*, 230
2. Ibid. 229
3. Eliade, *A History of Religious Ideas* Vol I, 41
4. Van Buren, *The Sacred Marriage in Early Times in Mesopotamia*, 2–3
5. Ibid. 45
6. Ibid. 46
7. Frankfort, *Kingship and the Gods*, 297
8. Kramer and Wolkstein, *Inanna*, 107–10
9. Kramer, *Sacred Marriage Rite*, 92
10. Ibid. 65

11. Ibid. 63–4
12. Black, *The New Year's Ceremonies in Ancient Babylon*, 49
13. Ibid. 42
14. Hooke, *Babylonian and Assyrian Religion*, 105
15. Black, op. cit. 44
16. Ibid. 46
17. Parke, *Festivals of the Athenians*, 111
18. Ibid.
19. Harrison, *Prolegomena*, 536
20. Parke, op. cit. 112
21. Ibid. 113
22. Kerenyi, *Zeus and Hera*, 165
23. Pausanias, *Guide to Greece*, 1, VII, 4.4
24. Kerenyi, op. cit. 161

13 – *The Voice of the Oracle*
1. Flaceliere, *Greek Oracles*, 1
2. Hooke, *Babylonian and Assyrian Religion*, 92
3. James, *The Varieties of Religious Experience*
4. Avedon, *In Exile from the Land of the Snows*, 239
5. Farnell, quoted in Fontenrose, *The Delpic Oracle*, 196
6. Ibid. 208
7. Ibid. 210
8. Aeschylus, *The Eumenides* l. 1–7
9. Fox, *Pagans and Christians*, 214
10. Ibid. 216
11. Ibid. 217
12. Ibid.
13. Ibid. 222
14. Ibid. 223
15. Ibid.
16. Ibid. 227
17. Ibid. 229
18. Ibid.
19. Fontenrose, *The Delphic Oracle*, 43
20. Ibid. 142
21. Ibid. 251
22. Ibid. 225

23. Pausanias, Guide to Greece, 1, I, 9.3
24. Meier and Kerenyi, *Asklepios; Archetypal Image of the Physician's Existence*
25. Virgil, *Aeneid* Book VI, l. 96–102
26. Ellis-Davison, *Myths and Symbols in Pagan Europe*, 159
27. Ibid.
28. Apuleius, *The Golden Ass*, 244
29. Ibid. 239
30. Hall, *The Moon and the Virgin*, 1

14 – The Mantle of the Goddess
1. Richardson, *Dancers to the Gods*, 117
2. Report in the possession of the author
3. Report kindly given to the author
4. Report kindly given to the author

APPENDICES

APPENDIX 1

The Priestesses of Nanna

Priestess	Relationship to King	Length of Service
Enheduanna	daughter of Sargon	?
Enmenana	daughter of Naramsin	?
Enanepada	daughter of Urbau	32 years
Ennirjalana	daughter of Urnammu	?
Ennirziana	daughter of Sulgir	28 years
Enburziana (also called Enmahagalana)	sister of Amarsuen	33 years
Ennirsiana	daughter or sister of Ibbisin	19 years
Ninziana	daughter of Isbierra	47 years
Enanatuma	daughter of Ismedagan	?
(possibly followed by Enanatum 11 or even an unknown priestess)		
Enmegalana	?	31 years
Ensakiagananna	daughter of Sumulium	43 years
Enanedu	daughter of Kudur Mabag sister of Waradsin	?

The information collated here is incomplete. Future research may hopefully fill in the gaps.

APPENDIX 2

Inscriptions made relating to the cult of Isis and Serapis

Place	Total number	Number made by women	%
Athens	35	17	48.6
Rome	97	36	37.1
Rhodes	75	0	0
Delos	247	28	11.3
Pompeii	14	2	14.3

Vidman, *Sylloge Inscriptionum religionis Isiacae et Serapiacae* include 1099 inscriptions relating to the cult of Isis and Serapis. Some 200 (18.2%) mention women who were priestesses, members of cult associations or ordinary devotees.

APPENDIX 3

Number of Inscriptions (see Vidman) mentioning Priestesses by Century

1st or 1st–2nd AD: 4
2nd or 2nd–3rd AD: 9
3rd AD : 2
4th AD : 1

Undated inscriptions bring the total number to 26.

APPENDIX 4

Number of Priestesses by Location

Athens	5
Rome	7
Greek mainland	4
other cities in Italy	3
other provinces of Europe and Africa	4
island of Imbros	1
cities of Asia Minor	2

APPENDIX 5

Useful Addresses

The Fellowship of Isis
Clonegal Castle
Enniscorthy
Eire

The Fellowship has shrines and temples throughout the world.
Offers liturgy, newsletter and a large number of publications.
Send four first class stamps (within UK) for further details or two
international reply paid coupons (overseas).

The House of Net
BCM Box 6812
London
WCIN 3XX

Offers a priestess training programme through a postal course,
based in the Egyptian Mysteries. Send two first class stamps for
further details.

SELECTED BIBLIOGRAPHY

LIST OF ABBREVIATIONS USED IN THIS BIBLIOGRAPHY

A.B.S.A. Annual of the British School at Athens
A.E. Ancient Egypt
A.J. American Journal of Archaeology
C.Q. Classical Quarterly
E.R.E. Encyclopeadia of Religion and Ethics
H.Th.R. Harvard Theological Review
J.C.S. Journal of Cuneiform Studies
J.B.S. Journal of Biblical Studies
J.H.S. Journal of Hellenic Studies
J.R.S. Journal of Roman Studies
J.R.H. Journal of Religious History
J.N.E.S. Journal of Near Eastern Studies

Ashcroft-Nowicki D. (ed.) *The Forgotten Mage* The Aquarian Press, 1986
Ashcroft-Nowicki D. *First Steps in Ritual* The Aquarian Press, 1982
Armstrong A.H. (ed.) *Classical Mediterranean Spirituality* Routledge, 1987
Apuleius *The Golden Ass* Penguin Classics, 1950
Astour M.C. 'Tamar the Hierodule' *J.B.S.* Vol. 85, pp 185–96, 1966
Beard M and North J. (eds.) *Pagan Priests* Duckworth and Co, 1990
Beard M. 'The Sexual Status of Vestal Virgins' *J.R.S.* pp 12–27, 1980
Beckman G. *Hittite Birth Rituals an Introduction* Undena Publications, Malibu, California, 1974

Bell H. *Cults and Creeds in Graeco-Roman Egypt* University of Liverpool Press, 1953

Bernhardt I. and Kramer S. N. *Enki und die Weltordnung* Wissenschaftliche Zeitschrift der Frederich-Schiller Universität Jena, 1959

Bettleheim B. *Symbolic Wounds Puberty Rites and the Envious Male* Thames and Hudson, London, 1955

Black J.A. 'The New Year Ceremonies in Ancient Babylon' *Religion*, Vol. II, pp 39–59, 1987

Blacker C. *The Catalpa Bow: A study of Shamanic Practices in Japan* George Allen and Unwin, 1975

Blackman A.M. 'On the Position of Women in the Ancient Egyptian Hierarchy' *J.E.A.* Vol. 7, pp 8–30, 1921

Blackman A.M. 'The Temple of Horus at Edfu' *J.E.A.* Vol. 36, pp 63–81, 1959

Blackman A.M. 'Priest, Priesthood (Egyptian)' *Hastings E.R.E.* 10, pp 292–302, 1918

Blackman A.M. 'Oracles in Ancient Egypt' *J.E.A.* Vol. 10, pp 176–185, 1926

Blackman A.M and Fairman 'Consecration of an Egyptian Temple according to the use of Edfu' *J.E.A.* Vol XXXII, pp 75–91, 1946

Blackman A. 'A Temple of Horus at Edfu' *J.E.A.* 36, pp 63–81, 1959

Bleeker C.J. *Egyptian Festivals* Leiden, E.J. Brill, 1967

Bleeker C.J. 'Initiation In Ancient Egypt' *Initiation*, Leiden, E.J. Brill, 1965

Bleeker C.J. *Hathor and Thoth–Two Key Figures of the Ancient Egyptian Religion* Leiden, E.J. Brill, 1973

Bleeker C.J. 'Isis as a Saviour Goddess' *The Saviour God: Comparative Studies in the Concept of Salvation* edited by S.G.F. Brandon, Manchester University Press, 1963

Bleeker C.J. 'Isis and Nephthys as Wailing Women' *The Sacred Bridge–Researches into the Nature and Structure of Religion* Leiden, E.J.Brill, 1963

Bleeker C.J. *Egyptian Festivals of Religious Renewal* Leiden, E.J. Brill, 1967

Bleeker C.J. 'The Position of the Queen in Ancient Egypt' in *The Sacral Kingship* Leiden, E.J. Brill, 1959

Bolen. J.S. *Goddesses in Everywoman* Harper Colophon Books, 1984

Boserup E. *Women's Role in Economic Development* Allen and Unwin, 1970

Brady T.A. 'The Reception of the Egyptian Cults by the Greeks' *University of Missouri Studies* Vol. 10, pt. 1, 1935

Brugsch H. *Egypt under the Pharoahs* 1902

Burkert W. *Ancient Mystery Cults* Harvard University Press, 1987

Cameron A. and Kuhrt A. (eds.) *Images of Woman in Antiquity* Croom Helm, 1983

Cameron D.O. *Symbols of Birth and Death in the Neolithic Era* Kenyon-Deane, 1981

Cannandine D. *Rituals of Royalty: Power and Ceremonial in Traditional Societies* Cambridge University Press, 1987

Castleden R. *The Knossos Labyrinth* Routledge, 1990

Cles-Reden S.V. *The Realm of the Great Goddess.* Thames and Hudson, 1961

Cottrell L. *Queens of the Pharoahs* Bobbs-Merrill & Co, 1967

Corbett P.E. *Greek Temples and Greek Worshippers* Bulletin by Institute of Classical Studies, University of London no. 17, pp 149–158, 1970

Crawford O.G.S. *The Eye Goddess* London, Phoenix House, 1957

Cumont. F. *The Oriental Religions in Roman Paganism* Dover, 1956

Dames M. *The Avebury Cycle* Thames and Hudson, 1977

Dames M. *The Silbury Treasure* Thames and Hudson, 1977

Davison H.R. *Myths and Symbols in Pagan Europe* Manchester Press, 1988

Davison J.A. 'Notes on the Panathenaea' *J.H.S.* Vol 78, pp 23–42, 1958

Dennis J.T. (trans.) *The Burden of Isis: Wisdom of the East* series London, 1992

Dow S. 'The Egyptian Cults in Athens' *H.T.R.* pp 183–232, 1937

Dow S. and Healey R.F. *A Sacred Calender of Eleusis* Cambridge, 1965

Dowden K. *Death and the Maiden–Initiation Rites in Greek Mythology* Routledge, 1989

Downing C. *The Goddess–Mythological Images of the Feminine* New York Crossroad, 1980

Easterling P.E. and Muir J.V. *Greek Religon and Society* University of Cambridge Press, 1985

Edgar C.C. 'An Ionian Dedication to Isis' *J.H.S.* p 337, 1904

Ehrenberg M. *Women in Prehistory* British Musuem Publications, 1989

Eliade M. *Shamanism-Archaic techniques of Ecstacy* Arkana, 1988

Eliade M. *Birth and Rebirth: The Religious Meaning of Initiation in Human Cultures* New York, 1958; reprinted as *Rites and Symbols of Initiation* New York, 1965

Ellis L.B. 'The Sistrum of Isis' *A.E.* pt 1, pp 19–26, 1927

Engelsman J.C. *The Feminine Dimension of the Divine* Chiron Publications, 1987

Erman A. *A Handbook of Egyptian Religion* Longwood Press, 1977

Evans A. *The Palace of Minos* 4 Vols. Macmillan 1921–35

Fairman H.W. *Worship and Festival in an Egyptian Temple* Bulletin of the John Rylands Library, Vol. 34, pp 165–203, 1954/5

Farnell L.R. *The Cults of the Greek States* Vols. I, II, III, IV, V Clarendon Press, 1896

Feaver D.D. *Historical Development in the Priesthood of Athens* Yale Classical Studies 15, pp 123–158, 1957

Fischer H.G. *Denderah in the Third Millennium* BC *Down to the Theban Domination* New York, J.J. Augustin, 1968

Fontenrose J. *Python-a Study of Delphic Myth and its Origins* University of California Press, 1959

Fortune D. *Aspects of Occultism* The Aquarian Press, 1978

Fox R.L. *Pagans and Christians* Penguin Books, 1986

Frankfort, H. *Kingship and the Gods* University of Chicago Press, 1948

Frankfort, H. 'State Festivals in Egypt and Mesopotamia' *Journal of the Warburg and Courtauld Institute*, 1952

Fraser P M. 'A Temple of Hathor at Kusae' *J.E.A.* Vol. 42, pp 197–8, 1956

Frantz A. 'From Paganism to Christianity in the Temples of Athens' *Dumbarton Oaks Papers*, pp 187–205, 1965

Freiderich P. *The Meaning of Aphrodite* University of Chicago Press, 1978

Gadd C.J. 'En-an-e-du' *Iraq* 13 pp 27–39, 1951

Gadon E.W. *The Once and Future Goddess* Harper and Row, 1989

Galvin M. 'The Hereditary Status of the Titles of the Cult of Hathor' *J.E.A.* Vol. 70, pp 42–9, 1984

Galvin M. *The Priestesses of Hathor in the Old Kingdom and First Intermediate Period* University Microfilms International no 8126877, 1981

Gardiner A.H. 'The House of Life' *J.E.A.* Vol. 24, pp 157-79, 1938

Gardiner A.H. 'Davies copy of the Great Speos Artimdos Inscription' *J.E.A.* Vol. 32, pp 43-56, 1946

Gardiner A.H. *The Astarte Papyrus Studies* presented to F.L. Griffith, pp 74-85, 1932

Greer M.K. *Magical Women of the Golden Dawn* Wingbow Press, California 1992

Garman D. *Greek Oracles* Elek Books, 1965

Gimbutas M. *The Language of the Goddess* Alfred van der Marck Editions, 1988

Gimbutas M. 'The Temples of Old Europe' *Archaeology* November-Decemebr 1980

Gimbutas M. *The Goddesses and Gods of Old Europe* University of California Press, 1982

Goldsmith E. *Ancient Pagan Symbols* G.P. Putnam & Sons, 1929

Gould J.P. 'Law, Custom, Myth: Aspects of the Social Position of Women in Classical Athens' *J.H.S.* pp 38-59, 1980

Grant F.C. *Hellenistic Religions* Bobbs Merrill Educational Publishing, 1953

Graves R. *The Greek Myths* Vols. 1 & 2 Pelican, 1955

Grigson G. *The Goddess of Love* Constable. 1976

Griffiths J.G. (ed.) *Plutarch's de Iside et Osiris* University of Wales Press, 1970

Griffiths J.G. *The Origins of Osiris and his Cult* Leiden, E.J. Brill, 1980

Grof S. *The Adventure of Self Discovery* New York State University, 1988

Hall N. *The Moon and the Virgin* Harper and Row, 1980

Harding E. *Women's Mysteries* Rider, 1989

Harris R. 'Biographical Notes on the Naditu Women of Sippar' *J.C.S.* 15 pp 117-20, 1962

Harris R. 'The Organization and Administration of the Cloister in Ancient Babylonia' *Journal of the Economic and Social History of the Orient* Vol. 6, pp 121-57, 1963

Harrison J.E. *Prolegomena to the Study of Greek Religion* Cambridge 1922

Harrison J.E. *Themis* Cambridge, 1927

Hallo W.W. and van Dijk J.J. *The Exaltation of Innana* Yale University Press, 1968

Hallo W. *Early Mesopotamian Titles* 1957

Hoch-Smith J. and Spring A. (eds.) *Women in Ritual and Symbolic Roles* Plenum Presss, 1978

Hornblower G.D. 'Predynastic Figures of Women and their Successors' *J.E.A.* Vol. XV, 1924

Heyob S.K. *The Cult of Isis Among Women in the Graeco-Roman World* Leiden, E.J. Brill, 1975

Hillman J. *Facing the Gods* Spring Publications, 1980

Hisako. H. 'Daughters of the Gods' *Monumenta Nipponica Monographs* no. 25 1966

Holtom D.C. *The Japanese Enthronement Ceremony* Tokyo, 1972

Hooke S.H. (ed.) *Myth, Ritual and Kingship* Oxford University Press, 1958

Hooke S.H. (ed.) *Myth and Ritual* Oxford University Press, 1933

Inglis B. *Trance, a Natural History of Altered States of Mind* Grafton Books, 1990

Jacobsen T. *The Treasures of Darkness* New Haven, Yale University Press, 1976

James E.O. 'The Saviour God' *Comparative Studies in the Concept of Salvation* edited by S.G.F. Brandon. Manchester University Press, 1963

James E.O. *The Cult of the Mother Goddess* Thames and Hudson, 1959

Johansen J.P. 'The Thesmorphoria as a Women's Festival' *Temenos* II pp 78-87, 1975

Johnson J.H. 'The Role of the Egyptian Priesthood in Ptolemaic Egypt' *Egyptological Studies in Honour of Richard Parker* presented on the occasion of his 78th birthday, edited by Lesko, University Press of New England, pp 70-84, 1986

Kerenyi C. *The Gods of the Greeks* Thames and Hudson, 1951

Kerenyi C. *Zeus and Hera* Routledege and Kegan Paul, 1975

Kramer R. *Meanads, Martyrs, Matrons-A Sourcebook on Woman's Religion* Fortress Press, 1988

Kramer S.N. *The Sacred Marriage Rite* Bloomington, Indiana University Press, 1969

Knapp A.B. *The History and Culture of Ancient Western Asia and Egypt* Wadsworth Pub. Co. 1988

Krzyszkowska O. and Nixon L. (eds.) *Minoan Society: Proceedings of the Cambridge Colloquim* Bristol Classical Press, 1981

Layard J. *A Celtic Quest: Sexuality and Soul in Individuation* Spring Publications, 1975

Latte K. 'The Coming of the Pythia' *H.T.R.* 33, pp 9–18, 1940

Lehmann K. 'The Mystery Cult of Samothrace' *Archaeology* Vol. 7, pp 91–5, 1954

Lerner G. *The Creation of Patriarchy* Oxford University Press, 1986

Lesko B. *The Remarkable Women of Ancient Egypt* Scribe, Berkeley, California, 1987

Levy G.R. *The Gate of Horn* Faber and Faber, 1948

Levy G.R. *Religious Conceptions of the Stone Age and their Influence upon European Thought* New York, Harper Torch Books, 1963

Lichtheim M. *Ancient Egyptian Literature* Vols. I, II, III, University of California Press, 1980

Lincoln B. 'The Rape of Persephone: A Greek Scenario of Women's Initiation' *H.T.R.* 72, pp 223–35, 1979

Lincoln B. *Emerging from the Chrysalis – Studies in Rituals of Woman's Initiation* Harvard University Press, 1981

Macurdy G. *Hellenistic Queens – A Study of Woman Power in Macedonia* John Hopkins Press, 1932

Marlow M.E. *Handbook for the Emerging Women* The Donning Company, 1988

Macmullen R. *Paganism in the Roman Empire* Yale University, 1981

Maringer J. *Gods of Prehistoric Man* Alfred A. Knopf, 1960

Maringer J. 'Priests and Priestesses in Pre-Historic Europe' *History of Religions* no. 17, pp 101–20, 1977

Marshak A. *The Roots of Civilization* Mcgraw Hill, 1972

Matthews C. *Sophia Goddess of Wisdom* Mandala, 1991

McEwan, Gilbert J.P. *Priest and Temple in Hellenistic Babylonia* Franz Steiner Verlag, 1981

Murray M. 'Priesthood of Women in Egypt' *History of Religions*, 3rd International Congress Proceedings, Vols. n/k, pp 220–4 1908

Mylonas G.E. *Eleusis and the Eleusinian Mysteries* Princeton University Press, 1961

Nadav Na'Aman 'The Ishtar Temple at Alalakh' *J.N.E.S.* Vol. 39, pp 209–14, 1980

Nicholson S. *The Goddess Re-awakening* Quest Books. Theosophical Publishing House, 1989

Oates J. 'Religion and Ritual in the Sixth Millennium BC in Mesopotamia' *World Archealogy* 10: 2, pp 117–24, 1978

Oates. J. *Babylon* Thames and Hudson 1979; revised edition 1985

Olsen C. (ed.) *The Book of the Goddess Past and Present* Crossroad Publishing Company, 1988

Oppenheim A.L. 'The Golden Garments of the Gods' *J.N.E.S.* Vol. 8, 1949

Otto W.F. *The Homeric Gods* Thames and Hudson, 1954

Otto W.F. 'The Meaning of the Eleusinian Mysteries 'in *The Mysteries* Eranos Yearbooks 2, pp 14–31, New York, 1955

Parke H.W. 'A Note on the Dephic Priesthood' *C.Q.* Vol. 34, pp 85–9, 1940(a)

Parke H.W. and Wormwell D. *The Delphic Oracle 1: The History* Blackwell, 1956

Patia R. *The Hebrew Goddess* New York, 1967

Peradotto J. and Sullivan J.P. *Women in the Ancient World, The Arethusa Papers* State University of New York, 1984

Pausanias. *Guide to Greece* Vols I & II. Penguin Classics, 1988

Pinches T.G. 'Priest, Priesthood (Babylonian)' *E.R.E.* Vol. 10, pp 284–88, 1918

Platon N. *Crete* Nagel, 1968

Pollard J. *Seers, Shrines and Sirens* Allen and Unwin, 1965

Pomeroy S. *Women in Hellenistic Egypt* Schocken Books, New York, 1984

Qualls-Corbett N. *The Sacred Prostitute* Inner City Books, 1988

Richardson A. *Dancers to the Gods* The Aquarian Press, 1985

Ringgren H. *Religions of the Ancient Near East* London, S.P.C.K. 1973

Robins G. 'The God's Wife of Amun in the 18th Dynasty in Egypt' *Images of Women in Antiquity* (eds. Cameron A. and Kuhrt A.) Croom Helm, 1983

Sabourin, L. *Priesthood* Leiden, E.J. Brill, 1973

Saggs H.W.F. 'The Encounter with the Divine in Mesopotamia and Israel' University of London, 1978

Sauneron S. *The Priests of Ancient Egypt* (trans. Morrisset A.) Evergreen Books, London, 1960

Scully V. *The Earth, the Temple and the Gods* Yale University Press, 1979

Sjoberg A. and Bergmann E. *The Collection of Sumerian Temple Hymns* New York, 1969

Skov G.E. 'The Priestesses of Demeter and Kore and their Role in the Initiation of Women at the Festival of the Haloa at Eleusis' *Temenos* II, 136–47, 1975

Slater P. *The Glory of Hera* Beacon Press, 1964

Solmsen F. *Isis among the Greeks and Romans* Harvard University Press, 1980

Solberger E. 'Sur la Chronologie des Roi d'Ur et Quelques Problèmes Connexés' *Archiv Für Orientforschung* Vol. 26, pp 10–48 1954

Souvinou-Inwood C. *Studies in Girl's Transitions – Aspects of the Arkteia* Kardamitsa, Athens, 1988

Souvinou-Inwood C. 'Persephone in Lokroi' *J.H.S.* pp 101–21, 1978

Stein M. 'Hera Bound and Unbound' *Spring*, pp 105–19, 1977

Spretnak C. (ed.) *The Politics of Women's Spirituality* Doubleday, 1982

Spence L. *The Mysteries of Egypt* Rider

Teubal S. *Sarah the Priestess: The First Matriach of Genesis* Swallow Press, 1984

Thompson D.J. *Memphis under the Ptolemies* Princeton University Press, 1988

Tran Tam Tinh. *Le cult d'Isis à Pompei* Paris, 1964

Todd I.A. *Catal Hüyük in Perspective* Brandeis University, Cummings Publishing Company, 1976

Uphill E.P. 'A Joint Sed Festival of Thutmose and Queen Hatsepsut' *J.N.E.S.* Vol. 20, pp 248–51, 1961

Van Buren D. 'The Sacred Marriage in Early Times in Mesopotamia' *Orienatalia* Vol. XIII, pp 1–72, 1944

Vidman L. *Sylloge Inscriptonium Religionis Isiacae Sarapicae* Berlin, 1969

Walbank M.B. 'Artemis Bear Leader' *C.Q.* pp 276–81, 1981

Warner M. *Alone of All Her Sex: The myth and the cult of the Virgin Mary* New York, Random House, 1976

Wente E. 'Hathor at the Jubilee' *Studies in Ancient Oriental Civilisation* Vol. 35, pp 83–91, 1969

Wehr D.S. *Jung and Feminism* Beacon Press, 1989

Wild R.A. *Water in the Cultic Worship of Isis and Serapis* Leiden, E.J. Brill, 1981

Willetts R.F. *Everday Life in Ancient Crete* Batsford, 1969

Willetts R.F. *Cretan Cults and Festivals* Routledge and Kegan Paul, 1962

Willetts R.F. *Aristocratic Society in Ancient Crete* London, 1955

Witte R.E. *Isis in the Graeco-Roman World* Thames and Hudson, 1971

Westendorf W. and Helck W. *Lexicon der -8e-gyptologie* Vol. IV, Wiesbaden, 1972–90

Whitehorne J.E.G. 'New Light on Temple and State in Roman Egypt' *J.R.H.* Vol. II, p 218–26, 1980

Wolkenstein D. and Kramer S.N. *Inanna Queen of Heaven and Earth* Rider, 1984

Worsfold T.C. *The History of the Vestal Virgins* Rider & Co, 1932

Woodhouse W.J. 'Priest, Priesthood, Greek' *E.R.E.* 10, pp 302–7, 1918

Zabkar L. 'Six Hymns to Isis in the Sanctuary of her Temple at Philae' 3 pts: *J.E.A.* Vol. 66, pp 127–36, 1983; *J.E A.* Vol. 69, pp 115–37, 1985; *J.E.A.* Vol. 71, pp 189–90, 1987

Zuntz G. *Persephone* Clarendon Press, 1971

INDEX

327

THE PILLAR OF ISIS

A PRACTICAL MANUAL ON THE MYSTERIES OF THE GODDESS

Vivienne O'Regan

The Pillar of Isis is a revolutionary new guide which allows you to experience the path of the Goddess: a path of positive union on all levels, including healing our relationship with others and with the Earth herself.

The combination of theory and practice eases the reader into an active, personal relationship with the Goddess in her various forms, and provides a complete course of development from basic skills to more advanced techniques of meditation, visualisation and ritual. Progressive creative visualisation techniques guide the reader to make individual contact with the Inner Temple of Isis: a place of teaching and a repository of her love and wisdom. The key to the Goddess mysteries is to 'know thyself'. Exercises in gentle self-exploration serve to balance the energies contacted through the main meditational sequences and aid the reader in coming to a better rapport with those about us and with the world we inhabit.

In Part Two the author examines the synthesis of the Pillar and its temples with the Kabalah, Tarot, chakras and auras, and gives guidance for further work on the Pillar for those wishing to enter into training for ordination.

Vivienne O'Regan has studied esoteric and psychological disciplines for twenty years. She is the founder and facilitator of a teaching centre within the Fellowship of Isis, of which she is an ordained Priestess. The Pillar of Isis is the culmination of her courses of meditation on the Goddess.

DAUGHTERS OF EVE

THE MAGICAL MYSTERIES OF WOMANHOOD

Dolores Ashcroft-Nowicki

'Of course, Daughter of Eve,' said the Faun.
'The further up and the further in you go, the bigger everything
gets. The inside is larger than the outside.'
Lucy looked hard at the garden and saw that it was not
really a garden but a whole world, with its own rivers and woods
and sea and mountains. But they were not strange:
she knew them all.
C. S. LEWIS, *THE LAST BATTLE*

As the seasons change and the year runs through its eternal cycle from spring to winter, birth to death, so too do we follow the cycle of life. As we pass through each transitional stage – our own changing seasons – Dolores Ashcroft-Nowicki eases our passage from Childhood to Cronehood with her own versions of the ancient rites of womanhood, adapted specifically for our modern age. With the compassion and understanding of a true Wise Woman, the author guides us through the maze of life from the mysteries of first menstruation and menopause, to the trauma of rape and severing painful emotional ties.

These rituals, pathworkings and meditations are for every Daughter of Eve, whatever her age, so that she may have the chance to rediscover her true self and be reunited finally with the Great mother in the womb of the Goddess.

Dolores Ashcroft-Nowicki, successful author and leading light in the occult world, is co-founder and Director of the Servants of the Light. She lives in Jersey.

JOURNEY OF THE PRIESTESS

THE PRIESTESS TRADITIONS OF THE ANCIENT WORLD
A JOURNEY OF SPIRITUAL AWAKENING
AND EMPOWERMENT

Asia Shepsut

The issue of female priesthood has now moved to the forefront of public debate within the Christian Church. Yet many influential women working outside orthodox religion are already operating as priestesses, often at a very high level. This book traces the remains of a submerged tradition of priestesses, whose characteristics have remained constant for millennia.

In the ancient world, throughout the rise and fall of Sumer, Egypt, Babylonia and Persia, women held great power. Their influence gradually spread westwards until it finally took root in Greece and Rome. Through an examination of history, ancient stories and images, Asia Shepsut links age-old ritual to modern conditions. The worship of the goddess in her many forms, with the yearly cycle of festivals and the celebration of the sacred marriage, still has striking relevance for today's priestess striving to blend everyday life with spiritual service.

Women still have much to learn about reclaiming and using their spiritual powers. Through drawing on the mythological cycle of life and death, with its interplay between male and female energies, we find a unique opportunity to rebalance the sexes, and lay the foundations of a common spiritual practice.

Asia Shepsut is an art historian and archaeologist, who has participated in many spiritual traditions. She has travelled and researched widely in the Middle East. She has co-authored and edited several books, including The Year of the Goddess.

THE PILLAR OF ISIS	1 85538 236 9	£9.99	☐
DAUGHTERS OF EVE	0 85030 977 8	£7.99	☐
JOURNEY OF THE PRIESTESS	1 85538 282 2	£12.99	☐
HER BLOOD IS GOLD	1 85538 312 8	£9.99	☐
THE YEAR OF THE GODDESS	0 85030 859 3	£6.99	☐
VOICES OF THE GODDESS	0 85030 965 4	£7.99	☐
SOPHIA: GODDESS OF WISDOM	1 85538 275 X	£7.99	☐

All these books are available from your local bookseller or can be ordered direct from the publishers.

To order direct just tick the titles you want and fill in the form below:

Name: _____

Address: _____

_____

_____ Postcode: _____

Send to: Thorsons Mail Order, Dept 3, HarperCollins*Publishers*, Westerhill Road, Bishopbriggs, Glasgow G64 2QT.

Please enclose a cheque or postal order or your authority to debit your Visa/Access account —

Credit card no: _____

Expiry date: _____

Signature: _____

— up to the value of the cover price plus

UK & BFPO: Add £1.00 for the first book and 25p for each additional book ordered.

Overseas orders including Eire: Please add £2.95 service charge. Books will be sent by surface mail but quotes for airmail despatches will be given on request.

24 HOUR TELEPHONE ORDERING SERVICE FOR ACCESS/VISA CARDHOLDERS — TEL: 041 772 2281.